WOMEN'S UNIVERSITY NARRATIVES, 1890–1945

CONTENTS OF THE EDITION

VOLUME 1
General Introduction
In Statu Pupillari

VOLUME 2
The Girls of Merton College

VOLUME 3
A College Girl

VOLUME 4
The Pearl

WOMEN'S UNIVERSITY NARRATIVES, 1890–1945

Volume 3
A College Girl

Edited by
Anna Bogen

PICKERING & CHATTO
2015

Published by Pickering & Chatto (Publishers) Limited
21 Bloomsbury Way, London WC1A 2TH

2252 Ridge Road, Brookfield, Vermont 05036–9704, USA

www.pickeringchatto.com

BRITISH LIBRARY CATALOGUING IN PUBLICATION DATA

Women's university narratives, 1890–1945. Part I.
1. College stories, English – History and criticism. 2. Women college students
in literature. 3. Universities and colleges in literature. 4. English fiction – 20th
century – History and criticism. 5. Literature and society – Great Britain – History – 20th century.
I. Bogen, Anna, editor.
823.9'12093557-dc23

ISBN-13: 9781848935228
Web-PDF ISBN: 978178447550

This publication is printed on acid-free paper that conforms to the American
National Standard for the Permanence of Paper for Printed Library Materials.

Content Management Platform by Librios™
Typeset by Pickering & Chatto (Publishers) Limited
Printed and bound in the United Kingdom by CPI Books

CONTENTS

Introduction   vii
A Brief Note on Editorial Practices   xvii

A College Girl   1

Editorial Notes   185

INTRODUCTION: *A COLLEGE GIRL*

When Mrs George de Horne Vaizey's novel *A College Girl* was serialized in the *Girl's Own Paper* in 1911, the first installment was illustrated by real-life photographs from Newnham College, which the novel's heroine Darsie attends. When the book was republished in complete form in 1913, the cover featured an attractive drawing of a Newnham student holding up a kettle. Both of these illustrations, as well as the title of the novel, highlight the importance of the college experience to the novel's plot, despite the fact that only a little less than half of it actually takes place at Newnham. They also showcase *A College Girl*'s role as a 'new' type of women's university fiction, less muted and careful than earlier works like *In Statu Pupillari* or *The Girls of Merton College*, with their disguised names like 'Castlebridge' and 'Hypatia'. Although Vaizey, like Johnson and Meade, was a generation too old to attend Cambridge herself, *A College Girl* operates confidently within the world of 'real' Cambridge, taking it for granted that fictional 'everygirl' heroines like Darsie, and the ordinary readers of the *Girl's Own Paper*, not only could but should access the delights of Newnham. *A College Girl* thus moves beyond the Victorian vision of Oxbridge suggested by Johnson and Meade, providing an Edwardian bridge between these older accounts and post-war narratives of women's university life.

Vaizey's own life also spanned this divide. Born Jessie Bell in 1856 in Liverpool, she came from a large Scottish family of seven children and grew up in a happy Victorian household that she recalled fondly in the novel *Salt of Life* (1915).[1] Like Johnson and Meade, she did not attend university, instead studying at home with governesses and tutors. She married Henry Mansergh in 1883 and gave birth to a daughter in 1886. Interestingly, however, her writing career really only started after her husband died of kidney failure in 1894.[2] She quickly became a popular success after the publication of her first book[3] *A Girl in Springtime* in 1897, and continued to publish many other novels under her new name of Mrs George de Horne Vaizey – she remarried in 1898 after romantically meeting her new husband on a Mediterranean cruise. In 1900 she introduced her most popular heroine, Pixie O'Shaughnessy, a plucky schoolgirl who fit the common school-story stock character of the 'wild Irish girl'.[4] Vaizey also wrote more serious books for young women, most notably *The Independence of Claire* (1915), which focuses on the difficulty of finding employment for young women in London. Despite struggling with rheumatoid arthritis, Vaizey wrote steadily up to her death in 1917, resolutely setting her tales in the modern Edwardian world.

A College Girl is therefore one of Vaizey's latest books, and shows her as a writer at the height of her powers. It is also her only book set at university. Nevertheless, it shares many important characteristics with her other fiction that gives it a particularly interesting viewpoint on Cambridge, especially its serialization in the *Girl's Own Paper*. The *Girl's Own Paper* has important connections to women's university narratives. Started in 1880 and running until 1956, its reign spanned the era of women's fight for inclusion at Oxbridge, from being allowed to take examinations at Cambridge (1881) to the final granting of degrees in 1948. Like the narratives in this collection, the *Girl's Own Paper* had to adapt to the rapidly changing cultural definitions of both femininity and feminism. The magazine was originally started in 1880 by the Religious Tracts Society in response to a perceived threat to girls' morality by the explosion of sensationalistic stories in the press and 'penny dreadfuls' – the canny editors had also noticed that many girls were avidly reading their brothers' magazines, particularly the highly successful *Boy's Own Paper,* started in 1879.[5] The first editor, Charles Peters, who was at the helm from 1880 to 1908, was very definite about his vision for the magazine, which he expected to 'foster and develop that which was highest and noblest in the girlhood and womanhood of England ... putting the best things first and banishing the worthless from his pages'.[6] This religious dimension meant that the *Girl's Own Paper* always had a complex relationship with women's rights. As many scholars have pointed out, it showed a continuing ambivalence towards issues such as higher education, employment and marriage. This is at least partially due to the paper's ambitious targeting of a very broad middle- and lower-middle class audience whose diversity the paper continually tried to smooth over with what Beth Rodgers has called 'a coherent textual identity ... that attempts to reconcile competing definitions of girlhood'.[7] The paper thus contained material that to readers today may feel contradictory or ill-matched; the serialization of *A College Girl*, for example, was surrounded by articles such as 'The Mistress of the Little House: Some Things She Ought to Know When her Maid is Inexperienced' and 'A Rosebud Outfit for Baby', along with pictures of kittens, puppies and quilt patterns.

The *Girl's Own Paper*'s wide audience means that it can give us valuable clues as to how university life for women was being portrayed in the public sphere. As early as 1897 the paper was publishing factual articles about higher education for women, usually profiles designed to show the audience what life was really like for female students.[8] Claire Hughes' '"Up"': A Magic Word', dating from 1929, is a typical example; accompanied by real photographs (like *A College Girl*) it presents the college experience as both exciting and accessible for women.[9] The *Girl's Own Paper* also featured fiction about university life, although more rarely; a little later than Vaizey's novel, for example, the paper published a short sequence entitled 'Bits in the Life of a Missionary Student'.[10] A wide audience was ensured for *A College Girl* through its initial serialization and later publication in book form, including magazine readers, parents and the 'reward' market – my own copy bears a stamp proclaiming that the book was a 1929 prize for proficiency in Biblical Knowledge. As we can see from this example, the novel remained in print for a long time and was even publicized in America in 1916 as a 'new book for young people'.[11] *A College Girl* was probably therefore one of the most widely read of university novels, encompassing the juvenile audience of Meade but also reaching a wider reading public, almost certainly including young mothers who might one day send their own daughters to college.

The story of *A College Girl* is a relatively simple one. As I pointed out at the beginning, the title is somewhat deceptive; the heroine, Darsie Garnett, spends the first half of the book at home in an anonymous provincial town, and only goes to Newnham halfway through the narrative. Nevertheless, it is clear that Vaizey uses the first part of the book to set up the second; the formative events of Darsie's childhood are carefully picked to emphasize her journey towards becoming the 'college girl' of the title: the nurturing friendships with the Vernon family next door, whose father 'is richer than ours, and he believes in higher education';[12] the kindly bequest from Great-Aunt Maria; and, above all, Darsie's sober awareness that despite her beauty and charm, she will have to earn her own living one day: 'work, work, work – teaching by day, correcting exercises by night, in a deserted schoolroom, with three months' holiday a year spent at home'.[13] This dire prediction isn't entirely fulfilled by the end of the book – instead we find Darsie safely engaged to Dan Vernon – but it sets up a comfortable connection between the unfortunate need for women to work and the justification for higher education. The final plot event of the early half of the book, the development of Darsie's relationship with the flighty and irresponsible Ralph Perceval, also contributes directly to the college section, with his early rescue of Darsie from the river foreshadowing his eventual drowning in the Cam. Thus although Vaizey's ending is relatively conservative, with Darsie burying her disappointment at a second-class degree in the 'beatific content' brought on by Dan's love, the overall structure of her novel, which sympathetically and realistically shows the struggles facing those with the ambition to become 'college girls', is more progressive than it first appears.

Also progressive in *A College Girl* is Vaizey's treatment of class, an issue which lurks beneath the surface of many women's university novels but rarely takes centre stage, usually because it is eclipsed by concerns about gender. Unlike the heroines of *In Statu Pupillari* and *The Girls of Merton College*, Vaizey's heroine is lower-middle-class and urban, characteristics that rarely appear in earlier women's university fiction. Meade's heroine Katherine Douglas, for example, is not rich, but we are told that her mother is of aristocratic birth and has merely fallen on hard times.[14] Vaizey is unapologetic and, indeed, celebrates her heroine's humble origins, signalling them from the book's opening words, which identify the novel as 'the tale of two terraces'.[15] We learn early on that the family inhabiting the terrace has six children and that money is scarce: Darsie's 'parents were not rich enough to pay for the modern plethora of nurses and governesses' and her mother's evenings are spent with her 'stocking-basket' by the fire.[16] The terrace they live in is dark and cramped with only a few yards of lawn that the children jokingly call 'the Grounds'.[17] Vaizey provides early descriptions of Darsie's urban life that are rare in college fiction of the period and make it clear that the neighborhood is not prosperous:

> From the eerie of the top landing window one could get a bird's-eye view of the Napier Terrace gardens with their miniature grass plots, their smutty flower-beds, and the dividing walls with their clothing of blackened ivy. Some people were ambitious, and lavished unrequited affection on struggling rose-trees in a center bed, others contented themselves with a blaze of homely nasturtiums; others, again, abandoned the effort after beauty, hoisted wooden poles, and on Monday mornings floated the week's washing unashamed. In Number Two the tenant kept pigeons; Number Four owned a real Persian cat ... When the lamps were lit, it was possible also to obtain glimpses into the dining-rooms of the two end houses, if the maids were not in too great a hurry to draw down the blinds.[18]

Vaizey's use of free indirect discourse here gives us a fascinating glimpse of Darsie's worldview and the narrow strip of respectability that her family inhabits, which stretches to cover both the expectation of having a maid and the 'unashamed' public hanging out of washing. Darsie's lower-middle-class status is established even more strongly when Vaizey introduces the aristocratic Perceval family, whose daughters are shocked that she lives 'in a street' and admit (with unintentional irony) that 'they had never met a prospective *working* girl before!'[19] As the novel continues, Vaizey continues to suggest that Darsie's origins are more of a boon than a hindrance. In the Cambridge section, we see this particularly through the figure of Ralph Perceval, the aristocratic pass-man who sees college life only as 'a rattling old place for sport and having a good time'.[20] By the time that *A College Girl* was written, the pass degree was rapidly falling out of favour, but still existed as an option chosen by many aristocratic young men who saw no need to work for an honours degree. Through Ralph's irresponsible behaviour and lack of motivation, Vaizey provides mild criticism of the class hierarchies at Cambridge, foreshadowing a change in the university through her championing of men of humbler origins like Dan Vernon, who comes up to Cambridge on a scholarship, receives a first-class degree, and goes off to teach in the provinces without a word of complaint. We can see in *A College Girl* the beginnings of a shift in the position of Cambridge from an expected rite of passage for public-school educated rich young men like Ralph who 'came to Cambridge, don't you know, because all one's people had been there, because it was the thing to do'[21] to an elite institution of higher education serving the best and brightest students from a diverse range of backgrounds. In 1913 this change was just beginning; after the two world wars, Oxbridge would be transformed. Norman Longmate points out that by 1950, for example, Balliol College at Oxford was admitting more students from state schools than from public schools.[22]

Another way in which Vaizey's novel breaks with its predecessors is in its clear connection of psychological maturity to college life. In *In Statu Pupillari* and *The Girls of Merton College,* Johnson and Meade are at pains to show how college life does not damage their protagonists, particularly in terms of physical health. Vaizey's vision in *A College Girl* is considerably more modern. Health scares are notably absent; Darsie's only bout of ill-health takes place after Ralph Perceval's death, and it is clearly cured, not caused, by college life. Instead, living at Newnham is clearly shown to aid psychological, social and mental growth. This *Bildungsroman* structure is remarkably less conflicted in Vaizey's texts than in the earlier two, and suggests a much stronger support for the college experience. Vaizey is careful to stress the girls' development in both mental and physical terms. Characters are carefully well-rounded; Darsie becomes Captain of the Fire Brigade and Prime Minister of the Newnham Political, while her brainy friend Hannah receives a first-class degree and captains the hockey team. Vaizey also explicitly connects the Cambridge experience to her characters' *moral* development – Ralph Perceval significantly drowns in the river, not hav-ing learned his lesson, while after the Tripos results Darsie finally understands the value of Dan Vernon. One gets the sense that Vaizey has to battle less against the 'New Woman' stereotypes that Johnson and Meade faced; instead, her novel reflects new thinking about the potential positive effects of institutions upon female adolescents. This reflects a shift in the discourse of adolescence that was beginning during this period; G. Stanley Hall, the seminal writer on adolescence during this period, had recently suggested that girls as well as boys would benefit from going away from home, and Vaizey's novel clearly agrees.[23]

Another important feature of *A College Girl* is its attitude towards academic work. This was a fraught subject in university fiction at the time, both in terms of the health scares in the earlier texts, and, as the century went on, in fierce debates over liberal education, gender and preparation for employment. Oxbridge during this period presented itself as the bastion of liberal and classically based educa-tion. Much of the university curriculum followed directly on from that of the public schools, which provided boys with a thorough classical and mathemati-cal background. For girls, however, the curriculum was more circumscribed. In

the early twentieth century, girls were beginning to be able to attend new High
Schools for girls, modelled on the North London Collegiate School, founded in
1850, that provided a much more rigorous classical education, and Vaizey sends
her heroine to one of these. Although Vaizey doesn't show us Darsie's school life,
we do get a glimpse of her classical training through her conversation with the
two Perceval girls. Noreen and Ida, who have a governess, represent a much more
traditional version of female education: 'mother doesn't approve of exams, for
girls. She wants us to be able to play, and sing, and draw, and speak German and
French, and she says that's enough.' Darsie, on the other hand, describes Latin
and mathematics as 'glorious' but is careful to explain her enthusiasm for these
subjects in economic terms: 'But you're rich, of course, and won't have to work.
I shall have to earn money myself, so I want to pass all the exams I can.'[24] This
strategy, defending classical education for women as a necessity for their future
employment, was a common one for advocates of women's higher education; the
fear at the end of the nineteenth century of the 'surplus woman' was at least partially appeased by the idea of more teaching jobs for women who did not marry.
As High Schools and public schools for girls flourished during the period, more
and more university-educated women were needed to teach them, developing a
circular employment system. Indeed, teaching has had a long association with
women's higher education in England; the first institutions that offered higher
education to women, Queen's and Bedford colleges, were specifically designed
to prepare women for teaching; during the period 1900–40, Janet Howarth has
pointed out that around 40 per cent of Oxford-educated women became teach-
ers.[25] Darsie's economic excuse is largely based on truth.

Despite this, however, when Darsie arrives at Cambridge Vaizey's book
continues to show her enjoying her studies. The girls are clearly excited to discuss 'shop', and Darsie bonds with her friend Margaret France over their shared
enthusiasm for Modern Languages:

> The two Modern Languages discussed work together eagerly, while mathemati-
> cal Hannah marched on a few feet ahead. Darsie felt a pang of remorse, because
> she could not help wishing that she would *stay* ahead, and so give the chance of a
> prolonged *tête-à-tête* with Margaret France.[26]

The girls, and Vaizey, identify and call each other by the names of their subjects
('Modern Languages groaned aloud'[27]) and leisure-time conversation focuses
around the intricacies of Historical French Grammar. In fact, Margaret France
strongly refutes the argument from necessity that Darsie used with the Perceval
sisters when she declares that she is not going to be a teacher after she leaves
Newnham, but plans to return home and live with her parents. The girls' initial
reaction to this bombshell is perhaps similar to a contemporary reader's: 'With
your brain! With your spirit! After this training! Such wicked waste...'[28] How-

ever, it is also possible to read Margaret France's decision as an endorsement of what is normally constructed during this era as a very 'male' version of liberal education: education as a means in itself, designed to improve the mind, not to prepare for a particular occupation, described by Arthur Waugh as the 'Oxford ethos': 'ideas not facts, judgments not index, life not death'.[29] While the novel still largely clings to the 'surplus women' excuse for female education, there is the beginning of a shift here to the idea that education for its own sake can be as valuable for women as it is for men.

Along with a shifting attitude towards education, we also see a shift in Vaizey's text around the concept of chaperonage and male–female relations. Although Vaizey's and Meade's texts are roughly contemporaneous, Meade's students clearly harken back to a pre-1900 version of Girton (probably based on her *Atalanta* articles from the 1890s) that makes Vaizey's students' free-and-easy behaviour seem strikingly modern by comparison. Not only do Darsie, Hannah and Margaret France freely come and go in Cambridge, but they frequently attend and give parties with men. Vaizey is careful to note that these parties are chaperoned by dons, but they still show a remarkable amount of mixing, perhaps even more than was allowed at the time. Moreover, Vaizey's text shifts the chaperonage focus from women to men through the figure of Mrs Reeves, the 'Professional Chaperon'.[30] Mrs Reeves argues that *male* students should be looked after and carefully watched; women, she suggests, are more mature and can even help in the process of chaperoning dangerous men: 'If one man is less admirable than another; if his friends and his entertainments are inclined to become rowdy and discreditable, does he need help *less,* or more?'[31] Although Mrs Reeves remains an ambiguous character in the novel, her concern for male students' wildness and general confidence in female students is borne out in the novel's plot, which sees the death of the badly behaved Ralph, but provides no female equivalent at Newnham, where the students appear on the whole much more sensible. At the end of the book, the contrast between 'the wildest fellows' rooms' and Darsie's demure 'Orchard picnic' makes an ironic comment on the chaperonage rules then in place, with Vaizey suggesting that male concern about female movement should perhaps better be redirected towards the students of their own gender.

If Vaizey's ideas about chaperonage are somewhat progressive, however, the book's foray into romance is less so. Chaperonage and romance are, of course, closely connected; Pauline Adams reports that at Somerville in 1912, a married overseas student caused a fierce debate in the common room over whether or not she should be allowed to have tea unchaperoned with her husband.[32] However, while Vaizey clearly suggests that her students are mature enough not to need much chaperoning, she still marries her heroine off. Sally Mitchell has suggested that during this period, a college setting could provide 'a pleasant set of new conventions for romantic fiction'.[33] The opening of *A College Girl* confirms this, explaining that the novel will tell of 'Darsie, her education, adventures, and ultimate romance'.[34] The word 'ultimate' foreshadows a depressing return to traditionalism at the novel's end when Darsie receives her second-class degree and is 'comforted' by Dan Vernon:

> Darsie! it's the day of my life, but it's all going to fall to pieces if you are sad! You've done your best, and you've done well, and if you are a bit disappointed that you've failed for a first yourself, can't you – can't you take any comfort out of *mine*? It's more than half your own. I'd never have got there by myself![35]

This ending, in which Darsie's disappointment with her lack of academic success is miraculously soothed by the 'beatific content' that she feels upon learning of Dan's love, seems to suggest that despite the book's earlier valorization of education for women, ultimately it is love and marriage, walking 'hand in hand' as the last sentence states, that is important for the female student. In this way, indeed, Vaizey seems less progressive than Meade or Johnson, who leave their heroines either resolutely single like Katherine Douglas or at the very least ambivalent like Eva. Nor is the fate of the other college girls particularly encouraging. 'Plain Hannah', for example, who does receive a first-class degree, becomes a teacher, which Vaizey tells us is more her 'métier' than domestic life, showing very clearly how few options there were for women post-college.

Overall, then, *A College Girl*, like *In Statu Pupillari* and *The Girls of Merton College*, presents a mixed view of Newnham life. As a typical Edwardian text, it occupies a key liminal position between the Victorian 'pioneer' days of women's higher education and the novels of the 1920s and 1930s in which women's place at the university was beginning to be taken for granted. For Vaizey, as for Johnson and Meade, telling the story of a college girl meant walking a tightrope between competing constructions of womanhood, education and class; if Vaizey goes a little farther than her predecessors, she is nevertheless very aware of the confines of what was still the very tenuous position of women at Cambridge. Despite its limitations, however, *A College Girl* remains a provocative and at times extremely progressive text, and one that, through its serialization in the *Girl's Own Paper*, reached what was probably one of the widest audiences for university fiction. For young girls (and their mothers!) poring over the photographs of 'real' Newnham rooms and halls, *A College Girl* had the potential to set in motion a life-changing dream.

Notes

1. *ODNB*; Mrs G. de Horne Vaizey, *Salt of Life* (London: Mills & Boon, 1915).
2. *ODNB*. I have found several references to Henry Mansergh struggling with alcoholism and/or drug addiction, but it is unclear where these suggestions originate.
3. According to Hilary Clare, this story was serialized in the *Girl's Own Paper* in 1894 before being published as a complete volume in 1897 (*ODNB*).

4. M. Cadogan and P. Craig, *You're a Brick, Angela! The Girls' Story 1839–1985* (London: Victor Gollancz, 1986), p. 86.
5. K. Moruzi and M. Smith, "'Learning What Real Work ... Means'": Ambivalent Attitudes towards Employment in the *Girl's Own Paper*', *Victorian Periodicals Review*, 43:4 (Winter 2010), pp. 429–45, on p. 430.
6. Quoted in H. Ward, *Girl's Own Guide: An Index of all the Fiction Stories Ever to Appear in the Girl's Own Paper from 1880–1941* (Colne, Lancashire: A & B Whitworth, 1992).
7. B. Rodgers, 'Competing Girlhoods: Competition, Community and Reader Contribution in the *Girl's Own Paper* and *Girl's Realm*', *Victorian Periodicals Review*, 45:3 (Fall 2012), pp. 277–300, on p. 277.
8. See, for example, 'One of them: Some Girl Graduates', *Girl's Own Paper*, 16 (1897), pp. 131, 219, reproduced in Volume 4 of this collection.
9. C. Hughes, '"Up": A Magic Word', *Girl's Own Paper*, 50 (1929), pp. 80–5.
10. Bits in the Life of a Missionary Student', *Girl's Own Paper*, 38 (1917), pp. 148–51.
11. 'Two New Books for Young People', *New York Times Book Review*, 1 October 1916, p. 887.
12. Mrs. G. de Horne Vaizey, *A College Girl* (London: Religious Tract Society, 1913), p. 73.
13. Vaizey, *A College Girl*, p. 58.
14. The one exception to this is perhaps the character of Betty Trowbridge in *The Girls of Merton College*, who is rich but who comes from a background in trade. However, despite Meade's obvious sympathy for Betty, she is not the novel's heroine and her origins are still presented as a disgrace to be overcome. The heroine of Meade's earlier novel *A Sweet Girl Graduate*, Priscilla, is, like Katherine Douglas, poor, but only in a romantic way.
15. Vaizey, *A College Girl*, p. 1.
16. Vaizey, *A College Girl*, pp. 27, 3.
17. Vaizey, *A College Girl*, p. 4.
18. Vaizey, *A College Girl*, p. 6.
19. Vaizey, *A College Girl*, p. 42.
20. Vaizey, *A College Girl*, p. 82.
21. Vaizey, *A College Girl*, p. 82.
22. N. Longmate, *Oxford Triumphant* (London: Phoenix House Ltd, 1954), p. 23.
23. Hall is careful to suggest that a 'family' atmosphere must prevail. G. Stanley Hall, *Adolescence: Its Psychology and its Relations to Physiology, Anthropology, Sociology, Sex, Crime, Religion and Education, Vol. 1* (1904; New York and London: D. Appleton & Co., 1925), p. 638.
24. Hunt, *Gender and Policy*, p. 42.
25. J. Howarth, 'Women', in B. Harrison (ed.), *The History of the University of Oxford, Vol. VIII* (Oxford: Clarendon Press, 1994), pp. 345–77, on p. 370.
26. Vaizey, *A College Girl*, p. 92.
27. Vaizey, *A College Girl*, p. 95.
28. Vaizey, *A College Girl*, p. 95.
29. 'The Oxford Ethos', in J. Morris (ed.), *The Oxford Book of Oxford* (Oxford: Oxford University Press, 1976), p. 283. I would argue that this definition could be expanded to the 'Oxbridge ethos'.
30. For another reading of Mrs Reeves, see A. Bogen, *Women's University Fiction, 1880–1945* (London: Pickering & Chatto, 2013).
31. Vaizey, *A College Girl*, p. 106.
32. P. Adams, *Somerville for Women: An Oxford College 1879–1993* (Oxford: Oxford Uni-

versity Press, 1996), p. 116.

33. S. Mitchell, *The New Girl: Girls' Culture in England, 1880–1915* (New York: Columbia University Press, 1995), p. 67.

34. Vaizey, *A College Girl*, p. 1.

35. Vaizey, *A College Girl*, p. 152.

A BRIEF NOTE ON EDITORIAL PRACTICES

The text of *A College Girl* presented here is the 1913 novel version published by the Religious Tracts Society. I decided to use this text in order to keep a parallel between *A College Girl* and the other novels in this volume, which all use the latest edition. Overall, Vaizey's language is extremely straightforward and should pose little challenge to the contemporary reader. Notably, however, Vaizey's use of names in *A College Girl* is inconsistent; although she uses real Cambridge locations in the Newnham section, the earlier section of the book appears to be set in an imaginary provincial city, Birchester. I have been unable to definitively identify any of the place names Vaizey uses in this section, with the exception of the village of Earley, which is in Berkshire. There is a small possibility that Vaizey is referring to Bicester in Oxfordshire and using an alternate spelling, but this seems unlikely; instead, Vaizey seems to be keeping these details deliberately ambiguous in order to highlight the importance of the Cambridge section. Once at Cambridge, Vaizey repeatedly refers to real locations, including many colleges (Newnham, King's, Caius, Catherine's), St Columba's Church and the Orchard Tea Room. Despite this use of real locations, Vaizey uses relatively little Oxbridge jargon (less than either Johnson or Meade), reflecting her young audience. The most challenging language in the text comes in the many references to popular trends of the early twentieth century, including Benger's Food, rinking parties and clock-golf. As such, it presents a fascinating picture of early twentieth-century leisure activities.

Every effort has been made to reproduce this text as closely to the original as possible without actually replicating the original typography. Original capitalization and punctuation have been retained and only the most significant typographical errors have been amended where they undermine the understanding of the text. Please note that there can be significant variances not only between different editions of texts but also differences between individual extant copies. We have proofed our text against a single original source. The original pagination of the text is indicated by the inclusion of / within the text at the exact point of the page break. Any sections omitted from the text are indicated by [...]. Any other editorial interventions are also contained within square brackets.

A COLLEGE GIRL

/

BY THE SAME AUTHOR

About Peggy Saville
Betty Trevor
Big Game
The Fortunes of the Farrells
A Houseful of Girls
More about Peggy
More about Pixie
Pixie O'Shaughnessy //

SHE RAINED ITS CONTENTS OVER THE GRASS.

A COLLEGE GIRL

BY

Mrs. GEORGE de HORNE VAIZEY

AUTHOR OF
"BETTY TREVOR," "ABOUT PEGGY SAVILLE," "PIXIE O'SHAUGHNESSY"
ETC., ETC.

LONDON
THE RELIGIOUS TRACT SOCIETY[1]
4 BOUVERIE STREET AND 65 ST. PAUL'S CHURCHYARD E.C.
1913 //

PART I

I. Boys and Girls   5
II. The Telegraph Station   9
III. Aunt Maria   15
IV. A Double Picnic   22
V. Left Behind!   27
VI. Dan to the Rescue   33
VII. Aunt Maria's Choice   39
VIII. First Days   44
IX. The Percivals   51
X. A Treaty   58
XI. A Dangerous Adventure   63
XII. Darsie's Suggestion   68
XIII. The Treasure Hunt   74
XIV. A Treasure Indeed!   81
XV. A Dream Fulfilled   85/

PART II

XVI. After Three Years   94
XVII. The Auction   101
XVIII. First Experiences   109
XIX. The Fancy Ball   117
XX. Undergraduate Friends   121
XXI. Mrs. Reeves Makes a Proposal   126
XXII. Christmas Day   129
XXIII. The Melodrama   138
XXIV. Dan and Darsie   142
XXV. New Year's Eve   146
XXVI. At the Orchard   156
XXVII. Disaster   161
XXVIII. Brighter Days   170
XXIX. Tripos Week   177
XXX. Farewell to Newnham   181/

Part I A College Girl

Chapter I

Boys and Girls

THIS is the tale of two terraces,[2] of two families who lived therein, of several boys and many girls, and especially of one Darsie, her education, adventures, and ultimate romance.

Darsie was the second daughter in a family of six, and by reason of her upsetting nature had won for herself that privilege of priority which by all approved traditions should have belonged to Clemence, the elder sister. Clemence was serene and blonde; in virtue of her seventeen years her pigtail was now worn doubled up, and her skirts had reached the discreet level of her ankles. She had a soft pink and white face, and a pretty red mouth, the lips of which permanently fell apart, disclosing two small white teeth in the centre of the upper gum, because of which peculiarity her / affectionate family had bestowed upon her the nickname of "Bunnie." Perhaps the cognomen had something to do with her subordinate position. It was impossible to imagine any one with the name of "Bunnie" queening it over that will-o'-the-wisp, that electric flash, that tantalizing, audacious creature who is the heroine of these pages.

Darsie at fifteen! How shall one describe her to the unfortunates who have never beheld her in the flesh? It is for most girls an awkward age, an age of angles, of ungainly bulk, of awkward ways, self-conscious speech, crass ignorance, and sublime conceit. Clemence had passed through this stage with much suffering of spirits on her own part and that of her relations; Lavender, the third daughter, showed at thirteen preliminary symptoms of appalling violence; but Darsie remained as ever that fascinating combination of a child and a woman of the world, which had been her characteristic from earliest youth. Always graceful and alert, she sailed triumphant through the trying years, with straight back, graceful gait, and eyes a-shine with a happy self-confidence. "I am here!" announced Darsie's eyes to an admiring world. "Let the band strike up!"

Some inherent quality in Darsie – some grace, some charm, some spell – which she wove over the eyes of beholders, caused them to credit her with a beauty which she did not possess. Even her / family shared in this delusion, and set her up as the superlative in degree, so that "as pretty as Darsie" had come to be regarded a climax of praise. The glint of her chestnut hair, the wide, bright eyes, the little oval face set on a long, slim throat smote the onlooker with instant delight, and so blinded him that he had no sight left with which to behold the blemishes which walked hand in hand. Photographs valiantly strove to demonstrate the truth; pointed out with cruel truth the stretching mouth, the small, inadequate nose, but even the testimony of sunlight could not convince the blind. They sniffed, and said: "What a travesty! Never again to *that* photographer! Next time we'll try the man in C – Street," and Darsie's beauty lived on, an uncontroverted legend.

By a triumph of bad management, which the Garnett girls never ceased to deplore, their three brothers came at the end instead of the beginning of the family. Three grown-up brothers would have been a grand asset; big boys who would have shown a manly tenderness towards the weaknesses of little sisters; who would have helped and amused; big boys going to school, young men going to college, coming home in the vacations, bringing their friends, acting as squires and escorts to the girls at home. Later on brothers at business, wealthy brothers, generous brothers; brothers who / understood how *long* quarter-day[3] was in coming round, and how astonishingly quickly a girl's allowance vanishes into space! Clemence, Darsie, and Lavender had read of such brothers in books, and would have gladly welcomed their good offices in the flesh, but three noisy, quarrelsome, more or less grimy schoolboys, superbly indifferent to "those girls" – this was another, and a very different tale!

Harry was twelve – a fair, blunt-featured lad with a yawning cavity in the front of his mouth, the result of one of the many accidents which had punctuated his life. On the top story of the Garnett house there ran a narrow passage, halfway along which, for want of a better site, a swing depended from two great iron hooks. Harry, as champion swinger, ever striving after fresh flights, had one day in a frenzy of enthusiasm swung the rings free from their hold, and descended, swing and all, in a crash on the oil-clothed floor. The crash, the shrieks of the victim and his attendant sprites, smote upon Mrs. Garnett's ears as she sat wrestling with the "stocking basket" in a room below, and as she credibly avowed, took years from her life. Almost the first objects which met her eye, when, in one bound, as it seemed, she reached the scene of the disaster, was a selection of small white teeth scattered over the oilclothed floor. Henceforth for years Harry pursued his way minus / front teeth, and the nursery legend darkly hinted that so injured had been the gums by his fall that no second supply could be expected. Harry avowed a sincere aspiration that this should be the case. "I can eat as much without them," he declared, "and when I grow up I'll have them false, and be an explorer, and scare savages like the man in Rider Haggard,"[4] so that teeth, or no teeth, would appear to hold the secret of his destiny.

Russell had adenoids, and snored. His peculiarities included a faculty for breaking his bones, at frequent and inconvenient occasions, an insatiable curiosity about matters with which he had no concern, and a most engaging and delusive silkiness of manner. "Gentleman Russell," a title bestowed by his elders, had an irritating effect on an elder brother conscious of being condemned by the contrast, and when quoted downstairs brought an unfailing echo of thumps in the seclusion of the playroom.

Tim played on his privileges as "littlest," and his mother's barely concealed partiality, and was as irritating to his elders as a small person can be, who is always present when he is not wanted, absent when he is, in peace adopts the airs of a conqueror, and in warfare promptly cries, and collapses into a curly-headed baby boy, whom the authorities declare it is "cr-uel" to bully! /

For the rest, the house was of the high and narrow order common to town terraces, inconveniently crowded by its many inmates, and viewed from without, of a dark and grimy appearance.

Sandon Terrace had no boast to make either from an architectural or a luxurious point of view, and was so obviously inferior to its neighbour, Napier Terrace, that it was lacerating to the Garnett pride to feel that their sworn friends the Vernons were so much better domiciled than themselves. Napier Terrace had a strip of garden between itself and the rough outer world; big gateways stood at either end, and what Vi Vernon grandiloquently spoke of as "a carriage sweep" curved broadly between. Divided accurately among the houses in the terrace, the space of ground apportioned to each was limited to a few square yards, but the Vernons were chronically superior on the subject of "the grounds," and in springtime when three hawthorns, a lilac, and one spindly laburnum-tree struggled into bloom, their airs were beyond endurance.

The Vernons had also a second claim to superiority over the Garnetts, inasmuch as they were the proud possessors of an elder brother, a remote and learned person who gained scholarships, and was going to be Prime Minister when he was grown up. Dan at eighteen, coaching with a tutor preparatory to going up to Cambridge, was / removed by continents of superiority from day-school juniors. Occasionally in their disguise of the deadly jealousy which in truth consumed them, the Garnett family endeavoured to make light of the personality of this envied person. To begin with, his name! "Dan" was well enough. "Dan" sounded a boy-like boy, a manly man; of a "Dan" much might be expected in the way of sport and mischief, but – oh, my goodness – *Daniel!* The Garnetts discussed the cognomen over the play-room fire.

"It must be so *embarrassing* to have a Bible name!" Lavender opined. "Think of church! When they read about me I should be covered with confusion, and imagine that every one was staring at our pew!"

Clemence stared thoughtfully into space. "I, Clemence, take thee Daniel," she recited slowly, and shuddered. "No – really, I couldn't!"

"He wouldn't have you!" the three boys piped; even Tim, who plainly was talking of matters he could not understand, added his note to the chorus, but Darsie cocked her little head, and added eagerly –

"Couldn't you, really? What *could* you, do you think?"

Clemence stared again, more rapt than ever.

"Lancelot, perhaps," she opined, "or Sigismund. Everard's nice too, or Ronald or Guy – –" /

"Bah! Sugary. *I* couldn't! Daniel is *ugly*," Darsie admitted, "but it's strong. Dan Vernon will fight lions like the Bible one;[5] they'll roar about him, and his enemies will cast him in, but they'll not manage to kill him. He'll trample them under foot, and leave them behind, like milestones on the road." Darsie was nothing if not inaccurate, but in the bosom of one's own family romantic flights are not allowed to atone for discrepancies, and the elder sister was quick to correct.

"Daniel didn't fight the lions! What's the use of being high falutin' and making similes that aren't correct?"

"Dear Clemence, you *are* so literal!" Darsie tilted her head with an air of superiority which reduced the elder to silence, the while she cogitated painfully why such a charge should be cast as a reproach. To be literal was to be correct. Daniel had *not* fought the lions! Darsie had muddled up the fact in her usual scatterbrain fashion, and by good right should have deplored her error. Darsie, however, was seldom known to do anything so dull; she preferred by a nimble change of front to put others in the wrong, and keep the honours to herself. Now, after a momentary pause, she skimmed lightly on to another phase of the subject.

"What should you say was the character and life history of a woman who could call her eldest / child 'Daniel,' the second 'Viola Imogen,' and the third and fourth 'Hannah' and 'John'?"

Clemence had no inspiration on the subject. She said: "Don't be silly!" sharply, and left it to Lavender to supply the necessary stimulus.

"*Tell* us, Darsie, tell us! You make it up – –"

"My dear, it is evident to the meanest intellect. She was the child of a simple country household, who, on her marriage, went to live in a town; and when her first-born son was born, she pined to have him christened by her father's name in the grey old church beneath the ivy tower; so they travelled there, and the white-haired sire held the infant at the font, while the tears furrowed his aged cheeks. *But* – by slow degrees the insidious effects of the great capital invaded the mind of the sweet young wife, and the simple tastes of her girlhood turned to vanity, so that when the second babe was born, and her husband wished to call her Hannah after her sainted grandmother, she wept, and made an awful fuss, and would not be consoled until he gave in to Viola Imogen, and a christening cloak trimmed with plush. And she was christened in a city church, and the organ pealed, and the godmothers wore rich array, and the poor old father stayed at home and had a slice of christening cake sent by the post. But the years passed on. Saddened and sobered by the discipline of life, / aged and worn, her thoughts turned once more to her quiet youth, and when at last a third child – –"

"There's only two years between them!"

Darsie frowned, but continued her narrative in a heightened voice –

"– was laid in her arms, and her husband suggested 'Ermyntrude'; she shuddered, and murmured softly, 'Hannah – *plain* Hannah!' and plain Hannah she has been ever since!"

A splutter of laughter greeted this *dénouement,* for in truth Hannah Vernon was not distinguished for her beauty, being one of the plainest, and at the same time the most good-natured of girls.

Lavender cried eagerly –

"Go on! Make up some more," but Clemence from the dignity of seventeen years felt bound to protest –

"I don't think you – *ought!* It's not your business. Mrs. Vernon's a friend, and she wouldn't be pleased. To talk behind her back –"

"All right," agreed Darsie swiftly. "Let's crack nuts!"

Positively she left one breathless! One moment poised on imaginary flights, weaving stories from the baldest materials, drawing allegories of the lives of her friends, the next – an irresponsible wisp, with no thought in the world but the moment's frolic; but whatever might be the fancy of the / moment she drew her companions after her with the magnetism of a born leader.

In the twinkling of an eye the scene was changed, the Vernons with their peculiarities were consigned to the limbo of forgotten things, while boys and girls squatted on the rug scrambling for nuts out of a paper bag, and cracking them with their teeth with monkey-like agility.

"How many can you crack at a time? Bet you I can crack more than you!" cried Darsie loudly. /

Chapter II

The Telegraph Station

THE Garnetts' house stood at the corner of Sandon Terrace, and possessed at once the advantages and drawbacks of its position. The advantages were represented by three bay windows, belonging severally to the drawing-room, mother's bedroom, and the play-room on the third floor. The bay windows at either end of the Terrace bestowed an architectural finish to its flattened length, and from within allowed of extended views up and down the street. The drawback lay in the position of the front door, which stood round the corner in a side street, on which abutted the gardens of the houses of its more aristocratic neighbour, Napier Terrace. Once, in a moment of unbridled temper, Vi Vernon had alluded

to the Garnett residence as being located "at our back door," and though she had
speedily repented, and apologized, even with tears, the sting remained.

Apart from the point of inferiority, however, the / position had its charm.
From the eerie of the top landing window one could get a bird's-eye view of
the Napier Terrace gardens with their miniature grass plots, their smutty flower-
beds, and the dividing walls with their clothing of blackened ivy. Some people
were ambitious, and lavished unrequited affection on struggling rose-trees in a
centre bed, others contented themselves with a blaze of homely nasturtiums;
others, again, abandoned the effort after beauty, hoisted wooden poles, and on
Monday mornings floated the week's washing unashamed. In Number Two the
tenant kept pigeons; Number Four owned a real Persian cat, who basked majestic on the top of the wall, scorning his tortoiseshell neighbours.

When the lamps were lit, it was possible also to obtain glimpses into the
dining-rooms of the two end houses, if the maids were not in too great a hurry
to draw down the blinds. A newly married couple had recently come to live in
the corner house – a couple who wore evening clothes every night, and dined in
incredible splendour at half-past seven. It was thrilling to behold them seated at
opposite sides of the gay little table, all a-sparkle with glass and silver, to watch
course after course being handed round, the final dallying over dessert.

On one never-to-be-forgotten occasion, suddenly and without the slightest
warning, bride and bridegroom had leaped from their seats and begun / chasing
each other wildly round the table. She flew, he flew; he dodged, she screamed
(one could *see* her scream!), dodged again, and flew wildly in an opposite direction. The chase continued for several breathless moments, then, to the desolation
of the beholders, swept out of sight into the fastnesses of the front hall.

Never – no, never – could the bitterness of that disappointment be outlived.
To have been shut out from beholding the *dénouement* – it was *too* piteous! In
vain Darsie expended herself on flights of imagination, in vain rendered in detail
the conversation which had led up to the thrilling chase – the provocation, the
threat, the defiance – nothing but the reality could have satisfied the thirst of
curiosity of the beholders. Would he kiss her? Would he beat her? Would she triumph? Would she cry? Was it a frolic, or a fight? Would the morrow find them
smiling and happy as of yore, or driving off in separate cabs to take refuge in the
bosoms of their separate families? Darsie opined that all would *seem* the same on
the surface, but darkly hinted at the little rift within the lute, and somehow after
that night the glamour seemed to have departed from this honeymoon pair, and
the fair seeming was regarded with suspicion.

As regards the matter of distance, it took an easy two minutes to cover the
space between the front doors of the two houses, and there seemed an endless
number of reasons why the members of the different families should fly round to
consult each other a dozen times a day. Darsie and Lavender, Vi and plain Han-

nah attended the same High School;[6] the Garnett boys and John Vernon the same Royal Institute, but the fact that they walked to and from school together, and spent the intervening hours in the same class-rooms, by no means mitigated the necessity of meeting again during luncheon and tea hours. In holiday times the necessity naturally increased, and bells pealed incessantly in response to tugs from youthful hands.

Then came the time of the great servants' strike.[7] That bell was a perfect nuisance; ring, ring, ring the whole day long. Something else to do than run about to open the door for a pack of children!

The two mistresses, thus coerced, issued a fiat. Once a day, and no oftener! All arrangements for the afternoon to be made in the morning *séance*, the rendezvous to be *out*side, not *in*side the house.

After this came on the age of signals; whistlings outside the windows, rattling of the railings, cooes through letter-boxes and ventilation grids, even – on occasions of special deafness – pebbles thrown against the panes! A broken window, and a succession of whoops making the air hideous during the progress of an extra special / tea party, evoked the displeasure of the mistresses in turns, and a second verdict went forth against signals in all forms, whereupon the Garnetts and Vernons in conclave deplored the hard-heartedness of grown-ups, and set their wits to work to evolve a fresh means of communication.

"S'pose," said Russell, snoring thoughtfully, "s'pose we had a telegraph!"[8]

"S'pose we had an airship![9] One's just as easy as the other. Don't be a juggins."[10]

But Russell snored on unperturbed.

"I don't mean a *real* telegraph, only a sort – of *pretend!* There's our side window, and your back windows. If we could run a line across."

"A line of *what?*"

"String. Wire. Anything we like."

"S'pose we *did* fix it, what then?"

"Send messages!"

"How?"

Russell pondered deeply. He was the member of the family who had a natural aptitude for mechanism; the one who mended toys, and on occasion was even consulted about mother's sewing-machine and escapes of gas, therefore he filled the place of engineer-royal and was expected to take all structural difficulties upon his own shoulders. He pondered, blinking his pale blue eyes.

"Can't send messages in the usual way – too / difficult. If the cord were double, we might have a bag and switch it across."

Ha! the audience pricked its ears and sat alert, seeing in imagination the tiny cord swung high in space above the dividing ground, stretching from window to window, fastened securely on the sills, "somehow," according to the girls, the boys critically debating the question of ways and means, strong iron hoops, for choice, clamped into the framework of the windows.

"How would the messages be sent?"

"In a bag, of course. Put the letter in the bag; then we'd pull and pull, and it would work round and round, till it arrived at the opposite end."

A stealthy exchange of glances testified to the general realization of the fact that it would take a *long* time to pull, a much longer time, for instance, than to run round by the road, and deposit the missive in the letter-box, a still unforbidden means of communication. Every one realized the fact, but every one scorned to put it into words. What was a mere matter of time, compared with the glory and *éclat* of owning a real live telegraph of one's own?

The first stage of the proceedings was to obtain the parental consent, and this was secured with an ease and celerity which was positively disconcerting. When mothers said, "Oh, yes, dears, / certainly – certainly you may try!" with a smile in their eyes, a twist on their lips, and a barely concealed incredulity oozing out of every pore, it put the youngsters on their mettle to succeed, or perish in the attempt. The mothers obviously congratulated themselves on a project which would provide innocent amusement for holiday afternoons, while they inwardly derided the idea of permanent success.

"We'll show 'em!" cried Harry darkly. "We'll let 'em see!"

The next point was to decide on the window in each house which should act as telegraph station. In the case of the Vernons there was obviously no alternative, for the third-floor landing window possessed qualifications far in excess of any other, but with the Garnetts two rival factions fought a wordy combat in favour of the boys' room and the little eerie inhabited by Lavender, each of which occupied equally good sites.

"Stick to it! Stick to it!" were Harry's instructions to his younger brother. "They can't put the thing up without us, so they're bound to come round in the end, and if we've got the telegraph station, it will give us the whip hand over them for ever. It's our room, and they've jolly well got to behave if they want to come in. If they turn rusty, we'll lock the door, and they'll have to be civil, or do without the telegraph. / Let 'em talk till they're tired, and then they'll give in, and we'll go out and buy the cord."

And in the end the girls succumbed as predicted. Lavender's pride in owning the site of the great enterprise weakened before the tragic picture drawn for her warning, in which she saw herself roused from slumber at unearthly hours of the night, leaning out of an opened window to draw a frozen cord through bleeding hands. She decided that on the whole it would be more agreeable to lie snugly in bed and receive the messages from the boys over a warm and leisurely breakfast.

These two great points arranged, nothing now remained but the erection of the line itself, and two strong iron hoops having been fixed into the outer sills of the respective windows a fine Saturday afternoon witnessed the first struggle with the cord.

Vi Vernon and plain Hannah unrolled one heavy skein, threaded it through their own hoop, and lowered the two ends into the garden, where John stood at attention ready to throw them over the wall. Darsie and Lavender dropped their ends straight into the street, and then chased madly downstairs to join the boys and witness the junction of the lines. Each line being long enough in itself to accomplish the double journey, the plan was to pull the connected string into the Garnett station, cut off the superfluous length, and tie the / ends taut and firm. Nothing could have seemed easier in theory, but in practice unexpected difficulties presented themselves. The side street was as a rule singularly free from traffic, but with the usual perversity of fate, every tradesman's cart in the neighbourhood seemed bent on exercising its horse up and down its length this Saturday afternoon. No sooner were lines knotted together in the middle of the road than the greengrocer came prancing round the corner, and they must needs be hastily untied; secured a second time, the milkman appeared on incredibly early rounds, reined his steed on its haunches, and scowled fiercely around; before there was time to rally from his attack a procession of coal-carts came trundling heavily past. By this time also the frantic efforts of the two families had attracted the attention of their enemies, a body of boys, scathingly designated "the Cads," who inhabited the smaller streets around and waged an incessant war against "the Softs," as they in return nicknamed their more luxurious neighbours.

The Cads rushed to the scene with hoots and howls of derision; white-capped heads peered over bedroom blinds; even the tortoiseshell cats stalked over the dividing walls to discover the cause of the unusual excitement. Clemence, with the sensitiveness of seventeen years, hurried round the corner, and walked hastily in an opposite direction, / striving to look as if she had no connection with the scrimmage in the side street. Darsie read the Cads a lecture on nobility of conduct, which they received with further hoots and sneers. Plain Hannah planked herself squarely before the scene of action with intent to act as a bulwark from the attack of the enemy. The three boys worked with feverish energy, dreading the appearance of their parents and an edict to cease operations forthwith.

The first lull in the traffic was seized upon to secure the knots, when presto! the line began to move, as Russell the nimble-minded hauled vigorously from the upstairs station, whence he had been dispatched a few moments before. The Cads yelled and booed as the first glimmering knowledge of what was on foot penetrated their brains; they grouped together and consulted as to means of frustration; but with every moment that passed yards of line were disappearing from view, and the skeins in the streets were rapidly diminishing in size. Presently there was not a single coil left, and a cheer of delight burst from the onlookers as they watched the cord rise slowly off the ground. Now with good luck and the absence of vehicles for another two minutes the deed would be done, and the Garnett-Vernon telegraph an accomplished fact; but alas! at this all-important moment one line of string caught in an ivy stem at / the top of a garden wall, and refused to be dislodged by tuggings and pullings from below. The Cads raised a derisive cheer, and to add to the annoyances of the moment a cab rounded the corner, the driver of which pulled up in scandalised amaze on finding the road barricaded by two stout lines of string.

His strictures were strong and to the point, and though he finally consented to drive over the hastily lowered line, he departed shaking his whip in an ominous manner, and murmuring darkly concerning police.

"On to the wall, John. Quick! Climb up and ease it over. If we don't get it up in a jiffy we shall have the bobbies after us!" cried Harry frantically, whereupon John doubled back into his own garden, and by perilous graspings of ivy trunks and projecting bricks scaled to the top and eased the line from its grip.

"Right-ho!" he cried, lifting his face to the opposite window. "Pull, Russell! *pull* for your life!"

Russell pulled; a second time the double thread rose in the air. Darsie jumped with excitement; Lavender clasped her hands, all white and tense with suspense, plain Hannah ran to and fro, emitting short, staccato croaks of delight; Harry stood in manly calm, arms akimbo, a beam of satisfaction broadening his face. That smile, / alas! gave the last touch of exasperation to the watching Cads. To stand still and behold the line vanishing into space had been in itself an ordeal, but Harry's lordly air, his strut, his smile – these were beyond their endurance! With a rallying shout of battle they plunged forward, grabbed at the ascending cord, hung for a dizzy moment suspended on its length, then with a final cheer felt it snap in twain and drag limply along the ground.

Alas for Harry and for John – what could they do, two men alone, against a dozen? The girls screamed, declaimed, vowed shrill revenge, but in the matter of practical force were worse than useless. Even with Russell's aid the forces were hopelessly uneven. Harry stood looking on gloomily while the Cads, chortling with triumph, galloped down the road, trailing behind them the long lengths of cord; then, like a true Englishman, being half-beaten, he set his teeth and vowed to conquer, or to die.

"They think we're sold, but they'll find their mistake! We'll get up at five on Monday morning and have the thing in working trig before they have opened their silly eyes."

This programme being duly enacted, the telegraph stations remained for years as an outward and visible sign of the only piece of work which Harry Garnett was ever known to accomplish before the hour of his belated breakfast. /

Chapter III

Aunt Maria

AMONG the crowd of relations near and far most families possess one relation *par excellence,* who stands out from all the rest by reason either of generosity, aggravatingness, or strength of character. Sometimes this relation is an uncle; more often it is an aunt; almost invariably he or she is unmarried or widowed, because the single state naturally allows more time and energy for interests beyond the personal household.

The Garnetts' relation *par excellence* was Aunt Maria – *Lady* Maria as they erroneously called her, being unsophisticated in the niceties of the peerage. Her rightful cognomen was Lady Hayes, and she was the elderly, very elderly, widow of an estimable gentleman who had been created a Baronet in recognition of services rendered to his political party. The Garnetts felt that it was very stylish to possess an aunt with a title, and introduced her name with an air when the Vernons grew / superior on the subject of "the grounds." Lady Hayes was an eccentric individual who inhabited a beautiful old country house in the Midlands, from which base she was given to suddenly swooping down upon her relations, choosing by preference for these visits the times when carpets had been sent away to be cleaned, or the maids granted days off to visit relations in the country. Then Lady Hayes would appear, announce her intention of staying a couple of nights, declare her unwillingness to give the slightest trouble, and proceed to request that her maid should be accommodated with a room next to her own, and that they should both be supplied with a vegetarian diet, supplemented by glasses of sterilized milk at intervals of every two hours. Sometimes the vegetarianism gave place to a diet of minced beef, but whatever might be the diet of the moment it was invariably something which no one else wanted to eat, and which took about three times as long to prepare as the entire rations for the household dinner of ten.

It was at the close of the Midsummer term, when the Garnett family were blissfully preparing for the yearly migration to the sea, that a letter from Aunt Maria fell like a bombshell upon the peaceful scene. This year the holiday promised to be even more blissful than usual, for the Vernons had secured a second farmhouse, not ten minutes' walk / from their own, and connected with the sea by the same fascinating fieldpaths. A farm and the sea! Could there possibly exist a more fascinating combination? The young people sniffed in advance the two dear, distinctive odours which, more than anything else, presented the scenes before them – the soft, cowy-milky scent of the farm, the salt, sharp whiff of the brine. From morn till night, at every available moment, they discussed the day's programme – feeding animals, calling the cows, bathing, picnicking on the sands, crab-hunting, mountain climbing. Excitement grew until it really seemed impossible to exist through the intervening days, and then the bombshell fell!

A letter arrived by an evening post, when Mr. and Mrs. Garnett were enjoying the one undisturbed hour of the day. It bore the Hayes crest, and was written in Aunt Maria's small, crabbed handwriting –

"MY DEAR EMILY, – I propose, all being well, to pay you a short visit from Tuesday to Thursday next, twelfth to fifteenth instant. Please let me have the same rooms as on my last visit. I am at present living on Benger's food,[11] and must ask you to see that it is made freshly for each meal, in a *perfectly clean, enamelled saucepan.*

"The chief object of my visit is to bring back one of your three daughters to stay with me during / the summer vacation. I have been feeling somewhat lonely of late, and my doctor recommends young society, so it has occurred to me that in obeying his instructions I might at the same time afford pleasure and benefit to one of your family. Should I become interested in the child it might be to her advantage hereafter, but it must be understood that I can make no promises on this point.

"The eighteen months which have elapsed since my last visit have somewhat dimmed my remembrance of your girls, so that I must see them again before deciding as to which of the three I should prefer as a companion.

"With love to William and yourself,

"Believe me, my dear Emily,

"Your affectionate Aunt,

"MARIA HAYES."

Mrs. Garnett read this communication in silence, handed it to her husband, and watched him flush and frown over the perusal.

"Does not even go through the form of asking our consent!"

"No! That's Aunt Maria all over. You could hardly imagine that she would. Oh dear! Oh dear! I'm afraid, Will – I'm *afraid* she will have to go!"

"Poor little kiddie, yes! How she will hate it! / Just at this moment when they are all wild with joy at the thought of their holiday with the Vernons. It seems positively brutal!"

"Oh, it does. I am so sorry for her – whichever it may be – but one must sometimes be cruel to be kind. We can't afford – I am not mercenary, as you know – but with our means we *can't* afford to refuse any possible advantage for our girls! The sacrifice of a summer holiday ought not to weigh against that."

"No, you're right, quite right. So be it then. Write and tell her to come, only I tell you plainly *my* holiday's spoiled.... With Darsie gone –"

"Dear! she has not chosen yet."

"Dear! you know perfectly well –"

They looked at each other, smiling, rueful, half-ashamed. It seemed like treason to the other girls, this mutual acknowledgment that Darsie was the flower of the flock, the child of the six to whom all strangers were attracted as by a magnet.

Clarence and Lavender were equally as dear to the parents' hearts, but there was no denying the existence of a special and individual pride in the fascinations of Darsie.

Mr. Garnett turned aside with an impatient shrug.

"There's one thing, Emily, *you* must tell her when it is settled! There'll be a tremendous scene. I flatly refuse – –" /

"Very well, dear, very well; I'll do it. But it's not decided yet, remember, and one can never be sure. I'd better break the idea to the girls before Aunt Maria comes, and let them get over the first excitement. To-night would be a good opportunity. You will be out late, so would be spared the scene!"

"Bless you, Emily! I'm a coward, I know, but I *should* be grateful. I can't answer for what I should do if Darsie cried, and begged my protection. Women have twice the pluck of men in these affairs!"

Nevertheless it was with a quaking heart that Mrs. Garnett broached the object of Aunt Maria's proposition over the schoolroom tea that afternoon, and her nervousness was not decreased by the smilingly unperturbed manner in which it was received. Never, never for a moment did it appear possible to the three girls that such a proposition could be seriously discussed.

"*So* likely!" sneered Clemence with a fine disdain. "Give up all the fun and excitement of the sea with the Vernons, to *browse* with Aunt Maria. *So* likely, to be sure!"

"Poor dear old love! She *is* deluded. Thinks it would be a pleasure and benefit, does she. I wouldn't take a thousand pounds –"

Thus Lavender. Darsie went a step farther in tragic declamation. /

"I'd drown myself first! To sit there – panting, in hot rooms, on Benger's food, and know that all the others were bathing and running wild on the shore – I'd burst! I'd run away in an hour –"

"Dears, it's a beautiful old place. There are gardens, and lawns, and horses, and dogs. Cows, too! I am sure there are cows – she used to keep a herd of Jerseys. You could see them being milked."

"Welsh cows are good enough for me. I don't need Jerseys. *Or* lawns! Give me the free, untrammelled countryside!

"'And to see it reflected in eyes that I love.'"

Darsie paraphrased a line of the sweet old ballad,[12] singing it in a clear, bell-like voice to a pantomime of clasped hands and rolling eyes. "It would be bad enough in an ordinary year, but to rend us apart from the Vernons – oh, no, it's unthinkable!"

"You have the Vernons near you all the year, dear. Aunt Maria only asks for eight weeks. There are occasions in life when it does not do to think only of our own pleasure."

Silence. A note in the mother's voice had startled her hearers into the conviction that the invitation must be regarded seriously, and not tossed aside as a joke. A lacerating suspicion that the authorities were in favour of an acceptance pierced like a dart. /

"Mother! What do you mean? You couldn't *possibly* be so cruel –"

"Mother, you don't mean –"

"Mother, what *do* you mean?"

"I mean that you ought to go, dears, which ever one of you is asked. Aunt Maria is an old lady, and she is lonely. Her doctor has ordered cheerful companionship. Moreover, she has been a kind friend to father in the past, and has a right to expect some consideration in return. If you went in the right spirit, you could be of real use and comfort, and would have the satisfaction of doing a kind deed."

Darsie set her lips in a straight line, and tilted her chin in the air.

"Couldn't pretend to go in the right spirit! I'd be in a tearing rage. Somebody else can have the 'satisfaction,' and I'll go to the sea."

"Darsie, dear, that's naughty!"

"I *feel* naughty, mother. 'Naughty' is a mild word. *Savage!* I feel savage. It's too appalling. What does father say? I'm sure he would never –"

"Father feels as I do; very disappointed for our own sakes and for yours that our happy party should be disturbed, but he never shirks a disagreeable duty himself, and he expects his children to follow his example."

Lavender instantly burst into tears. /

"It's always the way – always the way! It was too good to be true. We might have known that it was. She'll choose me, and Hannah will go without me. We'd planned every day – fishing, and bathing, and making hay, and I shall be mewed up in a close carriage, and have meals of nuts – and n-n-nobody to talk to. Oh, I can't – I can't bear it! I wish I could die and be buried – I *cannot* bear it –"

"You won't have to bear it. She'll choose me. I'm the eldest, and the most of a companion." Clemence spoke with the calmness of despair, her plump cheeks whitening visibly, her pale eyes showing a flush of red around the lids. "Of course, if it's my duty, I must go – but I'd as soon be sent to prison! I'm feeling *very* tired, and thought the holiday would set me up. Now, of course, I shall be worse. Eight weeks alone with Aunt Maria would try anybody's nerves. I shall be a wreck all winter, and have neuralgia[13] till I'm nearly mad."

"Nonsense, darling! If you are so tired, the rest and quiet of The Towers will be just what you need; and as we don't know yet which one of you Aunt Maria will wish as a companion, it is a pity for you all to make yourselves miserable at once. Why not try to forget, and hope for the best! Surely that would be the wiser plan."

The three girls looked at each other in eloquent / silence. Easy to talk. Forget, indeed. As if they *could*! Mother didn't really believe what she said. She was making the best of it, and there were occasions when making the best of it seemed just the most aggravating thing one could do.

It was a relief to the girls when Mrs. Garnett was summoned from the room on household business, and they were left to themselves. A craving for sympathy was the predominant sensation, and prompted the suggestion, "Let's wire to the Vernons," which was followed by a stampede upstairs. The telegraph was a sufficiently new institution to appear a pleasure rather than a toil, even though a message thus dispatched was an infinitely longer and more laborious effort than a run round the terrace, so to-day a leaf was torn from the note-book, a dramatic announcement penned and placed in the hanging-bag, with its jingling bell of warning, and the three girls took it in turns to pull at the cord till the missive arrived at its destination. Attracted by the sound of the bell, Vi and plain Hannah stood at the window awaiting the communication, read over its contents, and stood silent and dismayed. The Garnetts, watching from afar, realized the dramatic nature of that pause, and thrilled in sympathy.

"One of us is going to be sent to prison instead of to the country!"

"Prison!" Vi and plain Hannah wagged their / heads over the cipher, hesitated long, pencil in hand, and, finally, in a frenzy of impatience, which refused to be curbed even by loyalty to the telegraph itself, dispatched an urgent summons to speech –

"Come round and talk!"

The Garnetts flew. The Vernons, waiting upon the doorstep, escorted them upstairs to the scantily furnished room which had first been a nursery, then promoted to playroom, and, ultimately, when the more juvenile name wounded the susceptibilities of its inmates, had become definitely and proudly "the study." The bureau in the corner was Dan's special property, and might not be touched by so much as a finger-tip. The oak table with three sound legs and a halting fourth, supported by an ancient volume of *Good Words*,[14] was Vi's property; John and plain Hannah shared the dining-table, covered with the shabby green baize cloth, which stood in the centre of the room. There were a variety of uncomfortable chairs, an ink-splashed drugget,[15] and red walls covered with pictures which had been banished from other rooms as they acquired the requisite stage of decrepitude and grime.

The five girls surged into the room, faced each other, and burst into eager speech –

"Who's going to prison?"

"We don't know. Wish we did!" /

"What do you mean by prison?"

"Aunt Maria's!"

"Lady Maria's?"

"Lady Maria's! One of us has to go and stay with her for eight weeks instead of going with you to the sea."

Vi Vernon collapsed on to the nearest chair, and gasped for breath. "Stu-pen-dous!" she murmured beneath her breath. Vi had a new word each season which she used to describe every situation, good and bad. The season before it had been "Weird!" this season it was "Stupendous," and she was thankful for the extra syllable in this moment of emotion. "It's really true? You mean it in earnest? *Why?*"

"Thinks it would be a pleasure to us, and that we should be cheery companions. *So* likely, isn't it?"

"But – but surely your mother – What does she say?"

"Preaches! Oughtn't to think of ourselves. Ought to show a right spirit and go."

"Stu-pendous!" cried Vi once again. Plain Hannah hoisted herself on to the corner of the table, and hunched herself in thought. She really was extraordinarily plain. Looking at her critically, it seemed that everything that should have been a line had turned into a curve, and everything that should have been a curve into a line; she was / thick-set, clumsy, awkward in gait, her eyes were small, her mouth was large, she had a meagre wisp of putty-coloured hair, and preposterously thick eyebrows several shades darker in hue, and no eyelashes at all. Friends and relations lavished much pity on poor dear Hannah's unfortunate looks, but never a sigh did Hannah breathe for herself. She was strong and healthy, her sturdy limbs stood her in good stead in the various games and sports in which she delighted, and she would not have exchanged her prowess therein for all the pink cheeks and golden locks in the world. Hannah's manner, like her appearance, lacked grace and charm; it was abrupt, forceful, and to the point. She spoke now, chin sunk in her grey flannel blouse, arms wrapped round her knees –

"Is she coming to see you before she chooses, or will it be done by post?"

"She's coming! Two days next week. Isn't it too awful? We were so happy – the telegraph up, and the weather jolly, and holidays nearly here. 'All unsuspecting of their doom the little victims played.'[16] And then – *this!* Holidays with Aunt Maria! Even the third of a chance turns me cold with dismay. I couldn't bear –"

"You won't need to. She won't have you. She'll choose Darsie."

Darsie squealed in shrillest protest – /

"No, no! It's not fair. She won't! She can't! It's always the eldest or the youngest. I'm the middle – the insignificant middle. Why should she choose me?"

"You are not so modest as a rule! You know perfectly well that strangers always *do* take more notice of you than any one else. You are always the one who is fussed over and praised."

"Because I want to be! This time I shan't. I'll be just as sulky and horrid as I can for the whole blessed time."

"You'll be there anyway, and you can't alter your face."

"My fatal beauty!" wailed Darsie, and wrung her hands in impassioned fashion. Then she looked critically from one sister to another, and proceeded to candid criticisms of their charms.

"Clemence is not pretty, but she's *nice!* If she did her hair better, and sat up, and had a colour, and didn't poke her chin, she'd look quite decent. I should think it would be interesting to take some one who *needed* improving, and see what you could do. Lavender's gawky, of course, girls *are* gawky at her age, but I shouldn't wonder if she grew quite decent-looking in time. Rest and quiet would do wonders!"

"Thank you, indeed! You *are* kind!" The sisters bridled and tossed their heads, by no means appeased by such prognostications of their future / charms. "Certainly if she took *you,* she might teach you to be modest!"

"Oh, dear, oh, dear, I don't want *any* of you to go!" Vi, the peacemaker, rushed to the rescue. She was just sixteen, younger than Clemence, older than Darsie, attached almost equally to the two. Lavender, of course, was quite too young for a companion, but then Lavender and Hannah paired together; if she were absent, Hannah at a loose end would demand entrance into those three-sided conferences which made the joy of life. The fear of such an incursion made Lavender at that moment seem even more precious than her sisters. Vi continued her lament with bitter emphasis –

"*Too* bad – *too* hard – stupendous! Spoil everything. Horrid interfering old thing! If I were your parents I wouldn't – not for all the money in the world, I wouldn't sacrifice a child to an old ogre like that! I'd keep my own children and let them be happy while they could, but, of course, if she talks of duty...! If there's one thing more stupendous than another it's being put on one's honour! It gives one *no* chance. Well, you'll have to go, I suppose, and our holiday is spoiled. I've never been so disappointed in my life."

"Think of how *we* feel!" croaked Clemence tragically, but this time the tragedy did not ring so true, for since plain Hannah's verdict her spirits had risen considerably. Hannah was the shrewdest / and cleverest of all five girls, and her prophecies were proverbially correct. Clemence felt sufficiently reassured to reflect that as the eldest in years, she would do well to show an example of resignation. She lengthened her face, and added solemnly –

"I don't think you ought to talk like that about honour, Vi! It ought to be an incentive. If I go, the only thing that will console me most is the feeling that I am doing my duty!"

Vi stared, and the younger girls coughed in derisive chorus.

"Isn't it easy to be resigned for somebody else?" demanded plain Hannah of the ceiling. "You are *not* going, my dear, and you know it. Darsie likes well enough to queen it as a rule, and now she's got to pay the price. That's the cost of good looks. Thank goodness no one will ever want to run off with *me!* – not even a staid old aunt. Tell us about your aunt, by the way – you've talked enough about yourselves. Where does she live, and what is she like, and what does she do, and what will *you* do when you're there? Have any of you ever seen the place?"

"Not since we were old enough to remember, but mother has been and told us all about it. It's big, with a lodge, two lodges, and a park all round, very rich, and grand, and respectable, and dull. There are men-servants to wait at / table, and the windows are never open, and she drives out every day in a closed carriage, and plays patience at night, and wears two wigs, turn about, a week at a time. Her cheeks are red, the sort of red that is made up of little red lines, and never gets brighter or darker, and she likes to be quiet and avoid excitement. Oh, imagine what it would be like to *choose* to be quiet, and deliberately run away from a fuss! Can you imagine if you lived a thousand years ever reaching such a pitch as that?"

Darsie held out both hands in dramatic appeal, and her hearers groaned with unction. It was impossible, absolutely beyond the power of imagination to picture such a plight. Each girl hugged to herself the conviction that with her at least would remain immortal youth; that happen what might to the rest of mankind, no length of years could numb her own splendid vitality and *joie de vivre*.

Not even, and at the thought the three Garnetts sighed in concert, not even Aunt Maria! /

Chapter IV

A Double Picnic

ONLY four days before Aunt Maria arrived to make her great decision! The Garnetts were living in what Darsie graphically described as "the hush before the storm," adored, condoned, and indulged by parents who saw before them the pangs of separation, and by brothers shrewdly expectant of parting spoils.

Clemence, Darsie, and Lavender were acutely conscious of the rarified atmosphere by which they were surrounded, and only regretted its necessarily limited duration.

"Let's take advantage of it!" cried Darsie, the diplomat. "It's our chance; we should be noodles if we let it slip. Anything we ask now they'll let us have. It's like prisoners who can order what they like for supper the night before they're hanged. Let's think what we'd like, and go in a body and petition mother. She won't have the heart to refuse!" /

The sisters agreed enthusiastically, but were not rich in suggestions. It is one of the curious things in life that whereas every day one is brought up sharply against a dozen longings and ambitions, without the fulfilment of which it seems impossible to live, yet if the sudden question be put, *"What would you have?"* instantly the brain becomes a blank, and not a single suggestion is forthcoming. The Garnetts stared at one another in labouring silence. It was too late for parties; too early for pantomimes, a definite gift failed to meet the case, since each girl thought with a pang, "What's the use? I might not be here to enjoy it!" Extra indulgences, such as sitting up at night, or being "let off" early morning practising, did not appear sufficiently important, since, with a little scheming, these might be gained in addition. It was Lavender who at last succeeded in hitting the popular taste.

"A picnic! A real whole-day one this time. Lunch in the woods at Earley, tea' in our old woman's cottage, walk over the fields to the amphitheatre, and home by train from Oxholm.[17] Whoever goes with Aunt Maria will be cheated of her holiday, for the well-behaved country doesn't count. If you have to wear gloves and walk properly, you might as well be in town at once. For the victim's sake we ought to have one more day in the woods!" /

Clemence and Darsie sparkled, for the programme was an opulent one, combining as it did the two ordinary picnics into one. The yearly programme was that – "if you are good" – the Garnett family should be taken for two half-day excursions into the country on two summer Saturday afternoons, but though the woods and the amphitheatre were only separated by three short miles, never yet had the two places been visited together. An all-day picnic seemed a regal entertainment, worthy of the unique occasion.

"Ourselves and the Vernons! Mrs. Vernon to talk to mother, then they won't have as much time to look after us. When they begin on carpets and curtains they forget everything else, and we can do as we like. Do you suppose Dan would come?"

"Sure he wouldn't."

"Why?"

"My dear!" Clemence held out eloquent hands. "Does he ever come? He's a man, soon going to college, and you are only 'kids.' I'm older than he is really; a woman is always older than a man, but he doesn't like me. We are not *en rapport*." Clemence tried hard to suppress a smirk of self-consciousness at the use of the French term, while the two younger sisters jeered and booed with the callous brutality of their kind.

"Ha, ha! aren't we fine? Roll your r's a little / more next time, my dear. It will sound miles better. Your accent leaves much to be desired. Aren't we grown-up to-day? Aunt Maria *would* be impressed! A little stay in Paris just to put on the accent, and it's wonderful to think of what you might do! *En rapport!* Bet you daren't say that to Dan! Dare you to tell him that you are not *en rapport!*"

Clemence was seized with agitation, discerning through the innocent words a thinly veiled threat. If she didn't, Darsie *would!*

"Darsie!" she cried loudly. "You mustn't tell; you must *not!* It's mean. Only sneaky children repeat what is said in private. Promise this minute that you won't say a word!"

But Darsie, like her brothers, was keenly alive to the privilege of holding a rod in pickle over an elder member of the family. So long as Clemence lived in fear of humiliating disclosure, so long might she herself walk in safety, free from rebuffs. She laid her head on one side and smiled sweetly into her sister's face.

"I shouldn't like exactly, positively, to *promise,* don't you know, for I *am* such a creature of impulse. If it rushed over me suddenly, it might pop out, don't you know, bang! before I knew what I was about! Of course, on the other hand, I *might* not –"

"Very well," snapped Clemence sharply, "then / I stay at home! It would be no fun for *me* to go for a picnic with that sort of thing hanging over my head all the time. I know very well how you'd behave – rolling your eyes across the table, and beginning half-sentences, and introducing '*en rapport*' every other moment. If I'm going to be made miserable, I'll be miserable at home. You can go to our last picnic as an undivided family without me, the eldest of the family, and I only hope you'll enjoy it; that's all!"

"Oh, Darsie!" pleaded Lavender tragically, moved almost to tears by the pathos of those last words, and Darsie shrugged her shoulders, philosophically accepting her defeat.

"All right, I promise! I'll hug the remembrance secretly in my own breast. It will cheer me through the dullest hours!"

Clemence bridled, but made no further protest. To think of Darsie chuckling in secret was not agreeable, but it was as nothing compared with the humiliation of meeting Dan's grave stare, and seeing the curl of his lip at the repetition of her high-sounding phrase. As the quickest way of changing the conversation she suggested an adjournment to the morning-room, where mother sat busy over the eternal mending-basket, to broach the picnic project without delay.

Mother agreed instantly, eagerly, indeed, so that / there was something almost uncanny in the unusualness of the situation. To every demand, every suggestion came the unfailing, "Yes, darlings! Certainly, darlings!" Even the audacity of the double programme aroused no more notice than the remark that it was an admirable idea. Darsie, striking while the iron was hot, went a step farther and attacked the subject of lunch.

"Could we – for once – have something sub-stantialler than sandwiches? Chickens?" She gasped at the audacity of the request, for chickens were a state dish, reserved for occasions, and in summer for some inscrutable reasons just because they were smaller cost more than ever. "Chickens cut up are so easy to eat. We needn't have knives and forks. And little cobby dinner-rolls from the confectioner's, with crisp, browny crust, cut open and stuffed with butter and potted meat, and little green pieces of lettuce. They had them that way at supper at the Masons' party, and they were superb! And cakes and fruit! Do, mother, let us have a real swagger lunch just for once!"[18]

And mother said, "Yes, darling!" like a lamb, swallowing as it were spring chickens and cobby rolls at a gulp. It was impossible in giving the invitation to the Vernons to refrain from a hint at the magnificence of the preparations, though / good manners would, of course, have prompted silence on such a point.

The Vernons accepted with acclamation, all except Dan, who rudely declared that he "refused with pleasure," when Darsie bearded him in his den and proffered the invitation. He was seated at his desk, for the moment the only occupant of the workroom, and his manner was not expressive of welcome to the new-comer. He was a big, heavily built youth, with a face which was oddly attractive despite irregular features and a dull complexion. Dark eyes looked at you straight and square beneath bushy eyebrows; thin lips curved into the oddest, most expressive of lines, the square chin had a fashion of projecting until it seemed to become one of the most eloquent features in his face.

Close observation showed that there was a shadow of his upper lip, and rumour had it that he shaved, actually *shaved* every morning of his life. His huge hands had a grip of steel, but it was wonderful how deft and gentle they could be on occasion. Every album and collection in the house was labelled by Dan, indexed by Dan, embellished with ornamental flourishes and headlines, which Dan's big fingers alone had the power to produce. Now he leaned an elbow on the desk, turned round on his chair, and tilted that eloquent chin in scorn. /

"Picnic? Not much. Hate 'em like poison! You don't want me!"

"We *do* want you! We shouldn't have asked you if we didn't. Don't be unsociable, Dan. It's an extra special occasion, and it would be so much jollier to be complete. The boys will behave better if you're there."

Dan's chin tilted still an inch higher. That was of course, but –

"I hate a family crowd!" he pronounced tersely. "If there were only one or two, it wouldn't be so bad. Usual programme, I suppose – pick flowers and eat biscuits? Not much in my line – thank you all the same. Hope you'll have a good time!"

"We're going to have a *real* lunch – chickens and all sorts of good things, and walk to Oxholm across the fields. It will be much more exciting than the old picnics have been."

"It might easily be that! No, thank you, I'm off. Some other day –"

"But we want you, Dan! *I* want you to come."

"But *I* don't, you see. There's the difference. Sorry to disoblige."

Darsie regarded him silently, considered the point whether wrath or pathos would be the most powerful weapon, decided rapidly in favour of pathos, and sank with a sigh on to an opposite chair. /

"Very well. I *quite* understand. We wanted you especially because this may be the last, the very last time that one of us girls has any fun this summer, so of course it feels important. But you are so much older – it's natural that you shouldn't care. I think you've been very nice to be as much with us as you have been. . . . Dan!"

"Yes!"

"Hannah says it will be *me*! That Aunt Maria is sure to choose me when she comes. Do you think she will?"

"Ten to one, I should say."

"Oh, but why? *Why?* How can you be so sure?"

Dan's dark eyes surveyed the alert little head, poised on the stem of the graceful throat, his thin lips lengthened in the long, straight line which showed that he was trying not to smile.

"Because – er, you appear to me the sort of girl that an erratic old fossil would naturally prefer!"

"Ah-h!" – Darsie's dejection was deep – "Daniel, how cruel!" It was a comforting retaliation to address her tormentor by the name he so cordially disliked, but she remembered her rôle, and looked dejected rather than irate. "I suppose that's true. I *need* discipline, and she would naturally choose the worst of the three. / No one wants to be disciplined instead of having a good time, but it may be good for me in the end. All the time you are at sea, happy and free, I shall be being disciplined for my good. . . . Wednesday may be my last, my very last, glad day. . . ."

"Bah! Rubbish!" snapped Dan, but he looked at the curly head, and felt a pang of distaste. The idea of Darsie Garnett sobered and disciplined out of recognition was distinctly unpleasant. He wriggled in his chair, and said tentatively: "It will take more than one old lady to tame *you,* young woman! You'll have lots of fun yet – perhaps more than if you'd stayed at home."

Darsie smiled with angelic resignation.

"Perhaps so, but it won't be the same *kind* of fun. New friends can never be like old. If she chooses me, I must go, because of my duty to father and the rest, but it's going to *hurt!* I feel" – she waved her arms dramatically in the air – "like a flower that is being torn out by the roots! I shall not live long in a strange soil. . . . Well, goodbye, Dan; I won't bother you any more! Thank you very much for all you've done for me in the past."

Done! Dan searched his memory, found therein inscribed a number of snubs, rebuffs, and teasings, but nothing worthy of the thanks so sweetly offered. / He felt a stirring of reproach. Darsie was a decent kid – an amusing kid; if she went away she would leave behind her a decided blank. Looking back over the years, Darsie seemed to have played the leading part in the historic exploits of the family. She was growing into quite a big kid now. He glanced at her again quickly, furtively, and drummed with his fingers on the desk – hardly a kid at all, almost grown up!

"Oh, that's all right; don't worry about that," he mumbled vaguely. "What a grandiloquent kid you are! I hope you'll have a better time than you think, if you do go to visit your aunt."

"Thanks so much; I hope I may; and if at any time – *any* time – I can do anything to help you, or give you the least – the *very* least – pleasure, please let me know, Dan! I can understand now how one feels when one leaves home and faces the world!" said Darsie poignantly. "G-goodbye!"

"Bye," said Dan coolly. He leaned back in his chair, still thudding with his fingers on the desk. Darsie had reached the door and held it open in her hands before he spoke again. "What time did you say that blessed old picnic is to start?"

"Wednesday. Ten o'clock," said Darsie, and, like a true daughter of Eve, spoke not one more word, but shut the door and left him to his thoughts. /

"Dan's coming! You're not to say a word till the time, but he *is!*" she announced to her sisters that evening; but when they questioned and cross-questioned concerning the means whereby the miracle had been wrought, she steadfastly refused to satisfy their curiosity. That was not their concern. An inherent loyalty to Dan forbade that she should make public the wiles by which he had been beguiled. /

Chapter V

Left Behind!

WEDNESDAY dawned bright and fair; it had not seemed possible that it could be wet, and the party of twelve, with their baskets and hampers, drove economically and gaily to the ferry in a three-horse omnibus, so ostentatiously treating it as their own vehicle that the few alien passengers sat abashed, and plainly felt themselves *de trop*. Darsie's prophecy had been fulfilled, for Dan appeared at the starting-point, somewhat grim and sulky of demeanour, but obviously on picnic bent. He was the only member of the party whose hands were free of basket or bundle, and when the omnibus trundled into sight he walked forward to meet it and swung himself up to a place on top as though anxious to convince beholders that he had no connection with the noisy crowd at the corner, whereupon the two mothers smiled at each other in amused reminiscent fashion.

The girls were dressed in white; the boys wore / flannel trousers with school blazers and caps. Clemence had put on a veil to protect her complexion; plain Hannah's sailor hat left yards of forehead bleakly exposed. Darsie wore her little Kodak[19] swung across her shoulder in jaunty military fashion. She invariably carried a camera on such occasions, and never by any chance used it to take any photographs; the programme was so unalterable that it had ceased to attract any attention among her companions.

The omnibus conveyed the party to the ferry, from whence an hourly boat puffed several miles up the river to where the village of Earley stood on the opposite bank. It was an ancient and by no means luxurious barque, impregnated from bow to stern with a hot, oily, funnelly smell from which it was impossible to escape, and as travellers to Earley were almost invariably on pleasure bent, the usual satellites were in attendance. There was an old man in a long coat who had played the same ballads on the same old concertina with the same incredibly dirty fingers for as long as memory could recall; there was an old woman with a clean apron and a tray of gingerbread biscuits slung pendant from her shoulders, who presented them to you for three a penny, and exclaimed, "Bless yer little 'art!" when you paid for them yourself, because mother said it was a pity to spoil your lunch. Deary me! one *would* / have to be old to have one's appetite – and a picnic appetite at that! – spoiled by three gingerbread biscuits! The sail to Earley would have been shorn of one of its chief joys without these sticky sweets. The absence of the clean, smiling old woman would have been resented as a positive crime.

The ferry at Earley was an old-fashioned affair, sloping over the muddy shore to a little white pay-house with a clanky turnpike on either side. Once past these turnpikes, the visitor found himself in the midst of things with delightful suddenness. A wide green stretch of grass lay along the river bank, bordered by shady trees. To the right stood a stone hotel with gardens of brilliant flower-beds, and an array of white-covered tables dotted down the length of the veranda. Grand and luxurious visitors took their meals in the hotel, but such a possibility of splendour had never dawned upon the minds of the Garnetts or their friends – as well might a wayfarer in Hyde Park think of asking for a cup of tea at Buckingham Palace![20] To-day a young girl stood in the porch of the hotel and gazed at the procession as it passed. She was arrayed in a white serge coat and skirt, and wore a white sailor hat with a blue band. "Exactly like yours!" said Lavender easily, but Clemence shook her head in sad denial. *Her* coat and skirt had been bought / ready-made at a sale, was an inch too short in the waist, and cockled at the seams; her hat was last year's shape, while the girl in the porch had just – *the* – very – latest and most perfect specimen of both.

"Horrid thing, lunching in hotels in clothes like that! Some people have all the luck!" said Clemence grudgingly, as she moved the heavy basket from one hand to the other to screen it from the gaze of the aristocratic eyes; and the girl in the porch spied it all the same, and sighed to herself wistfully: "They are going picnicking – all those boys and girls! Oh, how lovely to be them. How I *wish* I were a big family . . ." after the manner of the ungrateful people of this world, who are so much occupied in envying the possessions of others that they have no time left in which to be thankful for their own!

The woods lay not a hundred yards from the ferry itself – real, natural, untrammelled woods, with grand old trunks standing up tall and straight like the columns of a cathedral, and dear old gnarled roots which ran along the ground, covered with lichens and soft green moss. To young people who spent their lives in one red-brick terrace looking out on another red-brick terrace across the road, it was like a voyage into fairyland to step within the cool, green shadow of the woods, to smell the sweet, sharp smell of the earth, / and watch the dapplings of sunlight through the leaves overhead. Even the boys succumbed to the spell, and for the first half-hour asked nothing better than to roll about on the grass, poke in the roots of trees, and speculate concerning rabbit-holes and nests; but the half-hour over, one and all were convinced that watches were wrong and they were right in deciding that it was beyond all manner of doubt full time for lunch; so the cloth was spread on a level piece of turf, and the good things were consumed with the lingering enjoyment which they deserved.

Every one felt that, as lunch marked what was perhaps the most enjoyable epoch of the whole day, it was his or her bounden duty to eat slowly and to go on demanding helpings so long as the supply endured; and a certain feeling of blankness descended when there was no longer any excuse for lingering, inasmuch as nothing remained to be eaten but a dozen jam puffs, which, as mother said, had been *meant* to be very nice, but had somehow failed to achieve success! The paste, hard enough on top, was inside of a damp and doughy consistence, and cook had used gooseberry jam for the filling, thereby taking a mean advantage of absence from home, when she *knew* that the family detested gooseberry in tarts, and steadily plumped for apricot instead.

"We'll give them to the little boy at the ferry. / *He* won't be so particular!" Mrs. Garnett said as she laid the rejected dainties on one side and proceeded to pack the oddments which had been required for the meal in one small basket, placing layers of paper in those left empty. The young people looked at each other with raised eyebrows as they watched these proceedings, the meaning of which they knew only too well. It was forbidden to gather roots from the woods, but no authority had dreamt of forbidding visitors to carry away *soil,* and this was just what Mrs. Garnett invariably insisted upon doing. The red-brown earth, rich with sweet fragments of leaf and twig, was too tempting to be resisted when she thought of her poor pot-bound plants at home; therefore, instead of swinging homewards with baskets light as air, the boys were doomed to bear even heavier weights than on the outward journey!

"Mother!" cried Clemence in a deep tone of protest. "Not *yet!* Remember the walk across the fields. Plenty of time to get soil in the Amphitheatre!" And Mrs. Garnett put down her trowel with quite a guilty air and resigned herself to wait.

"Well! Perhaps it would be best . . . Mrs. Vernon and I would like an hour's rest before going on. What are *you* going to do now?"

Every one waited for every one else, and no suggestion was forthcoming. The boys were once / more beginning to roll about on the grass, poking and pulling at each other in a manner which foretold the beginning of war. Clemence and Vi were gazing sentimentally through the branches. Plain Hannah, stretched flat along the ground, was barricading the movements of a tiny beetle, and chuckling over its persistent efforts to outwit her schemes. Dan sat with arms clasped around his knees, a picture of patience on a monument.[21] The sight of his twisted lips, his tilted, disconsolate chin fired Darsie to action. It was her doing that he was here at all; it was her duty to make the time pass as agreeably as possible.

"Sports!" she cried quickly. "Competitive sports. We'll each plan an event, and take them in turns. Dan shall be judge, and the one who gets most marks shall have a prize."

"What prize?"

That was a stumper. Darsie could suggest nothing better than a general subscription.

"If we each paid a penny entrance –"

"Oh, be bothered the pennies! I'll give a prize!" cried Dan loftily. Darsie saw with joy that he had brisked up at the prospect of sports and was already beginning to cast his eye around in professional manner, taking in the lie of the land, the outstanding features of the position. As judge and manager he was in his element, and each suggestion of an event was altered and / amended with a lordly superiority. It is somewhat difficult to introduce much variety into a programme of impromptu sports, but one or two of this afternoon's events had the advantage of novelty. A flower-gathering race, for instance, the object of which was to see how many varieties of wild flowers each competitor could gather in a given time, and a Roman water-carrier event, which consisted in balancing the hot-water jug on one's head and seeing how far one could walk without spilling its tepid contents over neck and shoulders. Plain Hannah was the only one of the girls who took part in this event, and to her joy succeeded in travelling a longer distance than any of the male competitors. The final and most elaborate event was the obstacle race, without which no competition of the kind is ever considered complete, and the united wits of the company were put to work to devise traps for their own undoing. Harry discovered two small trees whose trunks grew so close together that it seemed impossible that any human creature could squeeze between, and insisted upon it being done as a *sine qua non*.[22] Russell decreed that competitors should travel over a certain route without touching the ground, swinging themselves from branch to branch like so many monkeys, and as girls were plainly disqualified for this feat an alternative test was invented which should score / equally to their credit. Hopping races, races complicated by arithmetical and other such baffling problems, were also devised, and at the last moment Darsie came forward with a thrilling novelty.

"Run to the hamper, turn round three times, seize a jam puff, eat it in two bites, and hop back to the goal!"

"Good!" cried the judge approvingly, and after that the competitors might storm and lament as they would; the event was fixed!

The two mothers had retired from the scene of the fray and with backs resting against two friendly trees were peacefully discoursing on household trials; there was no one to preach concerning indigestion, and the perils of rapid eating; hot and gasping from their previous trials, the competitors ran, twirled, hopped and gobbled, and finally subsided in paroxysms of laughter on the mossy bank. The sports were over; the prize had fallen to Russell, as every one had known from the start that it must inevitably do; he sat snoring with pride, waving aside Dan's inquiries as to the nature of his prize in a gentlemanly manner worthy of his reputation, until the two mothers, becoming conscious that the afternoon was passing away, rose heavily from their seats and announced that it was time to start on the second half of the day's expedition. /

The three-mile walk lay for three parts of the way through fields, which to the town-livers afforded a refreshing change from noisy and dusty streets, and when the little village was reached, "our old woman's cottage" was found to be as clean and neat and hospitably attractive as of yore. It was a tiny whitewashed cottage standing back from the lane in a garden bright with old-fashioned flowers, and the stone-floored kitchen boasted an old oak dresser and table which were the envy of all beholders.

"They're always after it!" our old woman would announce, chuckling. "Titled gentry I've had, driving up in their own carriage, a-coaxing and wheedling so as never was. '*No*,' I says, they was my mother's afore me, and her mother's afore that, and it's a poor tale if I can't have the pleasure of them while *I* live! If it's waluable to you, it's waluable to me, too. That's only common sense. . . .' And what's your fancy today, lovies? biled eggs and buttered toast, same as afore?"

Boiled eggs and buttered toast it was, despite the protests of the mothers, who thought that really, after such a lunch –! And after tea our old woman provided buttonholes for each member of the party, and hobbled to the gate to see them off, assuring them, as was her yearly custom, that "the gamekeepers was getting very crusty of late, but / you leave the roots alone and nobody can't say nothing about a few bits of flowers." That yearly threat of the gamekeeper lent a *soupçon* of excitement to the scramble over the sloping woods, which surrounded as an amphitheatre a deep green meadow through which meandered a tiny stream.

At any moment, as it appeared, a stalwart figure in velveteen bearing a gun over his shoulder might appear round the trunk of a tree, demanding your licence or your life. It was interesting to discuss exactly what you would do or say under the circumstances, and the very worst thing in punishments which could possibly be your fate!

To-day, however, no such interruption took place, and the dear old play-ground looked, if possible, more beautiful than ever. The ground was carpeted with buttercups, and when one stood on the top of the steep banks and looked down on the green and the gold, and caught glimpses of the blue sky beyond – well, it was as near an approach to fairyland as one could hope to find within twenty miles of a big manufacturing town.

Mrs. Garnett packed her basket full of the soft, loamy soil; the girls roamed up and down making up bouquets of wild roses, honeysuckle, and fragrant meadowsweet; the boys were blissfully happy, risking life and limb in an exciting endeavour to travel from top to bottom of the bank without once touching grass. An occasional tree-trunk / was permitted as a foothold, otherwise you swung yourself from one branch to another, or took flying leaps into space, and trusted to fate to catch hold of something before you fell.

Russell's hairbreadth escapes would have terrified his mother had she been there to see, but the boys were wise in their generation and had quietly worked their way round to the opposite bank before beginning their experiments. It took a considerable time to call them back and rally forces in time to catch the eight o'clock train, and it was a dishevelled and by no means aristocratic-looking party which climbed over the high stone stile leading into the high-road.

It seemed hard luck that this last mile, when every one was feeling tired and a trifle flat, should have to be traversed along a dusty, uninteresting road, and the straggly line grew even farther and farther apart as the distance to the station decreased. Dan led the way, walking in the middle of the road, his head flung back with the old proud air of detachment. The two mothers plodded steadily in the rear. Russell, scratched and dusty, and looking more like a street arab than a youth renowned for gentlemanly demeanour, scuffled in the gutter, kicking up the gathered dust which enveloped him as in a cloud; Harry and John bore the big hamper slung on a stick, the ends of which they frequently released for the / purpose of straightening their backs and rubbing their tired hands. Plain Hannah limped on the sideway, being afflicted with corns which, as she expressed it, always "came on" at the end of a day's pleasuring. Vi and Clemence, arm-in-arm, were deep in sentimental conclave. Darsie, the last of the line, hung back of intent until a curve in the road hid the others from sight. A shadow of melancholy had descended upon her spirit during the last hour; that fear of "the last time" which at times makes cowards of us all,[23] was strong upon her; the possibility of separation suddenly became a terror which gripped her breath and left her faint and weak.

Mother – Father – Home! The dear delights of the sea. Could she – could she *bear* to give them up? Darsie whimpered miserably, and stopped short in the middle of the road to pull out her handkerchief, and wipe a threatening tear. She really did not think she could, and yet every one seemed to take it for granted that Aunt Maria's choice would fall upon herself. Was there nothing, nothing that she could do to lessen the probability? Nothing to make herself look ugly, unattractive, unsuited for the post of lady's companion?

A stranger walking along the high-road at this moment would have been amused to see a pretty, disconsolate-looking young girl deliberately twisting / her features into one grimace after another, and critically examining the effect in the back of a small silver watch. Every new grimace necessitated a pause for inspection, so that the distance between Darsie and her companions increased more and more, until on turning the next corner of the winding road she was surprised to find no one in sight – surprised and a trifle startled, for the early dusk was already casting its shadow over the landscape, and the solitude of a country road has in it something eerie to a lifelong dweller in towns. Darsie forgot her grimaces and set off at a trot to make up lost ground, and even as she ran a sound came from afar which quickened the trot into a run – the scream of an engine! the engine of the approaching train which was to bear the picnickers back to town.

The next turn of the road showed that the rest of the party had taken alarm also, for the flying figures of Vi and Clemence could be seen disappearing in the distance, evidently following hastily after those in front.

"They'll catch it – they'll rush down the steps just as it's going to start, bundle in anyhow, into different carriages – never miss me – go off, never know I'm not there till they get out!" These thoughts rushed through Darsie's head as she ran gaspingly along the dusty road. It was imperative that she must catch up to her friends – to be / left behind, without a penny in her pocket to buy a ticket, would be too awful for words. The shriek of the engine had given place to a repeated snort which was momentarily growing slower and less pronounced; the train was slackening speed before drawing up at the platform.

Faster! Faster! One rush to reach the goal! Darsie set her teeth and put on a last desperate spurt, caught her foot on an outstanding stone of the roadway, and fell heavily to the ground. /

Chapter VI

Dan to the Rescue

THERE were no bones broken; she was not seriously hurt; but one has to try for oneself the experiment of running at full tilt, and while so doing to pitch forward at full length on the ground, to realize how extremely disagreeable and disconcerting it can be. Darsie dragged herself slowly to a sitting position, and sat dazed and stupefied, a forlorn, dust-encrusted figure, with hat tilted rakishly on one side, and the palm of her right hand scratched to bleeding where it had dragged along the stony ground.

She blinked and stared, and mechanically brushed at her blackened skirts, but it was several moments before remembrance of her position returned to her brain, and with it the realization of the consequences of delay. She scrambled to her feet, ran forward for a few paces, and stopped short with a sharp groan of pain. She had bruised her knees as well as her hand, and the rapid movement was quite startlingly painful; she fell into a limp, / straining her head upwards to peep over the hedgerow at the road beyond. And then, clear and distinct after the interval of silence, came another sharp whistle, another laborious puff, puff, puff.

The train was leaving the station, and she was left behind!

Darsie stopped short, and leaned against the hedge. There was no longer any need to hurry. Either her absence had been discovered or it had not, and a

few minutes' time would settle that question once for all. It soothed her to pretend that there was a chance that she might find some one waiting her arrival
on the platform, but at the bottom of her heart she had little hope of such a
possibility. As members of a large family whose parents were not rich enough
to pay for the modern plethora of nurses and governesses, the Garnetts and
Vernons had been brought up to be independent, and to fend for themselves,
hence the two mothers would not be so anxious to count the number of their
brood, to see that each member was safe and sound, as would have been the
parents of smaller, more indulged families.

There would be a rush for tickets, a hurried glance around on emerging from
the office, the signal of waving hands, and bobbing heads from half a dozen windows, a quick leap into the nearest seats, and off they would all steam, panting
and puffing, congratulating themselves on their escape. /

No, Darsie told herself, it was stupid to pretend; certainly, quite certainly she
was left behind; nevertheless, when two or three minutes later she reached the
top of the railway bridge and peered over the stone wall, it was with quite a big
pang of dismay that she beheld the empty platform. Not a soul! Not a single soul
except a cross-looking porter sitting astride a barrow, with his hands thrust into
his trousers pockets.

Anything less promising in the shape of a forlorn hope it would be difficult
to imagine, but the circumstances offered no alternative. Darsie took her courage in both hands and marched boldly towards him.

"Please will you tell me the time of the next train from town?"

The porter rolled his eye sideways, surveyed her up and down, formed an
evidently poor opinion, and without a change of position muttered a curt reply –

"Ten-thirty."

"Ten-thirty!" Dismay at the lateness of the hour struggled with wounded
pride at the man's lack of respect. Half-past ten before any one could come to
the rescue; three long hours of chill and darkness, with no one to speak to, and
nowhere to go! Darsie threw the thought aside with the impetuous incredulity
of youth.

"When's the next train to town?" /

"Nine-ten."

"That was better! Nine-ten. If she could manage to travel by that train she
would arrive at the terminus in abundance of time to prevent any one starting
by the next stopping train. It was all easy – perfectly easy, except for the want of
a miserable eightpence, but, alas! for the moment eightpence seemed as inac-
cessible as eighty pounds. Darsie bent a scrutinizing glance upon the porter's
downcast face. "He looks about as disagreeable as he can be, but he's a human
creature; he must have *some* heart! Perhaps he's in trouble, too, and it's soured

his disposition. It would mine! I just *hate* it when things go wrong. I don't in the least see why I shouldn't have a ticket on account! I'll see what I can do."

She coughed and ventured tentatively –

"I missed the last train."

"Did ye!" said the porter coldly. It was not a question; there was no flicker of the interest of a question in his voice, only a dreary indifference which seemed to demand what in the world you were thinking of to trouble him about a stupidity which had happened twenty times a day throughout twenty years of his service on the line. Darsie drew herself up with a feeling of affront. He was a rude, ill-mannered man, who ought to be taught how to speak to ladies in distress. She would ask her father to complain to the railway! / What were porters paid for but to make themselves useful to passengers? She drew herself up in haughty fashion, then as suddenly collapsed as her eye rested on her dusty boots and blackened, bloodstained skirt. Ridiculous to act the grand lady with such handicaps as these! She drew a sharp breath, and said in a voice of childlike appeal –

"I'm left behind! My friends have gone on. It's very awkward!"

"Are ye?" asked the porter indifferently. He took one hand out of his pocket and pointed woodenly to the right. "Waiting-room first door. Ye can sit there!"

Of all the callous, cold-blooded –! Darsie turned with a swing and marched forward into the bleak little cell which had the audacity to call itself a first-class waiting-room, seated herself on a leather-covered bench which seemed just the most inhospitable thing in the way of furniture which the mind of man could conceive, and gave herself up to thought. Never, never so long as she lived would she ever again leave home without some money in her pocket! How in the name of all that was mysterious could she contrive to possess herself of eightpence within the next hour? "Our old woman" would lend it with pleasure, but Darsie shrank from the idea of the darkening country road with the dread of the town-dweller / who in imagination sees a tramp lurking behind every bush. No, this first and most obvious suggestion must be put on one side, and even if she could have humbled herself to beg from the porter, Darsie felt an absolute conviction that he would refuse. At the farther side of the station there stretched a small straggling village. Surely somehow in that village –! With a sudden inspiration Darsie leaped to her feet and approached the porter once more. Into her mind had darted the remembrance of the manner in which poor people in books possessed themselves of money in critical moments of their history.

"Porter, will you please tell me the way to the nearest pawnshop?"

"P-p – !" Now, indeed, if she had wished to rouse the porter to animation, she had succeeded beyond her wildest dreams! He spun round, and gaped at her with a stupefaction of surprise. "PAWNshop, did ye say? P-awn! What do *you* want with a pawnshop, a slip of a girl like you?"

"That's my business!" returned Darsie loftily. Since he had been so unsympathetic and rude, she was certainly not going to satisfy his curiosity. Her dear little watch would provide her with money, and somehow – she didn't understand why – pawnbrokers gave things back after paying for them, in the most amiable and engaging of fashions. / "That's my business! If you would kindly direct me –"

"We haven't got no pawnshop," said the porter gruffly. He stared at her slowly up and down, down and up, appeared to awake to a suspicious interest, and opined gruffly, "You'd better go 'ome!"

"Just what I'm trying to do," sighed poor Darsie to herself. She turned and went slowly back to her leather seat, and a second disconsolate review of the situation. In time to come this experience would rank as an adventure, and became an oft-told tale. She would chill her listeners with hints of The Tramp, evoke shrieks of laughter at her imitation of the porter. Darsie realized the fact, but for the moment it left her cold. Summer evenings have a trick of turning chill and damp after the sun is set, and the vault-like waiting-room was dreary enough to damp the highest spirits. *How was she going to obtain that eightpence for a ticket?*

The station clock struck nine; the porter took a turn along the platform and peered curiously through the dusty window; a luggage train rattled slowly past, an express whizzed by with thunderous din. The station clock struck the quarter, and still the problem was as far as ever from solution.

"Well," sighed Darsie miserably, "I must just wait. I'm perished with cold already. In two / more hours I shall be frozen. Rheumatic fever, I suppose, or galloping decline. It will settle Aunt Maria, that's *one* good thing! but it's hard all the same, in the flower of my youth! To think of all that a human creature can suffer for the sake of a miserable eightpence!"

She got up stiffly and pressed her face against the pane. People were beginning to assemble for the nine-ten. An old man with a satchel of tools, two old women with baskets. "The poor are always generous to the poor. Suppose I ask them? Twopence three farthings each would not kill them!" But when one is not used to begging, it is extraordinary how difficult it is to begin. Darsie tried to think of the words in which she would proffer her request, and blushed in discomfort. No! she *could* not. Of the two disagreeables it really seemed easier to shiver two hours, and retain one's pride intact, and then, suddenly, the door of the waiting-room opened with a bang, and Dan's heavy figure stood on the threshold!

The cry of delight, of breathless incredulity with which Darsie leaped to her feet, must have been heard to the end of the platform. She rushed forward, clutched his arm, and hugged it fast in the rapture of relief.

"Oh, Dan – you angel – you angel! Have you dropped down straight from the skies?" /

"Not I! Nothing so easy. Scorched along bad roads on a rickety machine. Would you be kind enough to let go my arm and stop shrieking! You'll have the whole village here in a moment. So *you're* all right, I see! Sitting quietly here, after scaring us half out of our wits –"

"I think *I'm* the one to be scared! You were all ready enough to go on, and leave me stranded by myself. I've gone through a martyrdom. Dan! tell me, when did you miss me first?"

Dan gave an expressive grimace. He looked hot and dusty, and thankful to sit down on the. leather bench.

"Well, it was too much of a scrimmage to think of anything for the first few miles, but things have a way of printing themselves on one's brain, and when I *did* begin to think, there seemed something missing! I remembered Vi's face – the colour of a beetroot, and Clemence limping in the rear. I remembered John and Russell hauling up Hannah by her arms, and the two mothers were safely in their carriage – I'd made sure of that, but – I couldn't remember a thing about *you!* Then I asked Vi, and she said you were a long way behind, and I began to guess what had happened. At the first stop I did a rush round, and – there you weren't! So of course I came back."

"But how – how? There was no train. Did you cycle? Where did you get your machine?" /

"Borrowed him from the stationmaster, and left my watch in exchange, in case I never went back. Jolly good exchange for him, too. It's the worst machine I ever rode, and that's saying a good deal. I told your mother I'd bring you back all right, and persuaded her to go home. What on earth possessed you to be such a muff?"[24]

Darsie tossed her head, gratitude giving place to wounded pride.

"Muff, indeed! You don't know what you are talking about, or you wouldn't be so unkind. I ran like the rest, but I fell – caught my foot on something, and fell on my face. I believe I fainted." There was an irrepressible note of pride in her voice as she made this last statement, for fainting, being unknown in the healthy Garnett family, was regarded as a most interesting and aristocratic accomplishment. "I do believe I fainted, for for several minutes I didn't know where I was. And I hurt myself, too; look at my hand!"

Dan looked and whistled.

"Skinned it properly, haven't you! Reminds me of the days of my youth. Better sponge it clean with your handkerchief and some of that water. And when you *did* remember, the train had gone –"

"Yes – and not another until after ten, and not a halfpenny in my pocket to buy a ticket, and no one but a callous wretch of a porter to consult. / Oh, Dan, I *was* wretched – I'll bless you all my life for coming back like this!"

"Rot!" said Dan briskly. "I was the only man. Couldn't do anything else. I say, you know, it was your doing that I came to this blessed old picnic at all, and you *have* let me in for a day! Eleven to eleven before we've done with it – twelve solid hours! I've had about as much picnic as I want for the rest of my natural life."

"I'm sorry. I thought it would be so nice. I'm sorry I bothered you, Dan."
Darsie was tired and cold, in a condition of physical depression which made her
peculiarly sensitive to a slighting mood. She leaned her head against the ugly
wall, and shut her lids over her smarting eyes. Her cheeks were white. Her lips
quivered like a wearied child's, but she made a charming picture all the same, her
inherent picturesqueness showing itself even in this moment of collapse.

Dan's gaze grew first sympathetic, then thoughtful, as he looked. In a dim,
abstract way he had been conscious that Darsie Garnett was what he would have
described as "a pretty kid," but the charm of her personality had never appealed
to him until this moment. Now, as he looked at the dark eyelashes resting on the
white cheek, the droop of the curved red lips, the long, slim throat that seemed
to-night almost too frail to support the golden head, a feeling of tenderness
stirred at / his heart. She was such a tiny scrap of a thing, and she had been tired
and frightened. What a brute he was to be so gruff and ungracious!

"Buck up, Darsie! Only ten minutes more to wait. I'll get you a cup of coffee
when we arrive. Your mother said we were to take a cab, so all the worry's over
and nothing but luxury ahead."

But Darsie, quick to note the soothing effect of her prostration, refused to
"buck up," and looked only more worn and pathetic than before. The opportunity of lording it over Dan was too precious to be neglected, so she blinked at
him with languid eyes, and said faintly –

"I'll try, but I'm so *very* tired! Do you think you could talk to me, Dan, and
amuse me a little bit? That would pass the time. Tell me about yourself, and all
you are going to do when you go up to Cambridge."

And to his own astonishment Dan found himself responding to her request.
His was one of the silent, reserved natures which find it difficult to speak of the
subjects which lie nearest to the heart, but even silent people have their moments
of expansion, and when once Dan had broken the ice, he found it unexpectedly
easy to talk, with Darsie's big eyes fixed on his in eloquent understanding.

She was a capital little listener; never interrupted at the wrong moment,
indulged in senseless ejaculations, or fidgety, irritating movement. Nothing /
about her moved, hardly even the blue eyes, so fixed and absorbed was their gaze,
while Dan spoke in low, rapid tones of the course of work which lay ahead, of the
ambitions and dreams which were to crown his efforts. He must take first-class
honours at Cambridge; nothing less than first-class honours would do – honours so distinguished that he would have no difficulty in obtaining a good post
as schoolmaster to tide him over the next few years. "Teaching's the thing for me
– for it leaves four months over for my own work, the real work of my life – scientific study and research! That's the only thing worth living for from my point
of view, and I shall plump for that. I don't care for money, I don't want to marry,
I'd be content to make enough to keep body and soul together, if I could only

help on the cause of humanity. I am not going up to Cambridge for two years. I can do better grinding quietly at home, and the governor doesn't mind. In fact, he is just as well pleased to think I shall have more time to run when Hannah goes up to Newnham."[25]

Darsie drew her breath sharply.

"Oh, Dan! how fortunate you are – how fortunate Hannah is, to be able to do as you like! I would give my ears to go up to Newnham, too, but father says it's impossible. He can't afford it with the boys' education getting more expensive / every year. I shall have to stay at home, and turn into a miserable morning governess, teaching wretched little kids to read, and taking them for a walk round the park. Oh, oh! it makes me *ill* to think about it."

Dan laughed shortly.

"Excuse me! it makes you well. You look quite like yourself again. I'll give you a bit of advice if you like: don't believe that anything's impossible in this world, because it isn't! Put the nursery governess idea out of your mind, and fire ahead for Newnham. There's always the chance of a scholarship, and even if that didn't come off, who can tell what may happen in three years' time? The way may clear in a dozen ways; it probably *will* clear, if you get ready yourself. There are precious few things one can't gain by steady slogging ahead."

Darsie looked at him with a kindling glance, her lips set, a spot of red showed on either cheek.

"Right!" she said briefly, and at that moment the train steamed into the station and the conference was at an end. /

Chapter VII

Aunt Maria's Choice

AUNT Maria arrived on Tuesday night, bringing "my woman" in attendance. She was more like a parrot than ever, for her face had grown narrower, her nose bigger, and the roundness of her eyes was accentuated by gold-rimmed spectacles. When a richly coloured Paisley shawl was drawn tightly over her sloping shoulders the resemblance was positively startling to behold, and the terrors of an eight-weeks visit loomed larger than ever before the minds of the Garnett sisters.

The extraordinary thing was that Aunt Maria seemed to take no notice of the girls, whom, as everybody was aware, she had come to inspect. She talked to father, she talked to mother, she cross-questioned the boys as to their progress at school and expressed regret that they had not done better; she displayed an intelligent interest in the neighbours, the servants, and the new dining-room rug, but for the three daughters of the house / she had not a word, hardly, it was believed, a glance.

In the presence of such utter indifference it was impossible to keep up the various rôles which each girl had privately practised with the view of concealing her charms and diverting Aunt Maria's attention from herself. Clemence had decided that rounded shoulders and a lurching gait were defects which at seventeen threatened a painful permanence, and had therefore lurched persistently throughout the first evening, since which time she had slowly but steadily recovered her natural gait.

After long practice before the mirror Darsie had decided that an open mouth and falling under-jaw could work marvels in the way of stupidity of expression, and had nerved herself to sit agape for the period of forty-eight hours. Lavender had decided to sulk. "Every one hates sulks! It would be better to live alone on a desert island than with a person who sulks. I'll sulk, and she won't be paid to have me!" So one sister had sulked and the other gaped the whole of that first long evening, and then, becoming increasingly freed from their fears, began to smile secretly across the table, to nod and to nudge, to telegraph messages in the silent but eloquent fashions to which members of a large family resort when visitors are present and talking is not allowed. And Aunt Maria munched her food, and wrapped / the Paisley shawl more closely round her shoulders, and cast not a glance to right or left! A blissful possibility was broached that she had changed her mind, and did not desire a visitor after all!

Wednesday and Thursday passed in increasing calm, but on Friday morning certain alarming symptoms became visible. Mrs. Garnett came to breakfast with unmistakable signs of agitation upon her face. Mr. Garnett was silent and distrait, hid behind his newspaper, and answered at random the remarks of his family. Late arrivals were allowed to pass without reproach, and Tim's raids upon the marmalade received no further protest than a flickering smile.

The die was cast! The girls knew it without a word; in a stupor of misery they sat, ears cocked, hearts in their boots, waiting for a sign which should betray the truth, and decide once for all the identity of the victim.

It came at last, towards the end of the meal, in the midst of a ghastly silence.

"Darsie, darling," said Mrs. Garnett fondly, "won't you have some more coffee?"

"*Darling!*" Never were Mrs. Garnett's north-country lips known to use that term except under stress of the most poignant emotion. To be "darling" one was compelled to be very ill, very sad, angelically repentant, or in an extremity of fear, and Darsie, who this morning was not / afflicted in any one of these three ways, realized in a flash the awful significance of the term. She sat white and silent, too dazed for speech, and to do them justice Clemence and Lavender looked almost as perturbed as herself, relief on their own account being eclipsed for the moment by a realization of the loss which the holiday party was about to sustain. With a sudden and uninvited humility each sister mentally acknowledged that for the general good of the family it would have been better had the choice fallen upon herself!

Darsie braced her feet against a leg of the table, and struggled with a lump in her throat. Coffee? she never wanted to drink any more coffee so long as she lived! The sight, the smell of it would be for ever associated with this ghastly moment. She turned big, woeful eyes on her mother's face and stammered a breathless inquiry:

"Mother, you have something to say! Please say it. Don't break it to me, please; it's worse to wait. Say it bang out!"

"Oh, Darsie, darling; yes, darling, it *is* as you suppose! Aunt Maria has chosen you. She wants you to start with her on Saturday morning, but if it's too soon – if you would rather stay over Sunday, I will arrange . . ."

Darsie bit her lips in the desperate resolve not to cry, but to carry off the situation with a high air.

"If I'm to go at all, I'd rather go at once, / and get it over. There's nothing to be gained by delay. 'Better to die by sudden shock than perish piecemeal on the rock.'"[26]

"But you will want to say goodbye to your friends, dear; you will have little arrangements to make. . . ." Mrs. Garnett was all nervousness and anxiety to appease, but after the manner of victims Darsie felt a perverse satisfaction in rejecting overtures, even when by so doing she doubly punished herself.

"I don't mean to say goodbye. I don't wish to see any one before I go. I hate scenes."

"Well, well! just as you please, dear. After all, it is for a very short time. Eight weeks will soon pass."

Silence. Every youthful face at the table was set in an eloquent declaration that eight weeks was an eternity, a waste, a desert of space. Mr. Garnett put down his newspaper and hurriedly left the room. He had the usual male horror of scenes, and, moreover, Darsie was his special pet, and his own nerves were on edge at the thought of the coming separation. If the child cried or appealed to him for protection, he would not like to say what he might do. Flight appeared to be his safest course, but Darsie felt a pang of disappointment and wounded love at this desertion of her cause, and the smart did not help to improve her temper. /

"Aunt Maria wishes to see you, dear, as soon as you have finished your breakfast," continued Mrs. Garnett, elaborately conciliatory. "Father and I are very grateful to her for her interest in you, but you know, dear, how we feel about losing you, how we sympathize with your disappointment! We are convinced that in the end this chance will be for your benefit; but in the meantime it is very hard. We are sorry for you, dear."

"And I," declared Darsie coldly, "am sorry for Aunt Maria!"

She pushed back her chair and stalked out of the room, while her brothers and sisters stared after her agape. Along the narrow oilclothed hall[27] she went, up the steep, narrow staircase to the little third-floor bedroom, the only place on earth which was her very own. There was nothing luxurious about it, nothing of any intrinsic value or beauty, but in the eyes of its occupant every separate article was a pearl of price. All her treasures were here – her pictures, her ornaments, her books, mementoes of journeyings, offerings of friends. It was a shrine, a refuge from the cold outer world. Alone in "my room" one lost the insignificance of a member of a large family, and became a responsible human being face to face with personal trials and responsibilities. . . .

Eight weeks out of a life! To the adult mind a / sacrifice of so short a period may be a disappointment, but can hardly be deemed a trial; to schoolgirl fifteen it may seem a catastrophe which clouds the whole horizon. To Darsie Garnett the change of plan was the first real sorrow of her life, and these moments of reflection were full of a suffocating misery. Anticipated joys rose before her with intolerable distinctness. She saw her companions happily at play, and felt a stabbing dart of jealousy. Yes, they would forget all about her and feel no loss from her absence! Clemence and Vi would enjoy their *tête-à-tête,* would be unwilling to admit a third into their conferences at her return. Dan would take them for boating and fishing expeditions. Dan would grow to like Clemence better than herself! Darsie gave a little sob of misery at the thought. She had no sentimental feelings as regards Dan, or any one else at this period of her life, but as the one *big* boy, almost man, of her acquaintance Dan stood on a pedestal by himself as a lofty and superior being, whose favour was one of the prizes of life. That Dan should become more intimate, more friendly with Clemence and Lavender than with herself was a possibility fraught with dismay.

Darsie sobbed again, but her eyes were dry; she was angry, too angry to cry; her heart was seething with rebellion. Some one knocked at the door and received no answer, knocked again / and was curtly ordered to "go away"; then Mr. Garnett's voice spoke, in gentle and conciliatory tones –

"It's father! Let me in, dear; I've just a minute. . . ."

It was impossible to refuse such a request. Darsie opened the door, and there he stood, tall and thin, with the embarrassed *boy* look upon his face which always made him seem especially near to his children. It was the look he wore when they were in trouble and he essayed to lecture and advise, and it seemed to say, "I've been there myself; I understand! Now it's my part to play the heavy father, but *I'm not nearly so much shocked as I pretend!*" To-day his manner was frankly commiserating.

"Well, Kiddie, dear! I was running off to town like a coward, but at the last moment I was obliged to come up for a word. It's hard lines for you, dear, and I

want you to know that it's hard lines for me, too! The country won't be half so
jolly as if we'd all been together. I'll miss you *badly*, little lass!"

"*Don't!* I'll howl. *Don't* make me howl!" pleaded Darsie hastily, the tight feeling about her eyes and lips giving place to an alarming weepiness at the sound of
the tender words. "If you really care, father, couldn't you – couldn't you possibly
refuse?" /

Mr. Garnett shook his head.

"No! That's settled. We talked it over, mother and I, and agreed that it must
be done. It's a duty, dear, and we can't shelve duties in this life. I'm sorry for you
in your disappointment, and only wish I could help, but in this matter no one
can help but yourself. You can do a lot if you try. Shall I tell you, Darsie, how
you could get over your regret, and turn your visit to Arden[28] into something far
more agreeable than you can now imagine?"

Darsie cocked an eye at him, suspicious and hesitating. He was going to
preach! She knew the symptoms of old, and by way of counteraction put on her
most dour and sullen expression.

"Um!"

"Very well, then, here it is! Turn your back on the might-have-been, and
try with all your might to like what *is!* Aunt Maria will, I know, be all that is
kind and indulgent – in her own way! It won't be *your* way, however, and that's
the rub. If you begin your visit in a spirit of irritation, I'm afraid you are going
to have a pretty poor time, but if you try to enjoy every little thing that comes
along out of which enjoyment can be squeezed and to *laugh* at the rest, to laugh
instead of to cry – well, it's astonishing how the scene will change! Do you think
you could try?" /

Darsie pouted, sulky and unconvinced.

"Were *you* resigned when you were fifteen?"

"No, my lassie! I wasn't, indeed. Very far from it, I'm sorry to say. But when
one has travelled on for many years and come many a cropper on the way one
does long to show one's children the short cuts! That's *one* short cut, Darsie; I
wish you'd take it, and avoid the falls. If you can't have what you like, try to like
what you have. Expect good, not evil. Say to yourself every morning: 'This is
going to be a good day, a happy day, one of the happiest days of my life,' and
then you are half-way towards making it so. Poor little Kiddie! it sounds hard,
but try it – try it – and occasionally, just for a change, forget that you are Darsie
Garnett for five minutes or so at a time, and pretend instead that you are Maria
Hayes! Pretend that you are old and lonely and ailing in health, and that there's
a young girl staying with you from whom you are hoping to enjoy some brightness and variety! Eh? The other morning in church you were beside me when we
were singing 'Fight the good fight!'[29] You sang it heartily, Darsie; I enjoyed your
singing.... I thought you looked as if you really meant the words. Well, here's the

battlefield for you, dear! Are you going to play coward? I don't believe it. I think better of my girl!" /

He laid his hand on her shoulder with a caressing touch. Darsie wriggled and screwed up her little nose in eloquent grimace, but when the hand crept up to her chin she lifted her face for the farewell kiss, and even volunteered an extra one on her own account on the dear, thin cheek.

Mr. Garnett smiled contentedly to himself as he descended the staircase. Darsie had made no promises, but he was satisfied that his words had not been in vain. And Darsie, left alone in her room, fell instinctively to repeating the words of the grand old hymn –

"Run the straight race through God's good grace, Lift up thine eyes, and seek His Face...."[30]

A little sob punctuated the lines. To the blind eyes of earth the straight race appeared so very very crooked! /

Chapter VIII

First Days

DARSIE left home on the following Thursday, and in company with Aunt Maria and "my woman" took train for Arden, in Buckinghamshire. The journey was a nightmare, for Lady Hayes disliked travelling, and was in a condition of nervousness, which made her acutely susceptible to the doings of her companions. Within an hour of starting Darsie had been admonished not to sit facing the engine because of the draught, not to look out of the window in case she got a cinder in her eye, not to read in case she strained her eyes, not to rub her fingers on the pane, not to cross her knees because it was unladylike, not to shout, not to mumble, not to say "What?" not to yawn without putting her finger over her mouth, &c., &c., &c.

Being called to account so frequently was an exhausting process, and Darsie felt a thrill of joy at the announcement of lunch. A meal in a train would be a novel and exciting experience / which would go far towards making up for the dullness of the preceding hour, but alas! Aunt Maria refused with scorn to. partake of food, cooked goodness knew how, by goodness knew whom, and had supplied herself with a few Plasmon biscuits,[31] the which she handed round with the information that they contained more nourishment than ounces of beefsteak. They were very dull and very dry, however, and Darsie managed to get a crumb down the wrong way, and coughed continuously for the next hour in a tickling, aggravating manner, while Aunt Maria reiterated, "Really, my dear! *Most* unpleasant!" and seemed to consider herself personally aggrieved.

When Arden was reached the position improved, for stationmaster and porters alike flew to hover round the great lady of the neighbourhood, and Darsie sunned herself in the novel consciousness of importance. Outside the station a cart was waiting for luggage, and a large, old-fashioned barouche[32] with two fat brown horses, and with two brown-liveried servants upon the box. The village children bobbed curtsies as the carriage bowled through the village street, and Darsie smiled benignly and bent her yellow head in gracious acknowledgment. As niece and guest of the Lady of the Towers, these greetings were surely partly intended for herself. She felt an exhilarating glow of complacence, and determined to describe the / scene to Vi Vernon on the earliest possible opportunity.

The Towers was a large, very ugly, stucco house, surrounded by a beautiful rolling park. Inside, the rooms were huge and square, and one and all characterized by a depressing pitch of orderliness, which made it almost impossible to believe that they could be used as ordinary human habitations!

Darsie was escorted to a bedroom with ponderous mahogany furniture, so complete a contrast from her own shabby, cheery little den that the sight of it added the final touch to her depression. She refreshed herself by a long splash in hot water, brushed out her tangled mane, put on her Sunday dress, and descended in state to partake of dinner, which was served an hour earlier than usual in consideration of the travellers hunger and fatigue.

Despite her weariness and nervous exhaustion, Lady Hayes had made what appeared to Darsie's unsophisticated eyes a magnificent toilette for the meal, and she eyed the Sunday frock with a criticism which was anything but approving. "But it's the best I've got, except the party one, and I can't wear that for one old lady," said Darsie to herself as she followed meekly behind the *moire antique*[33] train, and seated herself at the end of the dining-table. Two men-servants stood at attention – two! one for each diner, solemn, immovable-looking / creatures who seemed to move on wheels and who kept their eyes glued upon every mouthful you ate, ready to pounce upon your plate and nip it swiftly and noiselessly away. They were stricken with dumbness also, if you were to trust the evidence of your senses, but had certainly ears, and could drink in every word you said.

For the rest, it might be soothing to one's pride to live in a big country house, but it was certainly abnormally dull. The day's programme never varied by a hair's breadth, and Aunt Maria, though kind, possessed the failing of all others most trying to the youthful mind. *She fussed!* She fussed about clothes, she fussed about food, she fussed about draughts, she fussed about manners, deportment, speech, the way you sat down, the way you got up, the way you laughed, yawned, sneezed, crossed the room, and did your hair. From morning to night, "My dear, *don't!*" or "My dear, *do!*" rang in Darsie's ears, till she was almost beside herself with irritation.

Honestly and laboriously she tried to practise her father's advice: to put the thought of the seaside party aside, make the most of the good points of her own position, and "fight the good fight," but the effort seemed to exhaust her physically, as well as mentally, until by the end of the day she looked white and drooping, pathetically unlike her natural glowing self. Aunt / Maria noticed the change, and fussed about that, too, but with an underlying tenderness that was upsetting to the girl's strained nerves.

"You look very tired to-night, my dear! Are you not well? Is there anything the matter?"

"Quite well, thank you. Only – lonely!" replied Darsie, with a plaintive accent on that last word which brought Lady Hayes's glance upon her in quick inquiry –

"Lonely! But, my dear, you haven't been a minute alone all day long."

"No," agreed Darsie meekly, and said no more, but the little monosyllable was more eloquent than any disclaimer. Lady Hayes flushed, and knitted her brows in thought.

"I must ask some young people to meet you. I have some nice young friends living about a mile away. They are visiting at present, but will soon be home. I will write. Naturally you miss the young society."

She was so kind, so considerate, that it seemed mean to feel bored and impatient; but, oh dear, how long the days *did* seem, how dull and monotonous the morning drive, the afternoon needlework, the evening game of patience or bezique!

The climax came one rainy afternoon when the ordinary two-hours drive could not take place, and the hostess and her young guest had spent / most of the day together in the library. Now it is trying for an old lady as well as for a young one to be deprived of the usual exercise, and if Darsie's impatience and rebelliousness of spirit were more acute than usual, Lady Hayes was also more nervous and exacting. In this instance the weight of the old lady's displeasure seemed to fall upon Darsie's unfortunate coiffure. Whatever turn the conversation might take, it returned with relentless certainty to "Your hair, my dear! When *I* was young, young girls wore their hair neatly braided. I intensely dislike all this puffing and elaboration. You would look a different girl if you brushed it smoothly."

"I should," agreed Darsie coolly. "I should look a sight. *My* pompadour is the best pompadour[34] in my class. The girls all say so. They ask me how I do it. I've taught lots of them to do their own."

"I'm sorry to hear it. Time enough when you come out to wear 'pompadours' as you call them. And your bow! Ridiculous size! If it were neat and small –"

"They wear them twice as big in America. And in France. Sash ribbons! I would, too, if I could afford. It's the fashion, Aunt Maria. Every one wears them big."

"Surely that is all the more reason why a sensible girl should set a good example by being / neat and moderate herself! I don't approve of hair being allowed to grow long at your age, but if it *is* long, it ought certainly to be kept in bounds.

Yours is hanging all over your shoulders at this moment. Most untidy! I am speaking for your own good."

There was a moment's chilly silence, then Darsie asked in a tone of extraordinary politeness –

"Just exactly *how* would you do my hair, Aunt Maria, if you were in my place to-day? "

Lady Hayes straightened herself briskly. "I should *brush* it," she said emphatically. "It is naturally curly, no doubt, but I cannot believe that a good brushing would not reduce it to order! I should damp it and brush it well, and then tie it back so that it would not hang loose over your shoulders like a mane. It would be pleasant to see what a difference it would make. A neat head is one of the things which every young gentlewoman should strive to possess."

Darsie folded her needlework, put it neatly away in her bag, and, rising from her seat, marched slowly from the room. It was nearing the hour for tea, when she usually went upstairs to wash and tidy-up generally, so that there was nothing unusual in her departure; it was only when she was safe inside her room that the extraordinary nature of to-day's preparations was revealed.

She took off the lace collar and pretty bead / necklace which gave an air of lightness to her plain dark dress, wrapped a dressing-jacket round her shoulders, and dipped her head deep into a basin of water. Then with a comb the wet hair was parted accurately in the centre, and brushed to the ears till it had the air of being painted rather than real, so smooth and plastered was the effect. The ends, plaited with merciless tightness, were looped together with a fragment of a broken shoelace, so tightly that from the front no sign of their presence could be suspected. When all was finished and the dressing-jacket thrown aside the effect was positively startling to behold. It did not seem possible to believe that this prim, demure damsel could be the same brilliant-looking creature who had entered the room but ten minutes before, and Darsie herself was half-shocked, half-triumphant at the completeness of the transformation.

"'Spose I had a fever and lost my hair! How simply awful!" she said to herself in terror. "If they could see me at home, they'd never call me pretty again. I think even Aunt Maria will jump!"

She skipped with delight at the possibility, and the gesture seemed so singularly out of keeping with her appearance that she laughed again, restored to good temper by the delightful experience of taking part in a prank once more.

Ten minutes later, accurately at the moment / when the tea equipage would be in course of arrangement in the drawing-room, Darsie composed her face into a "prunes and prism" decorum,[35] and slipped noiselessly into the room.

SHEER HORROR OF THE SITUATION TOOK AWAY
DARSIE'S BREATH.

To a certain extent all was as she had expected. Mason stood majestically over the tea-table; James, his satellite, approached with a tray of cakes and sandwiches; Aunt Maria sat waiting in her high-backed chair – so far all was just as she had planned; what she was all unprepared for, however, was the presence of three youthful visitors, two girls and a youth, who sat facing the door, staring at her in stunned dismay.

The Percivals! By all that was ill-timed and embarrassing, the Percivals themselves, returned from their visit, choosing a wet afternoon to drive over and pay their respects to Lady Hayes's young guest! Sheer horror of the situation took away Darsie's breath; she stood stock still in the middle of the floor, felt her lips gape apart, the crimson rush to her face, saw in a mental flash a vision of the country bumpkin she must appear – just for a moment, then Aunt Maria's voice said, in even, equable tones –

"Ah, here she is! Darsie, these are my young friends of whom I have spoken. I am pleased that you should become acquainted. My niece, Darsie Garnett. Noreen, Ida, and Ralph Percival.... Now we will have tea!" /

The voice, the manner, were absolutely normal. Was it possible that she had not *seen?* Darsie shot a quick glance at the old lady's face, met an unconcerned smile, and for the first time in the history of their acquaintance felt a thrill of admiration. Splendid to have such self-control, to show *no* sign of surprise or irritation! She shook hands awkwardly with the three visitors, and sat down on the nearest chair.

"So awfully pleased to meet you!" cried Noreen gushingly. She was a smart-looking girl of sixteen, with brown eyes and a deeply dimpled chin. Darsie knew exactly what she was thinking – understood that the gushing manner had been adopted to disguise dismayed disappointment in the aspect of a possible companion. Ralph was quite old – eighteen at least, with well-cut features, thin lips, and small grey eyes, a dandy wearing a fancy waistcoat and resplendent white spats. His whole aspect breathed a loud, "I told you so! You *would* drag me with you. *Told* you how it would be. Lady Hayes's grandniece! What could you expect?" Ida was bubbling over with curiosity. What a fine story she would have to tell to the family party on her return!

Conversation would have dragged pitifully if it had not been for Aunt Maria's efforts, for the visitors seemed smitten with dumbness, and beneath / the fire of their glances Darsie's embarrassment increased rather than diminished. She had no spirit left; a succession of monosyllables and an occasional "Oh, really!" made up the sum of her contributions to the conversation. It must have been a strong sense of duty which nerved Noreen Percival to offer the invitation which presumably was the object of her visit.

"We want to know if you will come to lunch with us on Thursday, and stay for the afternoon? If it's fine, we can have some tennis. We will drive you back after tea."

Darsie hesitated, but apparently the decision was not to be left to her. Aunt Maria accepted with a gracious acknowledgment of Mrs. Percival's kindness, and in answer to a scowl from Ralph his sisters rose and made a hasty adieu.

"We came in the governess cart.[36] The pony-gets restless – mustn't keep him waiting. Thank you *so* much! *Good*bye!"

They were gone; the outer door was shut behind them. Darsie, standing by the tea-table, caught a glimpse of her own reflection in a mirror at the opposite end of the room, a stiff, Dutch-doll of a figure, with plastered hair, crimson cheeks, and plain frock. She glanced at Aunt Maria reseating herself in her high-backed chair, and taking up the inevitable knitting. Now for it! now for the lecture! Well, after all, she had / only done what had been suggested, a trifle *more* perhaps than had been suggested, but that was erring on the right side, not the wrong. Besides, if a naughty impulse to annoy and humiliate Aunt Maria had really existed, in the end she had been a thousand times more humiliated herself. And now, if you please, she was to be scolded and lectured into the bargain!...

But Aunt Maria neither lectured nor scolded. All through that next hour when pride kept Darsie chained to her place, the older lady talked in her most natural manner, and even smiled at her companion across the patience-board without a flicker of expression to betray that the figure confronting her was in any way different from the one which she was accustomed to see.

Once more admiration vanquished irritation, and Darsie roused herself to join in the problem of "building," and ended in actually feeling a dawning of interest in what had hitherto appeared the dreariest of problems. When seven o'clock struck, and the old lady closed the board, and said, in her natural, every-day voice, "And now we must dress for dinner!" Darsie walked slowly across the room, hesitated, and finally retraced her steps and knelt down on a footstool by Lady Hayes' side.

"Aunt Maria – *please!* I should like to thank you!" /

"Thank me, my dear. For what?"

"For – for saying nothing! For not crowing over me as you might have done!"

The flushed, upturned face was very sweet – all the sweeter perhaps for the plastered hair, which gave to it so quaint and old-world an air. Lady Hayes laid a wrinkled hand on the girl's shoulder; her eyes twinkled humorously through her spectacles.

"No, I won't crow, my dear! That would be ungenerous. Circumstances have been pretty hard on you already. This – this little exhibition was not intended for an audience, but for my own private edification. It was unfortunate that the

Percivals should have chosen such a moment for their first call. I was sorry for your discomfiture."

"You oughtn't to have been! I *meant* to be naughty. Oh, you've scored – scored all the way. I apologize in dust and ashes, but please – if you will be very noble – *never* speak of it again!"

She reached the door once more, was about to make a bolt for the staircase, when Lady Hayes's voice called to her to return –

"Darsie?"

"Yes!"

"Come here, child!"

The thin hand was held out to meet hers, the kind old eyes looked wonderfully soft and tender. /

"I think it is only fair to tell you that... in your own language, you have scored also!... Oblige me by doing your hair in your ordinary fashion for the future!"

"Oh, Aunt Maria, you *duck!*" cried Darsie, and for the first time in her life flung her arms voluntarily around the old lady's neck and gave her a sounding kiss. /

Chapter IX

The Percivals

IT was really rather fun dressing for the visit to the Percivals on Thursday; trying to make oneself look one's *very* best, and imagining their surprise at the transformation! Aunt Maria, too, seemed quite to enter into the spirit of the thing, inquired anxiously *which* dress, and gave special instructions that it should be ironed afresh, so that it might appear at its freshest and best.

"My woman" had evidently been instructed to take the young guest's wardrobe under her care, since new ribbons and frilling now appeared with engaging frequency, giving quite an air to half-worn garments. Darsie in a blue muslin dress, with a white straw hat wreathed with daisies, and her golden locks floating past her waist, made a charming picture of youth and happiness as she sat in the old barouche, and when the hall was reached Aunt Maria cast a keen glance around the grounds, transparently eager to discover the / young people and share in the fun of the meeting.

Ralph was nowhere to be seen, that was *not* to be wondered at under the circumstances, but the two girls were on duty on the tennis-lawn in front of the house, ready to come forward and welcome their guest immediately upon her arrival.

The blank gapes of bewilderment with which they witnessed the alighting of the radiant blue and gold apparition afforded keen delight both to aunt and niece. They were literally incapable of speech, and even after Aunt Maria had driven away, coughing in the most suspicious manner behind a raised hand, even then conversation was of the most jerky and spasmodic kind. It was amusing enough for a time, but for a whole afternoon it would certainly pall, and Darsie *did* want to enjoy herself when she had a chance. She decided that it was time to put matters on a right footing, and looked smilingly to right and left, at her embarrassed, tongue-tied companions.

"I think," said Darsie politely, "that I owe you an explanation!"

She explained, and Noreen and Ida pealed with laughter, and danced up and down on the gravel path, and slid their hands through her arm, vowing undying friendship on the spot.

"How per-fectly killing! I do *love* a girl who is up to pranks. *What* a prank! How you / *must* have felt when you saw us sitting there! And Lady Hayes – what *did* she say? Was she per-fectly furious?"

"Aunt Maria behaved like an angel, a dignified angel! I never liked her so much. How did *you* feel? Tell me just exactly your sentiments when you saw me walking into that room?"

"I certainly did feel upset, because we *had* to ask you! Mother said we must, and we asked each other what on *earth* should we do with you all day long. Ida did say that your eyes were pretty. She was the only one who stuck up for you at all! I thought you looked too appalling for words."

"What did your brother say?" asked Darsie with natural feminine curiosity, whereupon Noreen answered with unabashed candour –

"He said you were 'a rummy[37] little frump,' and that he would take very good care to have an engagement for to-day as many miles as possible away from home!"

"Did he, indeed!" The colour rose in Darsie's cheeks. "Well, I'm very glad he did. I like girls best, and I thought *he* looked conceited and proud. My best friend has a big brother, too, but he's not a bit like yours. Rather shaggy, but *so* clever and kind! He promised to write to me while I was here, just because he knew I should be dull. It's really an honour, you know, for he is terrifically clever. Every one says he will be / Prime Minister one day. He's going to Cambridge. Your brother is, too, isn't he? I shouldn't think they would be at *all* in the same set!"

The Percival girls looked at each other and smiled.

"Poor old Ralph! Isn't she blighting? You don't know anything about him, you know. It's only because he called you a frump, but never mind, he has to be back to tea to look after some work for father, and then he'll see! If you are going to be friends with us, you mustn't begin by disliking our brother. He may be conceited, but he is certainly not 'shaggy,' and he is much nicer to his sisters than most big boys. He thinks we are really nicer than other girls."

Darsie regarded them critically.

"Well, I think you are!" she conceded graciously. "Oh, how thankful I am that there is some one *young* in the neighbourhood. I was beginning to feel so painfully middle-aged. Let's sit down and talk. Tell me about yourselves. Do you go to school? Which school? Do you go in for exams? What subjects do you like best?"

Noreen laughed, and shook her head.

"We have a governess. We are going for a year to a finishing school in Paris, but mother doesn't approve of exams, for girls. She wants us to be able to play, and sing, and draw, and speak German and French, and she says that's enough. / We don't bother about Latin or mathematics or any of those dull old things."

"They are not dull. They're glorious. I revel in them. But you're rich, of course, and won't have to work. I shall have to earn money myself, so I want to pass all the exams. I can."

The Percivals stared in solemn surprise. The idea was so strange it took some time to digest. All their friends were well off like themselves; really, when they came to think of it, they had never met a prospective *working* girl before! They regarded Darsie with a curiosity tinged with compassion.

"Do you mean it – really? Tell us about yourself? Where do you live?"

"In Birchester,[38] Craven Street, Sandon terrace – the corner house in Sandon Terrace."

"Craven Street. Really!" The girls were plainly shocked, but Ida rallied bravely, and said in her most courteous air: "It must be so *interesting* to live in a street! So much to see. And have you *very* interesting people living across the road?"

"No. Rather dull. Husbands and wives, and one old bachelor with a leg – lame leg, I mean. No one at all thrilling, but our friends – our *best* friends – live in a terrace at right angles with ours. We have great times with them. I'll tell you about our latest craze." /

Noreen and Ida sat breathlessly listening to the history of the telegraph, till it was time to go into the house for lunch, when Darsie was introduced to Mrs. Percival, a very smartly dressed lady, who looked astonishingly young to be the mother of a grown-up family. After lunch the three girls attempted tennis, but gave it up in deference to the visitor's lack of skill, visited stables and kennels and conservatory, and were again brought face to face with the different points of view existing between the town and the country dweller.

"Do all people who live in the country go and stare at their horses and dogs every day of their lives?" demanded Darsie with an air of patient resignation, as Noreen and Ida patted, and whistled, and rubbed the noses of their four-footed friends, fed them with dainty morsels, and pointed out good points in technical terms which were as Greek in the listener's ears. "Aunt Maria goes every single day; it's a part of the regular programme, like knitting in the afternoon and Patience at night. I get – *so* bored!"

The shocked looks which the Percival sisters turned upon her seemed ludicrously out of proportion with the circumstances.

"Don't you – don't you *love* animals?"

"Certainly – in their place. But I can*not* see the interest in staring in through a stable door at the same horses standing munching in the same / stalls day after day. It's no use pretending that I can," declared Darsie obstinately. "And the dogs make such a noise, and drag at your clothes. I'm always thankful to get away. Let's go back to the garden and look at the flowers. I could stare at flowers for ages. It seems too glorious to be true to be able to pick as many roses as you like. At home mother buys a sixpenny bunch on Saturday, and cuts the stalks every day, and puts them into fresh water to make them last as long as possible, and we have nasturtiums for the rest of the week. I love the fruit and vegetable garden, too. It's so amusing to see how things grow! Especially –" she laughed mischievously, showing a whole nest of baby dimples in one pink cheek, "I warn you frankly that this is a hint! – especially things you can *eat!*"

Noreen and Ida chuckled sympathetically.

"Come along! There is still a bed of late strawberries. We'll take camp-stools from the summer-house, and you shall sit and feast until you are tired, and we'll sit and watch you, and talk. We seem to have had strawberries at every meal for weeks past, and are quite tired of the sight, so you can have undisturbed possession."

"And I," said Darsie with a sigh, "have never in my life had enough! It will be quite an epoch to go on eating until I *want* to stop. That's / the worst of a large family, the dainties divide into such tiny shares!"

Ten minutes later the three girls had taken up their position in the kitchen garden in a spot which to the town-bred girl seemed ideal for comfort and beauty. The strawberry-bed ran along the base of an old brick wall on which the branches of peach-trees stretched out in the formal upward curves of great candelabra. An old apple-tree curved obligingly over the gravel path to form a protection from the sun, and it was the prettiest thing in the world to glance up through the branches with their clusters of tiny green apples, and see the patches of blue sky ahead. Darsie sat stretching out her hand to pluck one big strawberry after another, an expression of beatific contentment on her face.

"Yes – it's scrumptious to live in the country – in summer! If it were always like this I'd want to stay for ever, but it must be dreadfully dull in winter, when everything is dead and still. I shouldn't like it a bit."

"No! No!" the Percival girls protested in chorus. "It's beautiful always, and livelier than ever, for there's the hunting. Hunting is just *the* most delightful sport! We hunt once a week always, and often twice – the most exciting runs. We are sorry, absolutely sorry when spring comes to stop us." /

"Oh, do you hunt!" Darsie was quite quelled by the thought of such splendour. In town it was rare even to see a girl on horseback; a hunt was a thing which you read about, but never expected to behold with your own eyes. The knowledge that her new friends actually participated in this lordly sport raised them to a pinnacle of importance. She munched strawberries in thoughtful silence for several moments before recovering enough spirit to enter another plea in favour of town.

"Well, anyway – if you *don't* hunt, it must be dull. *And* lonely! Aren't you scared to death walking along dark lanes without a single lamp-post? I should live in terror of tramps and burglars, and never dare to stir out of the house after three o'clock."

"No you wouldn't, if you were accustomed to it. Our maids come home quite happily at ten o'clock at night, but if they go to a city they are nervous in the brightly lit streets. That's curious, but it's true. We used to leave doors and windows open all day long, and hardly trouble to lock up at night, until a few months ago when we had a scare which made us more careful. Till then we trusted every one, and every one trusted us."

"A scare!" Darsie pricked her ears, scenting an excitement. "What scare? Do tell me! I love gruesome stories. What was it? Thieves?" /

Noreen nodded solemnly.

"Yes! It's gruesome enough. Simply horrid for us, for so many other people lost their – but I'll tell you from the beginning. It was the night of the Hunt Ball at Rakeham, and the house was crammed with visitors. We were allowed to sit up to see them all start. They looked so lovely – the men in their pink coats, and the ladies in their very best dresses and jewels. Well, it was about half-past seven; the ladies had gone upstairs to dress about half an hour before, when suddenly there was a great noise and clamour, and some one shouted 'Fire!' and pealed an alarm on the gong. No one knew where it was, but you never heard such a hub-bub and excitement. Doors opened all down the corridors, and the ladies rushed out in dressing-gowns and dressing-jackets, with hair half done, or streaming down their backs, shrieking and questioning, and clinging to one another, and rushing downstairs. The men were more sensible; they took it quite calmly, and just set to work to put the fire out. It was in a little room on the second floor, and the strange thing was that it hadn't been used for months, and no one could account for there being a fire there at all. After a little time one of the men came out into the corridor, and said: 'There's something wrong about this – this is not the result of accident! I don't like the look of it at all.' Then he turned / to the ladies, who were all huddled together, gasping and questioning, with their maids and the other servants in the background, and said: 'Ladies! I advise you to go back to your rooms as quickly as possible. There is not the slightest danger, but it might be just as well to look after your jewellery!' –

"You should have heard them shriek! They turned and rushed like rabbits, and the maids rushed after them, shrieking too, but that was nothing to the noise two minutes after, when they got back to their rooms and found their jewels gone! They were laid out ready to be put on, on the dressing-tables, and the alarm had been cleverly timed to give the ladies enough time to get half dressed, but not enough to have put on their jewellery. Only one out of all the party had put on her necklace. She *was* pleased!

"Well, they shrieked, and shrieked, and some of the men left the fire and came upstairs to the rescue. Captain Beverley was the smartest, and he just tore along the corridor to a dressing-room over the billiard-room, and there was a man letting himself drop out of the window, and scrambling over the billiard-room roof to the ground! Captain Beverley gave the alarm, and the servants rushed out to give chase. It was very dark, and they could not tell how many men there were, for they kept dodging in and out among the trees. Some / people said there were only two, and some said they saw four, but only one was caught that night – an idle, loafing young fellow who had been staying at the village inn for a few weeks, pretending to be a city clerk convalescing after an illness. The worst of it was that he had only a few of the smaller things in his pockets, none of the really big, valuable pieces."

"Goodness!" Darsie's eyes sparkled with animation. "That *was* an excitement. I wish I'd been here. Go on! What happened after that?"

"Oh, my dear, the most awful evening! The visitors had all brought their very *best* things, as the Hunt Ball is a great occasion, and they almost all cried, and one poor lady went into hysterics. Her father had been an ambassador and had all sorts of wonderful orders and things which she had had made into brooches and pendants, and they could never be replaced, no matter how much money she spent. Dinner was the most weepy meal you can imagine, and only one or two of the sensible ones went on to the ball. The others stayed at home and moped, and mother had to stay, too. Poor dear! she had to keep calm, and comfort every one else, when she'd lost all her own pet things. There was one string of pearls which has been in our family for generations, and each new owner adds a few more pearls, so that / it gets longer and longer, and more and more valuable. It would have belonged to Ralph's wife some day. He was so funny about it, so disappointed! He kept saying: 'Poor little girl! it *is* rough luck!' We said: 'Why pity her, when you haven't the least idea who she is?' He said: 'Why not, when I know very well that I *shall* know some day!'"

Darsie smiled with politely concealed impatience. She was not in the least interested in Ralph's problematical wife, but she was devoured with anxiety to hear further particulars of the exciting burglary.

"Well, well! Go on! You said they only caught one man that night. That means, I suppose –"

"Yes!" Noreen sighed tragically. "That was the saddest part of it. The next morning they found another man lying just outside the walled garden. He had scrambled up, holding on to the fruit-trees, and had then jumped down and broken his leg, and he was not a stranger, but one of our very own men – an under-gardener whom we had all liked so much. Father believed that he had been bribed and led away by the man from London, and offered to let him off if he would tell all he knew, how many thieves there had been, and give the names and descriptions of the ones who had escaped, but he wouldn't. Nothing would make / him speak. We all tried in turns, and then the Vicar came and was shut up with him for an age, but it was no use. They say 'there's honour among thieves,' and it's true. He wouldn't give the others away, so the two were sent to prison together, and they are there still. Father says they won't mind a few months' imprisonment, for when they come out they will get their share of the money and be quite rich. They'll probably sail off for America or Australia and buy land, and live in luxury ever after. It *is* a shame! Father and mother feel it awfully. Such a dreadful thing to happen when you ask your friends to stay!"

"Yes! it's a comfort to have nothing to lose. Mother has one diamond ring, which she always wears above the wedding one, and there's nothing else worth stealing in the house, except watches and silver spoons, so that Aunt Maria need fear no qualms on account of her present visitor. No one will set her house on fire on account of *my* jewels – a few glass beads and a gold safety-pin, all told! You see them before you now!" Darsie tossed her head and pointed towards her treasures with an air of such radiant satisfaction that Noreen and Ida dropped the effort to be polite, and pealed with delighted laughter.

"You *are* a funny girl! You do amuse us. It's so nice to have a new friend. The girls / near here are so deadly dull. You seem so full of spirit."

"Too full. It runs away with me. I act first and think afterwards. *Not* a good principle for a working life," pronounced Miss Darsie sententiously as she searched among the green leaves for a strawberry sufficiently large and red to suit her fastidious taste. The Percivals watched her with fascinated gaze. An hour before they would have professed the most profound pity for a girl who lived in a street, owned neither horse nor dog, and looked forward to earning her own living, but it was with something more closely resembling envy that they now regarded Darsie Garnett, weighted as she was with all these drawbacks. There was about her an air of breeziness, of adventure, which shook them out of their self-complacence. It no longer seemed the all-important thing in life to belong to a county family, attend the hunt, and look forward to a presentation at Court; they felt suddenly countrified and dull, restricted in aim and interest.

It was while Darsie was still conversing in airy, discursive fashion, and her companions listening with fascinated attention, that footsteps were heard approaching, and Ralph's tall figure appeared at the end of the path. He was evidently taking a short cut through the grounds, and as Darsie was out of his line of vision, being planted well back / among the strawberry plants, he saw only his two sisters, and advanced to meet them with cheerful unconcern.

"Hulloa! Here's luck! Hasn't she come?"

"Oh, yes! But it is luck all the same. Look for yourself!" cried Noreen gleefully, pointing with outstretched hand to where Darsie sat, a pale blue figure among a nest of greenery, her little, flushed, laughing face tilted upward on the long white throat, her scattered locks ashine in the sun. With the air of a queen she extended finger-tips crimson with the strawberry juice towards the newcomer, and with the air of a courtier Ralph Percival stooped to take them in his own.

For a moment they stared full into each other's eyes, while the bewilderment on the young man's face slowly gave place to recognition.

"Glad to see you again, Princess Goldenlocks! Let me congratulate you on the breaking of the spell. Who was the kind fairy who set you free to appear among us in your rightful guise?"

He spoke like a book; he looked tall and handsome enough to be a prince himself. Darsie forgave him on the instant for his former lack of respect, and bent upon him her most dimpling smile.

"I freed myself. I wove my own spell, and when I was tired of it I broke loose."

Ralph looked down at her with a slow, quizzical smile. /

"You had better be careful! Spells are awkward things to move about. They might alight, you know, on some other shoulders, and not be so easily shaken off!"

His eyes, his voice, added point to the words. It was the first, the very first compliment which Darsie had ever received from masculine lips, and compared with the blunt criticisms of Dan Vernon, she found it wonderfully stimulating.

"Come along, girls!" cried Ralph with a sudden return to a natural, boyish manner. "There's a whole hour yet before tea, and we can't sit here doing nothing. Let's go down to the river and punt. Do you punt, Miss Garnett? I'll teach you! You look the sort of girl to be good at sport. You'll pick it up in no time."

The three girls rose obediently and followed Ralph's lead riverwards, while Noreen and Ida, gesticulating and grimacing in the background, gave the visitor to understand that a great honour had been bestowed upon her, and that she might consider herself fortunate in being the recipient of an unusual mark of attention. /

Chapter X

A Treaty

Iꜰ there were innumerable good points in an acquaintance with the Percival family, there was certainly the inevitable drawback, for on the days when she was alone with her great-Aunt, Darsie was rendered lonelier and more restless than before by the knowledge that a couple of miles away were three agreeable young companions who would be only too pleased to include her in their pastimes. The different points of view held by youth and age were, as usual, painfully in evidence. Darsie considered that it would be desirable to meet the Percivals "every single day"; Aunt Maria was glad that you had enjoyed yourself; was pleased that you should meet young friends, and suggested a return invitation, "some day next week!" pending which far-off period you were expected to be content with the usual routine of morning drive, afternoon needlework, and evening patience. Really – really – really, to have lived to that age, and to have no better understanding!

Letters from the seaside did not tend to soothe / the exile's discontent. It seemed callous of the girls to expatiate on the joys of bathing, fishing, and generally running wild, to one who was practising a lady-like decorum in the society of an old lady over seventy years of age, and although Dan kept his promise to the extent of a letter of two whole sheets, he gave no hint of deploring Darsie's own absence. It was in truth a dull, guide-booky epistle, all about stupid "places of interest" in the neighbourhood, in which Darsie was frankly uninterested. All the Roman remains in the world could not have counted at that moment against one little word of friendly regret, but that word was not forth-coming, and the effect of the missive was depressing, rather than the reverse. Mother's letters contained little news, but were unusually loving – wistfully, almost, as it were, *apologetically* loving!

The exile realized that in moments of happy excitement, when brothers and sisters were forgetful of her existence, a shadow would fall across mother's face, and she would murmur softly, "*Poor* little Darsie!" Darsie's own eyes filled at the pathos of the thought. She was filled with commiseration for her own hard plight.... Father's letters were bracing. No pity here; only encouragement and exhortation. "Remember, my dear, a sacrifice grudgingly offered is no sacrifice at all. What is worth doing, is worth doing well. / I hope to hear that you are not only an agreeable, but also a cheerful and cheering companion to your old aunt!"

Darsie's shoulders hitched impatiently. "Oh! Oh! Sounds like a copy-book. *I* could make headlines, too! Easy to talk when you're not tried. Can't put an old head on young shoulders. Callous youth, and crabbed age...."[39]

Not that Aunt Maria was really crabbed. Irritable perhaps, peculiar certainly, finicky and old-fashioned to a degree, yet with a certain bedrock kindliness of nature which forbade the use of so hard a term as *crabbed*. Since the date of the hair episode Darsie's admiration for Lady Hayes's dignified self-control had been steadily on the increase. She even admitted to her secret self that in time to come – far, far-off time to come, – she would like to become like Aunt Maria in this respect and cast aside her own impetuous, storm-tossed ways. At seventy one *ought* to be calm and slow to wrath, but at fifteen! Who could expect a poor little flapper[40] of fifteen to be anything but fire and flame!

Wet days were the great trial – those drizzling, chilly days which have a disagreeable habit of intruding into our English summers. Darsie, shivering in a washing dress,[41] "occupying herself quietly with her needlework" in the big grim morning-room, was in her most prickly and rebellious of moods. /

"Hateful to have such weather in summer! My fingers are so cold I can hardly work."

"It is certainly very chill."

"Aunt Maria, couldn't we have a fire? It would be *something* cheerful to look at!"

"My dear!" Lady Hayes was apparently transfixed with amazement. "A fire! You forget, surely, the month! The month of August. We never begin fires until the first of October."

"You'd be much more comfortable if you did."

There being no controverting the truth of this statement, Lady Hayes made no reply. But after the lapse of a few minutes she volunteered a suggestion.

"There is a grey Shetland shawl[42] folded up under the sofa rug. You had better put it over your shoulders, since you feel so cold."

"*I?*" Darsie gave an impatient laugh. "Fancy me wrapped up in a Shetland shawl! I'd sooner freeze."

Lady Hayes dropped her eyelids and tightened her lips. Her manner pointed out more eloquently than words the fact that her guest was wanting in respect, but as hostess it was her duty to consider the comfort of her guest, so presently she rang the bell and gave instructions that a cup of hot cocoa should be served at eleven o'clock instead of the usual glass of milk. She herself was never guilty of the enormity of eating between / meals, so that the listener knew perfectly well for whose benefit the order was given, but being at once cold, lonely, and cross, her heart was hardened, and she spoke no word.

Between that time and the appearance of James with the tray Aunt Maria made three successive attempts to open new topics of conversation, which were each time checkmated by monosyllabic replies. There was a tone of relief in her voice, as of one hailing a much-needed assistance, as she said briskly –

"Now, my dear, here is your cocoa! Drink it while it is hot. It will warm you up."

"Thank you, I don't drink cocoa. It makes me sick."

There was a moment's silence. James stood at attention, tray in hand. Lady Hayes tightened her lips, and the little red lines on her cheeks turned a curious bluish shade. Then she cleared her throat, and said in her most courteous tones –

"I am sorry. Would you kindly tell James what you would like instead. Tea – coffee – soup? A warm drink would be better than milk this morning."

"Nothing, thank you."

"Nothing, James! You may go."

James departed. Aunt Maria went on with her knitting, the click-click of the needles sounding startlingly distinct in the silent room. Darsie sat / shamed and miserable, now that her little ebullition of spleen was over, acutely conscious of the rudeness of her behaviour. For five minutes by the clock the silence lasted; but in penitence, as in fault, there was no patience in Darsie's nature, and at the end of the five minutes the needlework was thrown on the floor, and with a quick light movement she was on her knees by Lady Hayes's side.

"Aunt Maria, forgive me. I'm a pig!"

"Excuse me, my dear, you are mistaken. You are a young gentlewoman who has failed to behave as such."

"Oh, Aunt Maria, don't, *don't* be proper!" pleaded Darsie, half-laughing, half in tears. "I *am* a pig, and I behaved as much, and you're a duchess and a queen, and I can't imagine how you put up with me at all. I wonder you don't turn me out of doors, neck and crop!"

Lady Hayes put down her knitting and rested her right hand lightly on the girl's head, but she did not smile; her face looked very grave and sad.

"Indeed, Darsie, my dear," she said slowly, "that is just what I am thinking of doing. Not 'neck and crop' – that's an exaggerated manner of speaking, but, during the last few days I have been coming to the conclusion that I made a mistake in separating you from your family. I thought too much of my own interests, and not enough of yours." She smiled, a strained, pathetic / little smile. "I think I hardly realized how *young* you were! One forgets. The years pass by; one falls deeper and deeper into one's own ways, one's own habits, and becomes unconscious of different views, different outlooks. It was a selfish act to take a young thing away from her companions on the eve of a summer holiday. I realize it now, my dean; rather late in the day, perhaps, but not too late! I will arrange that you join your family at the sea before the end of the week."

Darsie gasped, and sat back on her heels, breathless with surprise and dismay. Yes! dismay; extraordinary though it might appear, no spark of joy or expectation lightened the shocked confusion of her mind. We can never succeed in turning back the wheels of time so as to take up a position as it would have been *if* the disturbing element had not occurred. The holiday visit to the seaside would have been joy untold *if* Aunt Maria had never appeared and given her unwelcome invitation, but now! – now a return to Sea-view would be in the character of a truant carrying within her heart the consciousness of failure and defeat. In the moment's silence which followed Aunt Maria's startling announcement the words of advice and exhortation spoken by her father passed one by one through Darsie's brain.

"If you cannot have what you like, try to like / what you have.... Put yourself now and then in your aunt's place.... A sacrifice grudgingly performed is no sacrifice at all.... What is worth doing at all, is worth doing well."

Each word condemned her afresh; she stood as judge before the tribunal of her own conscience, and the verdict was in every case the same. Guilty! She had not tried; she had not imagined; everything that she had done had been done with a

grudge; the effort, the forbearance, the courtesy, had been all on the other side....
There fell upon her a panic of shame and fear, a wild longing to begin again, and
retrieve her mistakes. She couldn't, she could *not* be sent away and leave Aunt
Maria uncheered, unhelped, harassed rather than helped, as the result of her visit!

"Oh, Aunt Maria," she cried breathlessly, "give me another chance! Don't,
don't send me away! I'm sorry, I'm ashamed, I've behaved horribly, but, I *want*
to stay. Give me another chance, and let me begin again! Honestly, truly, I'll be
good, I'll do all that you want...."

Lady Hayes stared at her earnestly. There was no mistaking the sincerity of
the eager voice, the wide, eloquent eyes, but the poor lady was plainly puzzled as
to what had wrought so speedy a change of front. With her usual deliberation
she waited for several moments before replying, studying the girl's face with serious eyes. /

"My dear, don't imagine that I am thinking of sending you back in disgrace.
Not at all. I will take all responsibility upon myself, and explain to your parents
that I have come to the conclusion that it would be a mistake to prolong your
visit. It has been very dull for you alone with an old woman, and I am sure that
though you have not always succeeded, you have at least had the intention of
making yourself pleasant and agreeable."

"No!" Darsie shook her bright head in vigorous denial. "I haven't! I can be
fifty times nicer than that, when I really try. Let me stay, Aunt Maria, and you'll
see.... It's quite true that I was cross at first. I hated giving up the holiday with the
Vernons, and there seemed nothing to do; but I've changed my mind. I didn't
know you, you see, and now I do, and I – I would like you to be pleased with me
before I go! Please, *please,* Aunt Maria, let me stay!"

"Certainly, my dear, I shall be most pleased." Lady Hayes still wore a somewhat puzzled expression, but she was undoubtedly gratified by the girl's appeal,
and Darsie bent forward and kissed her cheek with the feeling of one who has
narrowly escaped a great danger.

"That's settled, and now we are going to live happily ever after!"

"Ah, my dear, I am afraid that is too much to expect! I have no amusements
to offer you to / relieve the dullness. My health obliges me to live a quiet life,
and I have grown to dread change. Of course, there are plenty of books to read
– improving, well-written books, very different from the rubbish published to-
day. If you would like to have a little reading aloud, or I could give you lessons in
knitting and crochet...."

Darsie laughed, a bright, audacious laugh.

"I wouldn't like it a bit! I've another plan to suggest, fifty times nicer and
more exciting. Suppose" – she leaned her arms on the old lady's knee and looked
gaily into her spectacled eyes – "suppose, instead of your trying to make me old

with you, *I* tried, for a time, to make you young with *me?* Eh? What do you think? Wouldn't it be far more fun!"

"You ridiculous child!" But Lady Hayes laughed in her turn, and showed no signs of dismay. "That would be too difficult an undertaking even for you. To make me young again, ah, Darsie! that's an impossible task."

"Not a whit more impossible than to make me old!" cried Darsie quickly. "Suppose we took turns? That would be only fair. Your day first, when you would read aloud dull books with the blinds half down; and then *my* day, when I'd read funny ones, with the blinds drawn up to the top, and the sun streaming into the room; your day, when we drove the ordinary round and came back to lunch; and mine when we went / away over the hill and took a picnic basket and drew up at the side of the road, and ate it, and got milk from a cottage and drank it out of cups without saucers! Your night, when we played Patience; and mine when I showed you tricks and danced figure dances as we do at school. I'm *sure* you'd like to see me dance the Highland fling! Now – now – promise! I *know* you'll promise. I can see the softening in your eye!"

"Ridiculous child!" protested Lady Hayes once more, but Darsie was right; there was certainly a softening in her eye which bespoke a disposition to yield. In truth it was not so much of Darsie as of herself that Lady Hayes was thinking at that moment, for as the young voice spoke the old heart quickened with quite an agreeable sense of expectation. Years since she had read a "funny book," years since she had partaken of a picnic meal; years – many, many years since she had looked on while a young girl danced! Radical changes and innovations in the routine of life she could not face at this late day, but Darsie's girlish plan attempted nothing so ambitious. Let the child have her way! It would be interesting, undoubtedly interesting, to see how she behaved.

So Darsie gained her point, and for the next week she and her hostess played in turn the part of Mistress of the Ceremonies, to their mutual benefit and satisfaction. /

Chapter XI

A Dangerous Adventure

ONE of the privileges gained by the alliance between aunt and niece was that the former veto against bicycle riding[43] was withdrawn, and that Darsie was set free each afternoon for an hour's enjoyment of this favourite exercise.

In deference to Lady Hayes's nervousness and sense of responsibility the high-road was avoided as much as possible, and detours taken through quiet lanes, where traffic was reduced to a minimum; and it was along one of these lanes that Darsie rode joyously some five or six days after her visit to the Percivals, bearing in her pocket a return invitation to her new friends. She had been longing to meet them again, had keenly regretted a domestic upset which had delayed the invitation until now, but all the same the last days had passed wonderfully quickly and happily.

Afire with resolution to "begin again" and show herself in the light of a cheerful and cheering / companion, she had neglected no opportunity to make herself agreeable to her hostess, while Aunt Maria in return had been sweetly considerate, and on occasions quite startling in her divination of hidden wishes and desires. The eyes behind the gold-rimmed spectacles would rest upon the girl's face with an intent scrutiny which seemed to have the power to draw free confidences, till to her own surprise Darsie found herself discussing fluently the all-important subject of her own future, and setting forth her hopes and fears in relation to a scholarship for Newnham. On this, as on almost every topic which came up for discussion, the old woman and the girl held almost diametrically opposite opinions, but so far Darsie had contrived to subdue her impatience, and to listen with some appearance of humility to Lady Hayes's somewhat sententious criticism.

"But I wonder if it can last!" she was asking herself doubtfully this afternoon, as she pedalled through the sweet-smelling lanes. "I wonder if I can possibly go on being so unnaturally good without falling ill from the strain! How I hope the Percival girls will be at home! If I can let off steam for an hour, and make as much noise as I like, it will be no end of a relief, and help me to last out without a relapse. I'd hate to have a relapse and spoil it all, just when I'm trying so hard; and she's really a dear, *quite* an old / dear! I love to please her. Whenever I begin to feel scratchy I must make an excuse and get over to the Percivals for an hour to be soothed down. I do *hope* they are in to-day!"

But alas! the butler announced "Not at home," in reply to Darsie's inquiry, then, seeing the blank disappointment on the young face, he added graciously: "The young ladies are out for a ride. They will probably be home about four o'clock. Will you not step in and wait?"

Darsie brightened instantly. Four o'clock, and she had promised to be back by five. Yes, she could enjoy half an hour's talk, and still leave ample time for the ride home, but as it was now barely three o'clock she did not feel tempted by the prospect of sitting cooped in the house for so long a time.

"Thank you," she said briskly. "I should like to wait, but I think I'll stay in the garden. Perhaps you would be kind enough to tell them when they return."

The man bowed and withdrew, and Darsie strolled away in the direction of the rose pergola, the beauty of which had attracted her so greatly on her first visit. She wandered up and down the archways, sniffed at the fragrance of the late blooms which still remained, indulged in a little of the sentimental poetizing which seems to flow so readily when one is "alone among the roses,"[44] / began to grow bored, wandered aimlessly ahead, grew very bored indeed, and, consulting her watch, was dismayed to find that only fifteen minutes had passed away.

Fifteen! and there still remained forty-five before her companions were likely to arrive! What could she find to do to while away a whole forty-five minutes? As a matter of prudence Darsie put the suggestion of the fruit garden resolutely aside. It would not be *safe* to put herself in proximity with those tempting strawberries, since on a second visit to a house one was, unfortunately, not on sufficiently intimate terms to take without being asked.

She was contemplating getting on her bicycle and taking a short ride round the lanes, when the brilliant alternative of the river darted into her mind. Of course, the river! Nothing could be more delightful. She set off at a trot, taking in her inexperience many wrong turnings, but arriving at last at the river, or rather the peaceful backwater of the river which bordered the Percival grounds. To Darsie's mind the spot was the most picturesque on the whole estate, and a good many people could be found ready to agree with her in the conclusion; for the backwater though narrow was bordered by banks rich in reeds and bulrushes, while a hundred yards or so below the miniature jetty a pair of ancient wooden gates spanned the stream, through whose decaying beams could be / seen fascinating peeps of a baby waterfall, and a great moss-covered wheel which proclaimed the former use of the old grey building of which it was a part. In olden times this quiet backwater had been a busy centre of industry, but the modern inventions of machinery had left it hopelessly in the rear. The millowner had been ruined long ago, and the mill-house, with its great panelled rooms, was given up to the occupancy of the rats, while the disused wheel was green with moss, and the wooden gateway threatened every day to fall free of its hinges.

The young Percivals could not remember the day when the mill had been working, but from a personal point of view they deeply regretted its cessation, for, deprived of the healthy action of the wheel, the little backwater was becoming every year more choked with weeds, until at some points it was difficult to navigate the punt.

At long intervals strange men came to investigate the mill and its machinery, and the Percivals were cheered by rumours of a certain "let," but as one rumour after another died away without bringing any tangible result their hopes had reached a vanishing point, and they paid little attention to the occasional stirring into life of the dreamy backwater.

Darsie walked to the end of the jetty, stepped lightly into the punt, and sank down on the soft / red cushions. One might not eat one's neighbour's fruit, but one might sit in his punt, and arrange his cushions to fit comfily into the crick in one's back, without infringing the laws of hospitality. Darsie poked and wriggled, and finally lay at ease, deliciously comfortable, blinking up at the sunshine overhead, and congratulating herself on having hit on the spot of all others in which to spend the time of waiting. She could lie here for hours without feeling bored; it was the most deliciously lazy, drowsy sensation she had ever experienced. At the end of five minutes, however, the drowsy feeling threatened to become altogether too pronounced, and having no wish either to be discovered fast asleep, or to sleep on undiscovered till past the hour for her return. Darsie sat up hurriedly and began to look around for fresh distractions.

At the very first glimpse the usual temptation for idle hands stared her in the face, for there on the jetty lay, not only the long punt-pole, but also the dainty little paddle which she had handled under Ralph's instructions the week before. It had been quite easy, ridiculously easy; the girls declared that she took to it as to the manner born; she had paddled the whole boatload for quite a considerable distance. Naturally it would be much easier and lighter to paddle for oneself alone. The chain holding the punt to the jetty / could easily be slipped from its ring; there was not, *could* not be, any danger in paddling peacefully along a quiet little backwater. Of course, prudent people would say – Aunt Maria would say – But then if you waited until all the prudent people on earth approved of all that you did, you might sit with your hands crossed in your lap for the rest of your life!

Darsie tossed her head with the defiant little jerk which meant that she was *going* to do it, and she didn't care, and the consequences could look after themselves. In another moment the punt was free from the chain, and was being paddled slowly down the stream. Really, she told herself, the solid old craft was as safe as a house; so big, so heavily built was it that it seemed curious, not that its progress should be slow but that it should move at all in response to the efforts of one inexperienced girl!

Glancing over, Darsie could see the weeds rising from the bed of the stream, sometimes so high that they caught in the paddle as it worked and greatly impeded its force; still she was steadily moving along, and, fired with ambition, her eyes fell on a willow-tree standing out from the bank some hundred yards ahead, and she determined to persevere until the point should be reached. To declare she had paddled "some way" – "quite a long way" – would probably be discounted to / mean but a few yards by the Percival sisters, but "to the willow and back" was a definite feat which could not be gainsaid. So Darsie worked and strained till her arms ached and her cheeks flamed, till the punt, moving heavily through the weeds, ran at last beneath the willow branches and found a natural anchorage.

Well, it was good to lie back against the cushions and rest one's weary arms and back! Darsie peeped at her watch, saw with relief that she had still a good quarter of an hour to spare, and abandoned herself to a lazy enjoyment of the situation.

And then the inevitable happened, for the soothing influence of the shaded light lulled the tired senses into deeper and deeper unconsciousness, until at last the fringed eyelids ceased to flicker, and remained peacefully closed, and, like a happy, tired child, Darsie rested her cheek on her hand and slept.

Subsequent comparisons pr· ved that her doze might have lasted for half an hour or more, before a sudden movement of the punt roused her with a start. She sat up, blinked sleepily around, and discovered to her surprise that the punt had moved from its anchorage and drifted into the centre of the stream. It had appeared so safely moored against the tree that she was puzzled to understand how this had come about, but as the movement / had roused her from sleep she was glad that it had occurred, and, seating herself steadily, lifted her paddle to work her way back to the jetty.

As she settled herself, however, Darsie's attention was arrested by the manner in which the banks seemed to be slipping past; she turned her head over her shoulder, and discovered that in the minute which had elapsed since she had awakened from sleep the willow-tree had been left several yards behind. Some mysterious change seemed to have passed over the surface of the still, almost stagnant, waters; they were flowing as with a tide, the rippling movement stirring the weedy banks. Darsie used her paddle automatically, but its puny force seemed superfluous, for the punt was moving of itself, quickly and still more quickly, swinging broadside to the stream in defiance of her efforts to keep it straight. Darsie ceased to struggle and leaned forward on the paddle to consider the situation. Then, for the first time, she became aware that the former stillness of the stream was replaced by a harsh, continuous noise, which seemed momentarily to increase in volume. What could it be? She stared around with puzzled eyes, but there was no hint of alarm in her bewilderment. A child of the city, she was inured to sudden and inexplicable noises; it was only when the punt swung / heavily round a bend that she realized the seriousness of her position. The mill was working! One of the infrequent experimental trials of which she had heard was even now in process, the great moss-covered wheel was revolving creakily on its axle, waking the sleeping river into life, and the heavy punt was bearing down, more and more rapidly towards the crazy wooden gates!

In a second all that she had heard on this subject from the Percival family flashed through Darsie's brain. The gates were frail, so eaten by long action of water, that at the impact of a heavy mass they would almost certainly burst apart, and then – what would happen to the punt and to its hapless occupant? Would she be hurled against a broken boulder, wedged helplessly beneath the debris, or rushed forward into the swirl of the millpond itself? Whatever happened it seemed certain that danger – and serious danger – loomed close at hand, unless she could succeed in overmastering the current and landing the punt safely at the little jetty. At this moment it was not fear but rather an exhilarating tingling of excitement of which Darsie was most aware. Here was an adventure – a full-fledged adventure, such as came but seldom to break the monotony of life!

For the sake of her future credit she must bear herself bravely, be swift, resourceful, energetic. With all her strength she plied the paddle to and / fro, but for all the effect produced she might as well have sat still upon her cushions. It would have required an experienced hand to guide the heavy punt through the sweeping current, and under Darsie's unpractised strokes it twisted, and turned, and revolved in aimless and disconcerting circles.... No matter! she was determined to win; by hook or by crook she must make the left side of the stream and gain an anchorage. The jetty or the millpond – that was the alternative, and it was one to put power into the arm and give staying power to the laboured breath!

The moments were flying now, the banks seemed to be flitting past more quickly than ever. Darsie tried to convert the paddle into an oar, with which to steer more vigorously for the desired bank; then came a breathless second of suspense, followed by a sickening realization of failure. The punt had swept past the jetty at a distance just wide enough to make it impossible to grasp the chain, and was now bearing straight for the wooden gates! /

Chapter XII

Darsie's Suggestion

WITH the passing of the jetty, fear awoke for the first time in Darsie's breast – the fear which arises when the possibility of action is over and nothing remains but to sit still and await the end. In one moment of time an incredible number of thoughts flashed through her brain; she thought of her father and mother, of their grief and pain at the knowledge of her untimely end; she thought of her brothers and sisters, of Vi Vernon and plain Hannah, and Dan; she saw a vision of them all garbed in black, sitting round the study fire, enlarging upon her own virtues and graces; she thought of Aunt Maria and her responsibility; she saw a vision of herself, cold and still, being dragged out of the millpond,[45] with her hair floating like seaweed behind her, and at the thought a wild rebellion rose in her heart, a determination to fight on, to fight to the end for her precious life!

One or two large trees stood out from the bank. / Darsie leaped to her feet and, raising the paddle so high above her head that it caught against the branches, strove to delay the progress of the punt. The result was to upset her own equilibrium, and as she fell forward she screamed loudly, a shrill, penetrating scream of panic and appeal.

With almost startling quickness the answer came, in the form of an answering cry, close at hand. Round the corner of the next clump of bushes dashed the figure of Ralph Percival, bareheaded, eager-faced, and, thank Heaven! unhesitating in action. Not for one fraction of a second did he hesitate, but with the assurance of one who knows every inch of the land rushed forward waist-deep into the river; halted there, and called out a sharp command –

"Your paddle! Stretch out your paddle towards me! Hold hard! Lean out as far as you can! . . ."

Darsie fell on her knees, and, leaning forward to the utmost extent of her body, held out the paddle as directed. There was a moment of sickening suspense, then came a halt, a jerk that seemed to pull her arms half out of the sockets, and the punt swung heavily towards the shore. The danger was over; she was helped on to the bank, where she collapsed in a little heap, while Ralph worked the punt slowly along to the jetty and fastened it to its chain. /

The short breathing space had allowed Darsie to recover her self-possession, to master the overpowering temptation to cry, and to swallow the lump in her throat sufficiently to be able to say in a weak little voice –

"You've saved my life!"

"You've spoiled my trousers!" retorted Ralph in a matter-of-fact manner calculated to put an instant check on sentimentality. He sat down on the bank, unfastened his mud-soaked gaiters, and threw them on one side. "The river's beastly dirty, and the mud sticks like the Dickens. A new suit, too! It will never look the same again."

"I'm sorry."

"So you ought to be. Things are bad enough as they are, *but* . . . How on earth did you come to be careering about alone in that punt?"

"I was waiting to see your sisters. I wandered down here, and thought I'd just sit in it for a rest, then I thought I could just paddle up and down. I managed quite well going up the stream; I got as far as the willow!" Even at that moment a faint note of pride crept into Darsie's voice. "We grounded there, and I – I must have fallen asleep, I suppose, and that hateful old mill must needs choose the opportunity to begin working at that very moment. ... Just my luck!"

Ralph pursed his lips in eloquent comment.

"If it comes to that, I think you have had a / fair amount of luck in another way! I heard the noise of the mill and came down to look on. If I hadn't been there, you'd have been pretty considerably in Queer Street by this time. Nice thing it would have been for us to discover your drowned body in the millpond, and have had to tell your aunt!"

"I thought of that," agreed Darsie meekly. "It was one of my dying thoughts. Don't scold me, please, for I feel so shaky, and you wouldn't like it if I cried. It was my own fault, and I got what I deserved. I wasn't a bit frightened till I missed the jetty, but that one moment was like a hundred years. Did my yell sound very awful?"

"Pretty middling blood-curdling!" replied Ralph, smiling. "Good thing it did. Gave me a bit of a shock, I can tell you, to see the old punt dashing down to the gates, with you sitting huddled up in the bottom, with your hair hanging wild, and your face the colour of chalk. You looked like a young Medusa."[46]

"Sounds attractive, I must say! Medusa froze *other* people's blood, not her own," declared Darsie, tilting her chin with a little air of offence, at which her companion laughed triumphantly.

"Oh, *you're* better; you're coming round again all right! I was afraid you were going to faint. I don't mind telling you that you were jolly plucky. / Most girls would have started screaming miles before, but you held on like a Briton.[47] How do the arms feel now? Rather rusty at the hinges, I expect. The stiffness will probably spread to the back by to-morrow, but it'll come all right in time. It is a pretty good weight, that punt, and I had to pull for all I was worth.... Don't you think you'd better come up to the house and have some tea?"

"Yes, please. And you can change your clothes, too. I should feel so miserable if you caught cold."

"No fear of that. I'm used to splashing in and out of the water half a dozen times a day. You need have no anxiety about me."

"But – the trousers?"

"Oh, bother the trousers! I piled that on a bit, just to prevent you from getting sentimental. *They're* all right!" Ralph paused a moment, then, "I say!" he cried anxiously, "is this going to get you into trouble with the aunt? Need you say anything about it, do you think? I'll swear to secrecy, if you say the word, and not a soul need know."

Darsie debated the point thoughtfully while the two walked side by side along the gravelled paths, and finally arrived at a conclusion.

"I think, on the whole, I'll tell! Aunt Maria allowed me to go out alone as a great concession, / and it was mean to take advantage and run risks. So upsetting for her if I were killed in her house! So I'm in honour bound to confess, and promise not to do it again."

"You might do something else just as bad! Probably she'll withdraw her permission and keep you under her thumb as she did those first weeks."

"She *may;* but I don't think she *will!* I think she will appreciate my confidence," said Darsie, with a grandiloquent air, at which her companion whistled softly, his face twitching with amusement. He was much more natural and boyish in his manner than on either of the previous occasions on which Darsie had met him, and the agitation of the last few minutes seemed to have carried them in a bound past all the formalities of early acquaintance.

"Right you are!" he said briskly. "I like a straight girl. But if you don't mind we won't speak of it before the mater.[48] She's a bit nervous, and would be always imagining that the girls were going to have the same experience. You might warn Lady Hayes not to speak of it either. We'll keep it a secret between us."

"Just as you like! I *believe*," said Darsie shrewdly, "that you're afraid of being praised and fussed over, as you would be if people knew that you had saved my life! Men hate a fuss, but you can't escape my gratitude. I didn't want / to die. It came over me with a sort of horror – the thought of leaving the flowers, and the trees, and the blue sky, and all the people I love. Have you ever been so nearly dead to know how it feels?"

"Once – when I had enteric at school. It was a near squeak at the crisis."

"And how did you feel? What did you think?"

"I didn't care a whit one way or another. I wanted to have the pillow turned. That seemed a hundred times more important than life or death; I was too ill to think. . . . Well, thank goodness, you are *not* dead! I hope you'll live for many years to be a pride and glory to – er – er – the ranks of women blue-stockings!"[49]

Darsie looked at him sharply.

"The girls have been telling you of my ambitions! Mean of them! They might have known you'd scoff. All boys do, but I fail to see why if a girl has brains she should not use them as well as a man."

"The inference being –"

"Certainly! I'm unusually clever for my years!" returned Darsie proudly, whereupon they simultaneously burst into a peal of laughter.

"Well, you goaded me to it!" Darsie declared in self-vindication. "I can't stand it when boys are superior. Why must they sneer and jeer / because a girl wants to go in for the same training as themselves, especially when she has to make her own living afterwards? In our two cases it's more important for me than for you, for you will be a rich landowner, and I shall be a poor school marm. You ought to be kind and sympathetic, and do all you can to cheer me on, instead of being lofty and blighting."

Ralph Percival looked down at her with his handsome, quizzical eyes –

"I don't mind betting that *you'll* never be a school marm!" he said calmly; and at that very moment, round a bend of the path, the two girls came suddenly into view, trotting briskly towards the river. They waved their hands, and tore down upon the visitor in lively welcome.

"There you are! This *is* nice. Bates said you were in the garden, so we just flew and changed, and rushed off in pursuit. So glad you had Ralph to amuse you. The mill's working! We guessed you'd be there looking on. . . ."

"There's nothing to, see but the old wheel creaking round. Tea is far more to the point. I'm dying for some, and I'm sure – er – Miss – er – Garnett is, too! She's had a tiring afternoon."

"Er – Miss – er – Garnett's name is Darsie. You can always call a girl by her Christian name till her hair's up," said Darsie quickly, and Ralph immediately availed himself of the permission. /

"All right, Darsie. It's a jolly little name. Much easier to say."

Rather to Darsie's disappointment tea was served in the drawing-room in formal, grown-up fashion, Mrs. Percival presiding over the little table, with its shining silver and fine old-world china. There were hot, brown little scones, crisp buttered toast, iced cakes, thick cream, and other indigestible luxuries, which came as an agreeable change from Lady Hayes's careful dietary, and Darsie was acutely conscious of the beauty and elegance of the room. How small and poky and drab the home drawing-room would appear in comparison! How different the outlook on another row of red-brick houses, from the sweep of green lawns, and the avenue of great beech-trees seen through the four long French windows which broke the side of this long, low room!

How different her own life promised to be from those of the two girls by her side – the girls who had just returned from a ride on their own horses over their own land! ... They would never need to worry about money; their rôle in life for the next few years would consist in being pretty and agreeable, wearing charming frocks, visiting at friends' houses, travelling in summer, hunting in winter, and, finally, making suitable marriages, settling down as mistresses of other luxurious houses, and living happily ever after! /

She herself would study and cram for examination after examination; go through agonies of suspense waiting for results, and as she passed or failed, obtain a good or second-rate appointment in a suburban school. Henceforth work, work, work – teaching by day, correcting exercises by night, in a deserted schoolroom, with three months' holiday a year spent at home among brothers and sisters whose interests had necessarily drifted apart from her own! As the years passed by she would become staid and prim; schoolmistressy manner; the girls would speak of her by derisive nicknames. ...

A knifelike pang of envy pierced Darsie's heart; she dropped the dainty morsel of cake on to her plate with a feeling of actual physical nausea; for the moment her old ambitions lost their savour, and appeared grey and dead; she was pierced with an overpowering pity for her own hard lot.

The sensation was, perhaps, as much physical as mental, for no one can pass through a moment of acute mental tension without suffering from a corresponding nervous collapse, but being too young and inexperienced to realize as much, Darsie mentally heaped ashes on her head, and shed tears over her blighted life. The signs of her emotion were noticeable, not only in an unusual silence but in whitening cheeks, which brought upon her the quick attention of her friends. /

"Aren't you feeling quite well, dear?" Mrs. Percival asked kindly. "You look pale. Would you like to lie down?"

"Darsie, you are *green!* What's the matter? You were all right a moment ago."

"I'm all right now. Please, please, take no notice. I'm perfectly all right."

Noreen was beginning to protest again, when Ralph called her sharply to order –

"That's enough, Nora! Awfully bad form to fuss. Talk about something else. What about that garden-party you were discussing? I thought you wanted to ask suggestions."

Instantly both sisters were sparkling with excitement and animation.

"Oh, yes, yes. Of course! We must ask Darsie. She has such lovely ideas. Darsie, we are going to have a garden-party. The invitations are going out to-morrow. Hundreds of people are coming – mother's friends, our friends, everybody's friends, every bowing acquaintance for miles around. The question of the hour is – *What shall we do?* Garden-parties are such monotonous occasions, always the same over and over again – people sitting about in their best clothes, eating ices and fruit, listening to a band, and quizzing each other's best clothes. We want to hit on a brilliant novelty. What shall it be?" /

Darsie mused, her face lighting with pleasure and anticipation.

"I know nothing about garden-parties. There aren't any in town. What have you done before?"

"Tennis, croquet, clock-golf, pingpong, archery, yeomanry sports, blue bands,[50] red bands, black and yellow bands, glee-singers, Punch and Judy," Ida counted off one item after another on the fingers of her left hand. "And now we seem to have come to the end of our resources. We can't think of anything else. Do, like a darling, give us an idea!"

The darling deliberated once more, head on one side, lips pursed, eyes on the ceiling, while the Percival family looked on, and exchanged furtive glances of admiration. She *was* pretty! prettier by far than ordinary pretty people, by reason of some picturesque and piquant quality more readily felt than defined. It didn't seem to matter one bit that her nose turned up, and that her mouth was several sizes too large. "If you described me on paper, I'd sound far nicer, but I look a wur-r-rm beside her!" sighed Noreen mentally, just as Darsie lowered her eyes to meet those of her hostess, and inquired gravely –

"How much may it cost?"

It was the question which accompanied every home plan, and on which hung a momentous importance, but the Percivals appeared quite taken / aback by the suggestion. The girls stared, and their mother smilingly waved it aside.

"Oh-h, I don't think we need trouble about that! It's only once a year, and we must do the thing well. If you have a suggestion, dear, please let us have it!"

"I was thinking," said Darsie hesitatingly, "of a treasure hunt!"

Instantly all four hearers acclaimed the idea with such unanimity and fervour that the proposer thereof was quite overpowered by the thanks lavished upon her.

"The *very* thing! Why did we never think of it ourselves? Every one will like it, and it will keep them moving about, which is always the great problem to solve. Presents, presents, lots of presents, stowed away in odd corners. . . ."

"We'll each take a certain number and hide them in our *own* pet corners when no one else is in the garden. We'll make the parcels up in *green* paper, so as to be less easy to find. . . ."

"Every one must be told to bring them back to the lawn for a grand public opening, so that the disappointed ones may join in the fun. . . ."

"We may take part ourselves, mother? We *must* take part! Get lots and lots of presents, and let us hunt with the rest!"

"Certainly, dears, certainly. It is your party as much as mine; of course you must hunt. I'll / run up to town and buy the presents at the stores. You must help me to think of suitable things. Bags, purses, umbrellas, blotters, manicure-cases –"

"Boxes of French bonbons, belts, scarfs –"

"Cigarettes, brushes –"

"Nice little bits of jewellery –"

Suggestions poured in thick and fast, and Mrs. Percival jotted them down on a little gold and ivory tablet which hung by her side unperturbed by what seemed to Darsie the reckless extravagance of their nature. It was most exciting talking over the arrangements for the hunt; most agreeable and soothing to be constantly referred to in the character of author and praised for cleverness and originality. Darsie entirely forgot the wave of depression which had threatened to upset her composure a few minutes before, forgot for the time being the suspense and danger of the earlier afternoon.

Some one else, it appeared, however, was more remindful, for when she prepared to depart the dog-cart[51] stood at the door, and Ralph announced in his most grand seigneur manner –

"We're going to drive you back, don't you know! Too awfully fagging[52] to bicycle on a hot afternoon. Put on your hats, girls, and hurry up."

The girls obediently flew upstairs, and Darsie's / protestation of "My bicycle!" was silenced with a word.

"The stable-boy shall ride it over to-morrow morning. You're a bit jumpy still and can't be allowed to run any risks. I mean to see you safely back in your aunt's charge."

Darsie scrambled up to her high seat and leaned back thereon with an agreeable sense of importance.

"I feel like a cat that's been stroked," she said to herself, smiling. "When you're one of a large family you are not used to fussing. It's most invigorating! I'd like to go in for a long course!" /

Chapter XIII

The Treasure Hunt

THE invitations for the garden-party arrived in due course: one for Lady Hayes, another for Miss Darsie Garnett, and in the corner of each, beside the name of a celebrated military band, appeared the magic words "*Treasure Hunt.*" Darsie felt something of the proud interest of the author who beholds in print the maiden effort of his brain, as she gazed upon those words, and reflected that but for her own suggestion they would never have appeared. Lady Hayes also seemed to feel a reflected pride in her niece's ingenuity, which pride showed itself in a most agreeable anxiety about the girl's toilette for the occasion.

After a survey of the few simple dresses which composed Darsie's wardrobe, it was pronounced that nothing was suitable for garden-party wear, and a dress-maker was summoned from the country town to take measurements for a dainty white dress and hat to match. The dress was made to / reach right down to the ankles, in deference to Lady Hayes's ideas of propriety, and Darsie felt prodigiously fine and grown-up as she peacocked about before the long glass of her bedroom wardrobe on the day of the garden-party itself. Never in her life before had she possessed a gown made by an expert dressmaker, and the result was surprisingly flattering. She expatiated on the same with a candour startling to the audience of aunt and her maid.

"Don't I look s-weet? So slim! I'd no idea I was such a nice shape. I don't know which looks nicest, the frock on me or me in the frock! Aren't I tall? Isn't it graceful when I stand like this, and show the pleats? The hat's a duck! I must say I do look most scrumptiously nice!"

"My dear!" Lady Hayes looked both shocked and alarmed. "My dear, how *can* you? I shall begin to regret my purchases if they encourage a spirit of vanity. I was always taught to allow others to praise me and to keep silent myself."

"But you *thought* all the time, Aunt Maria, you couldn't help thinking, and it's worse to bottle it up. I'm always quite candid on the subject of my appearance," returned Darsie calmly. "On principle! Why should you speak the truth on every other subject, and humbug about that? When I've a plain fit I know it, and grovel accordingly, and when I'm nice I'm as / pleased as Punch. I *am* nice to-day, thanks to you and Mason, and if other people admire me, why shouldn't I admire myself? I *like* to admire myself! It's like the cocoa advertisements, 'grateful and comforting.' Honest Ingin,[53] Aunt Maria! Didn't *you* admire yourself when you saw yourself in the glass in that ducky grey bonnet?"

Evidently the question hit home, for Lady Hayes made a swift change of front.

"My dear, my dear, moderate your language! Your expressions are unsuitable for a young gentlewoman. You are growing up. Try, I beg, to cultivate a more ladylike demeanour!"

Darsie made a little face at the charming reflection in the glass, the which Lady Hayes wisely affected not to see, and presently aunt and niece were seated side by side in the big old barouche, forming one of a concourse of vehicles which were converging together out of every cross road, and turning in a seemingly endless string in the direction of the Hall. Shut carriages, open carriages, motors of different sizes and makes, dog-carts, pony carriages, governess carts – on they came, one after another, stirring up the dust of the road till the air seemed full of a powdery mist, through which unhappy pedestrians ploughed along in the shadow of the hedgerows, their skirts held high in white-gloved hands. /

Darsie thought it inhuman of her aunt not to fill the carriage to overflowing with these unfortunates, but she made no attempt to do so, but sat up stiff and straight in her seat, a typical old lady of the olden times, in her large bonnet, grey satin gown, and richly embroidered China crape shawl.[54]

"If you're not proud of yourself, I'm proud of you!" the girl declared, smoothing the satin folds with an approving hand. "You look just what you are, a dear old fairy godmother who pretends to be proud and fierce, and is really a lump of kindness and generosity. All the other old ladies look dowds beside you."

"Don't flatter me, my dear. I dislike it extremely," returned Lady Hayes with such an obvious look of satisfaction the while that Darsie laughed in her face, and laughed unreproved.

Arrived at the Hall, the guests were escorted through the perilously slippery hall, on which the mats seemed to turn into fresh pitfalls and slide beneath the feet; then through a side-door on to a miniature lawn, in the centre of which stood Mrs. Percival, sweetly smiling, and ejaculating endlessly: "Delighted to see you! *So* nice of you to come!" before passing the visitors on to her husband and children who were ranged at discreet intervals along the sweep of the lawn. The girls whispered dramatically to Darsie that / for the time being they were tied, literally tied by the heels, so she sat demurely by her aunt's side under the shade of a great beech-tree, listened to the band, spilt drops of hot tea down the front of her white dress, buttered the thumbs of her white kid gloves, and discovered the unwelcome but no doubt wholesome fact that there were other girls present who appeared just as attractive, or even more so than herself!

Then the band began to play item number four on the programme, and Noreen Percival came forward with a sigh of relief.

"At last I am free! They've all come, or practically all, and we can't wait for the laggards. The Hunt begins at three o'clock., Mother thought we'd better have it early, as it would shake them up and make them more lively and sociable. You'll have to search by yourself, Darsie, for as we have all done some of the hiding, it wouldn't be fair to us to go about in pairs. There are piles of presents, and your eyes are so sharp that you are sure to find two or three. You mustn't open them on the spot, but bring them up to the cedar lawn, where mother will be waiting with the old fogies who are too old to run about, but who would like to see the fun of opening. I *do hope* I find the right thing! There's the sweetest oxydized buckle with a cairngorm in the centre[55] that would be the making of my grey dress. I / have set my heart upon it, but I haven't the least notion where it's stowed. It may even have been among my own parcels, and of course I can't go near those. . . ."

"If I get it, we'll swop! I wish I knew the garden better. I don't know of *one* good hiding-place except those I made myself. . . . Perhaps I shan't find anything at all."

"Oh, nonsense! Keep your eyes open and poke about with your feet and hands, and you can't go wrong. The paper's just a shade lighter than the grass. Remember!"

Noreen flew off again to move a chair for an old lady who wished to escape the rays of the sun, and once more Darsie was left to her own resources. By her side Lady Hayes was deep in conversation with another old lady on the well-worn subject of a forthcoming agricultural show, and the town-bred visitor, failing to take an intelligent interest in prize carrots and potatoes, turned her attention to the group on the right, where Ralph Percival was making himself agreeable to three fashionable-looking girls of about her own age.

He wore an immaculate grey suit and a Panama hat, and regarding him criti-cally, Darsie felt another shock of surprise at being compelled to admire a *man!* Hitherto she had regarded the race as useful, intelligent creatures, strictly utili-tarian in looks, as in attire, but to-day it was / impossible to deny that the beauty was on Ralph's side more than on that of his companions. The poise of the tall, slim figure was so graceful and easy that it was a pleasure to behold; the perfect lines of aquiline nose, and dented chin, the little kink and wave which refused to be banished from the clipped hair, the long narrow eyes, and well-shaped lips made up a whole which was quite startlingly handsome and attractive. The three girls looked back at him with undisguised admiration and vied with one another in animated conversation, in return for which he drawled out slow replies in a tone of languid boredom.

During the fortnight which had elapsed since the date of her misadventure on the river, Darsie had had frequent meetings with the Percivals, and now felt on the footing of a friend rather than an acquaintance. Concerning the girls, there was no question in her mind. They were dears, not dears of the same calibre as Vi and plain Hannah, dears of a less interesting, more conventional description, but dears all the same, lively, good-tempered, and affectionate. The only brother was a far more complex character, with regard to whom Darsie changed her mind a dozen times a day. At one time he was all that was delightful, full of natural, boy-like good-comradeship; at another he was a bored and supercilious dandy, looking down on schoolgirls from an intolerable / height of patronage, and evi-dently priding himself on a *blasé* indifference. The present moment showed him in the latter mood, and Darsie's lips curled as she watched and listened, and in her eyes there danced a mocking light. "Like a vain, affected girl!" was the mental comment, as her thoughts flew back to Harry and Russell, uncompromising and blunt, and to Dan Vernon in his shaggy strength. Even as the thought passed through her mind Ralph turned, met the dancing light of the grey eyes, and turned impatiently aside. He would not look at her, but he could *feel!* Darsie watched with a malicious triumph the flush creeping slowly over the smooth pale cheek, the hitch of the shoulders, the restless movement of the hands which betrayed the hidden discomfort. Presently some friends came forward to join the three ladies, when Ralph immediately joined her with an invitation which sounded more like a command –

"Come for a walk round the gardens!"

Darsie rose, nothing loath, conscious that she was about to be reproved, and finding an agreeable sense of support in her lengthened skirts, and the semblance of grown-upness which they imparted.

"What did you mean by staring at me like that?"

"Like which?" /

"You know very well. You did it on purpose to annoy me, and make me uncomfortable."

"Oh no, I didn't! I didn't do anything. It did itself. It was just the outward and visible expression of my inward and invisible thoughts."

"Pretty middling disagreeable thoughts they must have been!"

"Humph! Not disagreeable exactly. Hardly strong enough for that. Just amused!"

"Amused!" The flush deepened on the lad's cheek. Unwittingly Darsie had hit upon the most scathing of all indictments. To be an object of *amusement* to others! What could be more lacerating to the dignity of nineteen years. "I had no idea that I was being so funny. Will you have the goodness to point out what you found so amusing?"

"Your airs," replied Darsie bluntly. "And graces! You asked me, you know, so I'm bound to tell you. It's so odd to see a boy like that. But you needn't be cross. I'm speaking only for myself. Those other girls liked it very much . . . .You could see that for yourself."

"Just so. We are talking of *your* opinion at the moment, however, not of theirs. What sort of – er – *boys* are you accustomed to meet, if one may ask?"

The strong accent thrown on the word "boys" showed a fresh ground of complaint. Darsie felt / a twinge of compunction, remembering the episode of the punt and her own great cause for gratitude. The answer came with startling earnestness.

"Not a bit braver than you, nor quicker and cleverer in an emergency. Perhaps not so good. If you'd hesitated one moment I mightn't have been here to criticize. But, just big, simple boys, not an ounce of affectation between them. Of course, they are not handsome. That makes a difference. . . ."

But Ralph was not to be mollified by a compliment on his good looks. He was irritated, and considered that he had good reason for being so. Darsie Garnett was an unusually pretty and attractive girl, and having saved her from a perilous position but a fortnight earlier, it had been an agreeable delusion to imagine himself ensconced for life in her estimation as a gallant young rescuer, the object of her undying gratitude and admiration – a delusion indeed, since the criticism of those mocking eyes was more than equalled by the explicitness of her explanations!

Ralph looked injured and melancholy, and Darsie, with characteristic softness of heart, was instantly seized with compunction. She was finding out for herself what every one who came in contact with Ralph Percival discovered sooner or later – that it was exceedingly difficult to keep up a feeling of offence against any one who showed / his displeasure in so interesting and attractive a fashion.

He was so handsome, so graceful in movement, he had the art of concealing the most ordinary emotions behind a cloak of baffling superiority. To-day, as he paced the garden paths by Darsie's side, Ralph wore the air of a lovelorn poet, of a patriot sorrowing for his country, an artist wrestling over a life's masterpiece, like anything or everything, in fact, but just what he was – a sulky and empty-headed young gentleman, wounded in his own conceit!

To her own amazement Darsie presently found herself engaged in the humble position of "making it up," and in taking back one after another each disparaging remark which she had made, which, being done, Ralph graciously consented to "think no more about it!" and strolled off to speak to a friend, leaving her stranded by herself at the far end of the garden.

The position would have been an uncomfortable one had it not happened that just at that moment a bell rang loudly, followed by a sudden gathering together of the guests upon the cedar lawn. Mr. Percival was making some announcement which was greeted by bursts of approving laughter. The words of the announcement were inaudible to Darsie's ears, but the purport was unmistakable. The treasure hunt had begun! With one accord / the guests turned and streamed in the direction of the gardens, turning to right and to left, peering beneath bushes, poking delicately among the foliage of flower-beds with the ferules of walking-sticks and parasols. . . .

Darsie turned and fled like a lapwing along the path leading past the tennis-lawn and rose and vegetable gardens, to the shaded fern grotto which formed one of the boundaries of the grounds. The idea had come to her to begin, so to speak, at the end and have the field to herself, but, as is usually the case, she was to discover that others were as ingenious as herself, for she had soon quite a string of followers along the narrow paths.

The thickly growing ferns seemed to offer endless hiding-places, but a printed notice to the effect that "It is not necessary to walk upon the Beds!" seemed to limit the possible area to that within reach of hand or stick. Darsie poked and peered, lifted the hanging fronds which fell over the rockwork border of the lily pond, stood on tiptoe on the rustic seat to peer between the branches of surrounding trees, but could discover nothing in the semblance of a paper packet. It was the same story in the rose garden, though the thick foliage on the pergolas seemed to offer numberless hiding-places for dainty packets, containing great gear in little bulk; it was the same / story in the wide, herbaceous border, though pathways on either side offered double opportunities for search. For the first few minutes the search was pursued in almost complete silence, but as time went on there came the sound of one triumphant cry after another, as a busy searcher was rewarded by a sudden sight of the longed-for paper wrapping. Darsie's envious eyes beheld one young girl running gaily past, with no less than three trophies carried bag-like in the folds of a chiffon scarf. *Three!* And she herself had not yet discovered one! What would the Percivals say if at the end of the hunt she returned empty-handed? The surprised incredulity of the girls, the patronising condolences of Ralph, seemed in prospect equally unwelcome. Desire for a present itself became subservient to anxiety for the credit of her own sharp-sightedness and intuition. She *must* and would discover a parcel before the time limit was past!

The next half-hour passed in a search ever more eager and strenuous, as with every moment that passed the chance of success diminished. So many treasures had already been discovered that Darsie began to think with a pang that perhaps there were no more to be found. Every third or fourth visitor seemed to be carrying a trophy; some with airs of would-be modesty were wending their way back to the cedar lawn carrying as / many as three or four, declaring that really and really they must not look any more – it was altogether *too* greedy! As they passed by the spot where Darsie pursued her ceaseless search, they would pause with words of maddening advice or condolence.

"Not found anything yet? How unfortunate! Look beneath the leaves. . . ." Once Ralph passed by and arched his eyebrows in eloquent surprise. He seemed on the point of offering advice, but Darsie whisked off in the opposite direction, to take refuge in the least frequented portion of the grounds, the orchard.

Only ten minutes left! The bell of warning was pealing loudly from the cedar lawn, she could hear the merry chatter of the returning guests.

Darsie lifted her muslin skirts and ran quickly in and out between the trees, searching for some hiding-place as yet undiscovered. The gnarled branches seemed to offer endless convenient niches, but in none of them could anything in the shape of a parcel be discovered. She was on the point of abandoning the search and returning empty-handed, when, lifting up a heavy branch, her eyes suddenly lit upon a cavity in the trunk of one of the oldest trees. When the branch remained in its ordinary position, the hollow was completely hidden from sight; moreover its position facing the wall made it doubly invisible. It hardly / seemed possible that so very obscure a hiding-place would be chosen under the circumstances, but at this last moment no chance could be neglected.

Darsie rolled back her dainty net sleeve, plunged her hand deep into the hollow trunk, and flushed with triumph as her fingers came in contact with something loose and soft. It was not a paper parcel, it felt more like cloth – cloth with knotted ends all ready to pull. Darsie pulled with a will, found an unexpected weight, put up a second hand to aid the first, and with a tug and a cloud of dust brought to light nothing more exciting than a workman's handkerchief, knotted round a lumpy parcel which seemed obviously a midday meal.

It was a disappointment, but the next moment an inherent sense of humour had discovered its possibilities of the position and gallantly accepted a second best.

Since she might not possess a proper present, she could at least be the happy proprietor of a joke! Into the middle of the ring of guests she would march, handkerchief bundle in hand, and to her credit would remain, if not the greatest applause, at least the biggest laugh of the afternoon!

Darsie drew down her sleeve, brushed the top coating of dust from the handkerchief, and hurried onwards towards the cedar lawn. /

Chapter XIV

A Treasure Indeed

DARSIE was one of the last guests to arrive upon the final scene of the treasure hunt, and already the merry process of parcel opening had begun. The young girl who had captured three prizes was on her knees before a garden seat, laying them out in a row to be seen and admired of all. Gaily dressed women were running about appealing to their male friends for the loan of penknives to cut the encircling string, and the air was full of the sound of laughter and happy, triumphant voices.

"How lovely! How beautiful! Isn't it charming? *Just* what I wanted!"

Darsie stood in the background, her hands clasping her bundle behind her back, so as to screen it from view until the right moment arrived for its production. The prize-winners were one and all in such a desperate hurry to examine their "finds" that she would not have long to wait, and meanwhile the scene was delightful to witness. / Every one looked gay, and happy and smiling; the many-coloured frocks of the women made charming flecks of colour against the sombre green of the old cedar, as they moved to and fro with dazzling, kaleidoscopic effect. Darsie had never even imagined such a scene; it seemed to her more like fairyland than the dull work-a-day world.

She looked on, absorbed in delighted admiration, while one after another the coverings were torn from the dainty packages, and the brilliance of the scene was enhanced by the glitter of silver, and glass, and dainty patches of colour. It would take long, indeed, to write of the treasures which Mrs. Percival had amassed in that day in town; it seemed to Darsie that nothing less than the contents of an entire shop window could have supplied so bewildering a variety. Bags, purses, satchels, brushes, manicure-cases, blotters, boxes, cigarette-cases, photograph frames, fans, brooches, bracelets, buckles, studs, tie-pins, waistcoat buttons – wherever the eye turned there seemed something fresh and beautiful to admire.

After such an Aladdin's feast, would not her workman's bundle fall very flat? With a sudden access of humility Darsie was about to turn tail and put the poor man's dinner back in its hiding-place, when from across the lawn she met Ralph's eyes fixed upon her with an expression of patronizing commiseration. He was pitying her, / because she had come back empty-handed when sharper eyes had reaped so rich a harvest! That touch of superiority made short work of Darsie's hesitation. She would show that she was in no need of pity, that so far from being overpowered by failure, she remained jaunty and self-confident enough to turn her own disappointment into a joke for the amusement of others! With head thrown back she marched dramatically forward to the spot where Mrs. Percival stood, the gracious mistress of the ceremonies, and held the bundle towards her in extended hands.

"Dear child, what have you there? A bundle – a workman's bundle! Where in the world have you discovered that?"

"In the trunk of an old tree, in the orchard near the wall."

"In the orchard? It belongs most likely to one of the men. His dinner, I should say, but what an odd place to hide it! So dirty! She gave a dainty little shake of distaste. "I should put it away, dear, really! It is covered with dust."

"It's a very *lumpy* dinner," said Darsie, patting the surface of the bundle with curious fingers. "I thought perhaps it was a treasure done up in a different way from the others. It's heavy, too, far heavier than bread and cheese. I can open it, can't I? Just to make sure!"

"Oh, certainly, if you like –" assented Mrs. / Percival dubiously, and Darsie waited for no further permission, but promptly knelt down on the grass and set to work to untie the knotted ends of the checked handkerchief. The surrounding guests gathered around in a laughing circle, being in the gay and gratified frame of mind when any distraction is met halfway, and ensured of a favourable reception. What was this pretty girl about? What joke was hidden away in this commonplace-looking bundle?

The knot was strongly tied, but Darsie's fingers were strong also and in a minute's time it was undone, and the corners of the handkerchief dropped on the grass to reveal an inner bag of thick grey linen tied again round the mouth.

"It *is* lumpy!" repeated Darsie again; then with a tug the string came loose, and lifting the bag in her hands, she rained its contents over the grass.

* * * * *

Was it a dream? Was it some fantasy of imagination – some wonderful effect of sunshine shining upon hundreds and hundreds of dewdrops, and turning them into scintillating balls of light, catching reflections from the flowers in yonder beds, and sending dancing rays of red, blue, and green across the grass? Red and blue and green the rainbow drops gleamed upon the ground, vivid and clear as the loveliest among the blossoms, but / possessed of a radiance which no earth flower had inherited before.

Darsie sat back on her heels, her arms falling slack by her sides, her wide eyes fixed on the ground in a surprise too complete for speech. Nobody spoke; the stupor in her own brain must surely have communicated itself to the guests crowding around, for while one might have counted fifty there was blank, utter silence upon the lawn. Then suddenly came a dramatic interruption; a cry, almost a scream, in a high, feminine voice, and a tall, fashionably dressed woman grasped wildly at a dangling chain of stones.

"My rubies! My rubies! My beautiful, beautiful rubies! Found again! *Safe!* Oh, my rubies!" She burst into excited sobs, a gentleman came forward and led her gently aside, but her place was immediately taken by other women – white-faced, eager, trembling with anxiety.

"Oh! Oh-h – let me look! It's the jewels, the lost jewels – Are my diamonds among them? Do you see a diamond necklace with an emerald clasp? Oh, *do, do* look!"

"My sapphires! They were taken, too. My sapphires – !"

They fell on their knees, regardless of their filmy draperies, and grasped at one shining treasure after another. The delicate chains were knotted together; curved corners of gold had caught in / other curved corners, so that in some cases half a dozen different ornaments presented the appearance of one big, bejewelled ball, and it was no easy matter to disentangle one from the other. The different owners, however, showed a marvellous quickness in recognizing even a fragment of their lost treasures, and their exultation was somewhat undignified as they turned and twisted and coaxed the dainty threads, and finally clasped their lost treasures, safe and sound, and all the time Darsie sat back on her heels, with her golden hair hanging in heavy masses over her shoulders, her eyes fixed upon this extraordinary scene, staring – staring!

"Darsie, dear child, how can we thank you?" Mrs. Percival's low voice trembled with earnestness; she had lifted a long string of pearls from the grass, and now held it between both hands, with a transparent pleasure it was true, but without any of the hysteric excitement shown by her guests.

"Do you realize all that your workman's bundle contained, or the weight you have taken off our minds? It was the thief's bundle, the bundle of jewels which he stole from the house on the night of the Hunt Ball, which we have tried so hard to recover! To think – to think that all this time they have been hidden close at hand!"

"Hidden with a purpose, too! Look at this, Evelyn!" interrupted Mr. Percival, holding out / a corner of the checked handkerchief towards his wife, with a stern look on his handsome face – "'B. W.' That's Wilson's property! He was a worse offender than we thought."

"Wilson? That was the young gamekeeper, wasn't it?" asked another man – the husband of the lady who was still crooning over her recovered diamonds. "You thought he had been led away by smart London thieves, but this seems as if he had taken a leading part. Looks, too, as if there may have been only himself and Forbes in the affair!"

"Just so! No wonder Wilson refused to give the names of his colleagues. When the chase grew too hot he hid the spoils in this tree – evidently an old hiding-place – before climbing the wall. If he had made clear away that night we should never have suspected his share in the theft. He would have turned up as usual next morning, and expressed great surprise at the news. As it is he and Forbes are no doubt patiently waiting until their sentences are out, expecting to slip back some dark night and secure their prey. From such point of view it is a small business to serve a few months when there's a fortune waiting at the end! Well, this takes ten years off my back. I can't tell you how the whole business has preyed on our minds. My dear fellow, I am so thankful that your diamonds have turned up!" /

"My dear fellow, it was fifteen times worse for you than for us! A most uncomfortable position; I congratulate you a hundred times. Just in the nick of time, too. In a month or so there would have been no bundle to discover."

A general gasp at once of dismay and relief passed round the little inner circle of those most nearly interested in the recovered treasures, and the first excitement of recovery having passed, every one seemed bent on lavishing thanks and praises upon the girl through whom the happy discovery had come about.

"Who is she?" "What is her name?" "Where does she come from?" The questions buzzed on every side, and the answer, "Lady Hayes's grandniece," served only to enhance existing attractions. Darsie found herself kissed, patted, embraced, called by a dozen caressing names by half a dozen fine ladies in turn, during which process every eye on the lawn was turned upon her blushing face. Through a gap in the crowd she could see Lady Hayes holding as it were a secondary court, being thanked effusively for possessing a grandniece with a faculty for recovering jewels, and bowing acknowledgments with a bright patch of colour on either cheekbone. The position was so strange and bewildering that even yet it seemed more like a dream than reality; that sudden rain of jewels descending from the linen / bag was the sort of thing one might expect in an Arabian night adventure[56] rather than in the midst of a decorous English garden-party! It must surely be in imagination that she, Darsie Garnett, has been hailed as a good fairy to all these fashionably dressed men and women!

The almost hysteric effusion of the women who kissed and gushed around her must surely have something infectious in its nature, since she herself was beginning to feel an insane inclination to burst into tears or laughter, it was immaterial which of the two it should be. Darsie turned a quick look around, searching for a way of escape, and at that moment Noreen's hand pressed on her arm, and she found herself being led gently towards the house.

"Poor old Darsie, then! She looks quite dazed!" said Noreen's voice. "No wonder, after all that fuss. You've been kissed to pieces, poor dear, and howled over, too. Silly things! howling when things are lost, and howling again when they are found! I've no patience with them; but, oh, my dear, I *do* bless you for what you've done! You've no idea how relieved we shall be. It was such a *stigma* to have your guests robbed under your own roof, and by one of your own men, too. Mother has never been the same since – worried herself into nerves, and fancied every one blamed her, and thought she'd been careless. You can't / think *how* happy she'll be writing to the people who aren't here to-day telling them that their things are found! She'll feel a new creature."

"I'm so glad. She's a dear. Wasn't she sweet and dignified among them all? Oh, dear! I'm all churned up. I thought as I couldn't find a treasure I'd have a little joke on my own account, and after all I found the biggest treasure of all! Noreen! how much money were those things worth?"

"Oh, my dear, don't ask me! Mother's pearls alone are worth three thousand, and that's nothing to the rest. Mrs. Ferriers' rubies are the most valuable, I believe. Altogether it must be a fortune – to say nothing of the associations. Isn't it strange to think of? An hour ago you were a stranger whom scarcely any one knew even by sight, and now in a flash you have become a celebrity, a heroine – the pet of the county!"

"Am I? Really? It sounds agreeable. I'll write to-night and tell Vi Vernon, and sign myself 'The Pet of the County.' She *will* be impressed. Pity it wasn't my own county, where it would be of more use. I shall probably never see these good people again."

"Fiddle!" cried Noreen derisively. "No chance of that. Whether you like it or no, my dear, this day has settled your fate. You can / never be a mere acquaintance any more. You've done us a service which will bind us together as long as we live. Henceforth a bit of you belongs to us, and we'll see that we get it!" /

Chapter XV

A Dream Fulfilled

THE next week brought with it a succession of bewildering excitements. From morn till night, as it seemed, the bell rang, and visitors were ushered in to congratulate Lady Hayes and her niece on the happy episode of the jewel-finding, and to repeat *ad infinitum* the same questions, ejaculations, and remarks. People who had no personal interest in the theft seemed, strangely enough, quite as excited and curious as those who had; and even when their curiosity was satisfied there still remained the servants in the house, the tradesmen in the village, the very children in the roads, who seemed one and all possessed with a thirst to hear the romantic story from the lips of the heroine herself.

Then letters from relations and friends! However minutely one might retail every incident, there still seemed an endless number of details which remained to be told to people who could not be satisfied without knowing in each case what *he* / said, how *she* looked, how *you* yourself felt and behaved!

The first three days were spent in talk; on the fourth began a second and still more exciting stage. The bell rang, a small, daintily tied parcel was handed in for Miss Garnett, which being unwrapped revealed a red velvet jeweller's box, and within that a small heart-shaped pendant, slung on a gold chain, and composed of one large and several small rubies, set transparently, so as to show to advantage their glowing rosy light. An accompanying card bore the inscription, "A small expression of gratitude from Mrs. Eustace Ferriers"; but even this proof was hardly sufficient to convince Darsie that such splendour was really for her own possession.

"Aunt Maria! Can she *mean* it? Is it really to keep?"

"Certainly, my dear. Why not? It is quite natural that Mrs. Ferriers should wish to give you some little remembrance as you were the means of restoring a valuable heirloom. It is a good stone. You must be careful not to lose it."

"Is it valuable, Aunt Maria – worth a lot of money?"

"It is a pretty ornament, my dear. Do not look a gift horse in the mouth."

It was all very well for Aunt Maria, a titled lady with a box full of jewels of her own, to / take things calmly, but for a member of a poor large family to receive a ruby pendant was a petrifying experience, only to be credited by a continual opening of the box and holding of it in one's hand to gaze upon its splendours. And then the very next morning the bell rang again, and in came another parcel, another jeweller's box, and inside it a blue enamelled watch with an encircling glitter of light where a family of tiny diamonds formed a border round the edge. There was an enamel bow also to fasten it on to a dress, but Darsie fairly quaked at the thought of the responsibility of wearing so gorgeous an ornament.

"That will do for mother," she announced decidedly. "It wouldn't be *decent* for me to flaunt about in enamel and diamonds when she has an old gold thing that is always slow. Besides, if she wears it I can watch the diamonds flash, and that is the best part of the fun. Aunt Maria, that's two! Do you suppose, should you imagine, that they'll *all* –"

Lady Hayes looked shocked, as in duty bound.

"My dear, I don't suppose anything about it. That is not our affair. It is sufficient that these two friends have been most kind and generous, and that you ought to be a very grateful girl. Surmises as to future gifts are in the worst possible taste."

Darsie wrinkled her nose and sat in silence for / several moments, moving the little watch to and fro to catch the play of light upon the stones. Then suddenly she spoke again –

"Aunt Maria, what are your ideas with regard to *luck*?"

"I have none, my dear. I don't believe in its existence!"

"But you must, Aunt Maria. You must. It was the merest luck my seeing that hole, and thinking of feeling inside, but it seems as if it were going to have such big consequences. Just in a moment it has brought me more influential friends than most girls meet with in the whole of their lives. They are all grateful to me; they feel that I have helped them; they want to help me in return; but after all there's no credit to me, it was all done without one scrap of thought or trouble. It seems hard to think that many people work and slave for years, and fail to gain a quarter as much as I have done by just pure luck!"

"Don't be so sweeping in your assertions, child. These are early days yet to talk about results. When you come to my age, my dear, you will look back and realize that those who go through life in the right spirit are never left to the mercy of what you call 'luck.' 'Submit thy way unto the Lord, and *He* will direct thy path.'[57] I am an old woman, Darsie, but I can say from my / heart that goodness and mercy have followed me all the days of my life."[58]

Darsie sat gazing thoughtfully into her aunt's face. Within the last weeks a degree of intimacy had developed between the old woman and the girl, which made it possible for the latter to speak out more openly than she would have believed possible a short month before.

"Aunt Maria," she said slowly, "I wish you would explain.... You talk of goodness and mercy, but – don't be shocked! – it doesn't seem to me that you have so *much* to be thankful for!... You are rich, of course, but that doesn't count for much by itself, and your life must have been hard.... You are delicate, and your husband died, and you have no children – no one to live with you in this big house. Now when you *are* old you are so lonely that you are glad to have me – a girl like me – for a few weeks' visit! When I go away you will be lonely again...."

A tremor passed over Lady Hayes's face; the thin fingers crossed and uncrossed themselves on her lap, but she smiled, a brave and patient smile. "You are right, Darsie. I have had bitter trials, nevertheless I have gained the greatest treasure that is given to any one on this earth."

"What is that, Aunt Maria?"

"Peace in my soul, child – 'the peace of God, / which passeth understanding,'"[59] said the old woman solemnly.

There was silence in the room. Darsie bent her head, awed and touched by the sound of those wondrous words. A month ago, at home with her brothers and sisters, she would have scoffed at the idea of peace in connection with Great-aunt Maria, but a closer intimacy had altered her opinion. About the trifling affairs of every day Aunt Maria continued to fuss. No one could deny for a moment that she fussed; but the big demands of life found her calm, serene, prepared. On the surface the waters might dash occasionally into foam, but the deep, strong current bore steadily towards the sea!

Darsie pondered, and as though divining the course of her thoughts, Lady Hayes spoke once more.

"Perhaps that appears to you a serious statement for me to make, since there are times when I must appear a very unpeaceful person. I am apt to be unduly concerned about trifles, to my own exhaustion and that of others. I am aware of the fact, and also that to one of your impetuous disposition such a failing must be particularly trying. Nevertheless, Darsie" – the old voice deepened impressively – "*the peace is there!*"

Slowly, thoughtfully Darsie bowed her head.

"Yes, I know. I've *felt* it. It has made me / ashamed. The human part of you may get out of hand sometimes, but you are *very* nearly an angel, Aunt Maria. You haven't much more to learn!..."

Lady Hayes shook her head, but her hand fell on Darsie's head with a tender touch, and a light shone in the tired eyes. The lonely heart was grateful for those words of encouragement.

Darsie's surmise that still more presents might arrive was justified by the delivery of three more packets – a dainty little pearl necklace from Mrs. Percival, a turquoise and diamond ring (oh, the rapture of owning a real ring of one's very own!), and a combination present of a jewelled bangle from three other ladies who had benefited by the lucky find. Thus in one short week had Darsie's jewellery risen from a total which she herself described as consisting of "a few glass beads and a gold safety-pin" to five separate articles of real beauty and value.

She was fond of spreading her treasures in a row on the table and gazing at them *en bulk,* moving her head from side to side to enjoy the flashing colours of the stones, and as she did so Lady Hayes was more than surprised by a mercenary element which seemed out of keeping with the girl's natural character.

"Rubies are the most valuable stones, aren't / they, Aunt Maria – more valuable than diamonds?"

"If they are of the right colour and depth, and of sufficient size."

"You said this was a good stone. It's a ripping colour. I should think this must be a valuable stone, wouldn't you?"

"I prefer not to speculate on the subject, child."

Or again –

"I should think this watch was worth lots of money. I have just counted, and there are forty diamonds, teenies, of course, but still – And the enamel is so fine. My bracelet has five *big* diamonds, and a whole heap of pearls; and there's the necklace, too. Should you think, Aunt Maria, that they were worth a hundred pounds put together?"

Lady Hayes laid down her knitting, and stared with stony eyes into the girl's face.

"I have told you before, Darsie, that I excessively dislike surmises as to the value of presents. I am surprised and disappointed to discover signs of an avaricious and grasping nature!"

To her surprise and dismay the only reply to this serious aspersion was a good-natured laugh.

"Goodness gracious, mercy on us!" cried Darsie audaciously. "I'm bad enough, in all conscience, but I'm not *that!* Not a grasp in me! You ask any one at home, and they'll tell you / I'm quite stupidly generous. It's not the money for the money's sake, I think of, but for what it will *do!* I've no use for jewels, Aunt Maria – shan't ever have a chance of wearing them, like Noreen and Ida. Imagine a daily governess glittering with gems! But if only – only I could turn them into money, it might fulfil the big ambition of my life and send me to Newnham, without troubling father for a penny! Can you wonder that I feel impatient with watches and chains when I think of *that?*"

"I am sorry, my dear. I did not understand. I apologize!" said Lady Hayes promptly. It was this unfailing sense of justice, combined with the dignity which never forsook her under any stress of excitement or agitation, which had been most largely instrumental in attracting the girl's admiration. From the impetuous standpoint of youth it seemed an almost inhuman pinnacle of perfection, but Darsie was quite determined that at some far-distant elderly epoch – say, in thirty years' time – she would begin practising these virtues on her own account. They seemed the only decorous accompaniment of white hair and spectacles.

She stretched out a sunburnt hand and patted the old lady's shoulder with an affectionate touch.

"All right! Don't worry. It *did* seem greedy, and of course you couldn't guess. You see, it's / particularly hard because plain Ha – Hannah Vernon, I mean – is going up, and that seems to make it worse for me. Her father is richer than ours, and he believes in higher education, so it's all settled that she is to go to Newnham, and she talks about it all the time, and pities me when she's in a good temper, and brags when she's not. And Dan would be at Cambridge, too, and Ralph Percival, and, oh dear, oh dear, we'd have such *sport!* Balls, and picnics, and cocoa parties, and boating in summer – no end of lovely exciting pranks!"

"Excuse me, my dear" – Lady Hayes was frosty again, staring stonily over the rim of her spectacles – "excuse me, but would you kindly explain for what reason you are anxious to go to Cambridge? I had imagined that it was for education, now it appears that balls and picnics are the attraction. Which of the two is it of which you are really thinking?"

"Oh, Aunt Maria, I'm a human girl! Of *both!*" cried Darsie, laughing. "Education first, of course, because of the result, and all it will mean afterwards, but if you want the truth, I shouldn't be so keen if it wasn't for the fun! We know a girl who's just come down, and it sounds such a lovely life.... I'd work hard; I love work, and when there is any on hand there's no peace for me till it's done; but *wouldn't* I / just play, too! It would be the time of my life. Oh, Aunt Maria, when I look at the governesses at school, and think that I'm going to be like that all my days, it *does* seem hard that I shouldn't have just two or three years *first* of the life I want!"

The words, the tone, both bore a touch of real pathos; nevertheless Lady Hayes smiled, as if, so far from being pained by the sad prospect, she found something amusing in the contemplation.

"It is a mistake to look too far ahead in life, but of course if you contemplate teaching, you ought to be thoroughly equipped." She was silent for a moment, gazing thoughtfully through the window. Then in a level, perfectly commonplace voice she continued: "I shall be pleased, my dear, to defray the expenses of your course at Newnham...."

The manner in which our great ambitions in life meet their realization is always and inevitably other than we have imagined. Sometimes so many years have passed by since the dreaming of the cherished plans, that the eager spirit is transformed into a wearied and dispirited being, to whom fulfilment brings no joy; sometimes it comes freighted with complications which rob it of half its zest; sometimes it brings no charm at all, but only bitterness and disappointment; and again – oh, often again, thank God for His / mercies! – it comes at the moment of hopelessness, of renunciation, dazzling the eyes and heart with a very incredulity of joy.

Those few quiet words in an old woman's voice transformed for Darsie Garnett the whole path ahead, making what had seemed a far-away vision become a solid, tangible fact. Quietly, prosaically, without any flourish of trumpets, the great prize of life had been handed into her grasp.

She sat motionless, staring with distended eyes, while Lady Hayes continued to speak in calm, even tones.

"I should like to explain to you, my dear, that I am not as rich a woman as I appear. It was my dear husband's wish that I should continue to occupy this house for the term of my life, but after that it passes to his relations. It is an expensive place to keep up, and leaves little margin out of the income which goes with it. I cannot save as I should have wished, and my own property is not large. When it is divided among my various nephews and nieces, there will not be much for each. I should like to have done more for your father, as he has a large family to provide for, but it is impossible. In your case, however, you have done me a kindness in spending these weeks with me when I needed companionship – and, I think, we are good friends! I can spare a few hundreds to give you your training *and* your fun – / and it will be a pleasure to me to do so. I will make a formal arrangement in my will so that in the case of my – so that in any case the money may be forthcoming. So, my dear, you may look upon the matter as settled, and make your arrangements accordingly."

Darsie put her hands to her head. Her cheeks were white, but around her eyes and nose an increasing pinkness of hue betrayed the inward struggle of emotion.

"I'm going to cry! I'm going to cry!" she cried. And when Lady Hayes began a protest, "Oh, Aunt Maria, don't, *don't* be proper!" she pleaded piteously. "I can't bear it just now. Please, please let me thank you in my own way! I must howl! I *must!* I'm all seething and churning with emotion, and if I don't cry I shall burst; but oh, I *do* love you – I adore you – I shall worship you until my dying day.... You'll be like a saint to me. I'll put you up on a pedestal and burn incense to you every day of my life. If you *knew* what it meant! And I've been so mean and hateful – such a contemptible little worm! Oh, if I lived a hundred thousand years, I could never repay you for this!"

"My dear, does it strike you that you are talking in a very wild, exaggerated fashion?"

"I am, I am! Girls *do,* Aunt Maria, when they are off their heads with joy. Wild, I mean, not / exaggerated – I mean it, every word. Oh, I *must* hug you. Never mind your cap; I must give you a bear hug, if I die for it. Dear, dearest, kindest, best –"

The old lady's stiff, upright figure disappeared bodily within the swooping arms; she was squeezed, hugged, rocked to and fro, and pelted with kisses until she was speechless and gasping for breath. When she was released her cap was askew, and the muslin folds in the front of her gown crumpled out of recognition; but for a marvel she spoke no word of reproach, and Darsie saw, with a sobering thrill, a glitter as of tears in the old eyes, and the mental question which arose at the sight was answered with intuitive sharpness. It was so long since she had been hugged before, so many, many years since anything more than a conventional peck had been pressed upon her cheek! Old, stern, proper as she was, Aunt Maria loved to be loved!

For the rest of the morning Darsie was as subdued and gentle in manner as she had hitherto been boisterous. The future was discussed in detail, and plans made which revolutionized more and more her future life, for Lady Hayes seemed to take for granted that in taking upon herself the responsibility for the girl's education she had earned a certain right to her society. Such phrases as "And in the holiday-time we can discuss," / "When you are here in the summer vacation," "I shall look forward to hearing your descriptions," could not be mis-understood, but for the moment the big gain outweighed the loss, and Darsie smiled on unperturbed. In time to come the sacrifice of merry family holidays would of a certainty demand its toll of suffering, but why encourage trouble that lay ahead when the present was so blissfully full of contentment?

When lunch was over Darsie tucked her hostess on the sofa, and hailed with delight the opportunity of a free hour in which to dream uninterrupted over the wonderful development of the day.

"I'll go out and walk it off. I'll rush down to the village and telegraph home. I can't possibly wait to write. How can I put it so that it will be plain enough and not too plain? 'Newnham ahoy!' 'I'm off to Newnham College in the morning!' 'Plans for Newnham satisfactorily arranged. Break news to Hannah.' *Won't* they stare! It's a blessing that neither Clemence nor Lavender would care to go if they had the chance, so they won't be jealous, but Hannah *will* jump. And Dan – what will Dan say? It is good luck knowing the boys so well. We'll make them take us about. To think that I was so furious and rebellious about this visit, and that it should have ended like this! It will be a lesson to me for life!"

It was very pleasant to ride through the sweet-smelling / lanes on this bright summer afternoon; very pleasant work sending off that telegram to the parents at the seaside, and drawing mental pictures of the excitement and rejoicings which would follow its arrival; pleasant to meet on every side kindly, interested glances, and to realize that if she were, as Noreen had declared, "the pet of the county," she was assuredly also "the heroine of the village."

It was a temptation to linger in the quaint little streets; but on this afternoon of all others Darsie was anxious not to be late for tea, so, with a sigh of regret, she turned up a side lane leading to the field path to the Manor, and in so doing came face to face with Ralph Percival, who, in his lightest and most sporting attire, was escorting a pack of dogs for an airing. There was the big silky-haired collie whom Darsie loved, the splay-footed dachshund which she hated, the huge mas-tiff which she feared, with one or two terriers of different breeds – alert, friendly, and gentle-eyed. One and all came sniffing round her as their master stopped to shake hands, and she stood up stiff and straight, trying to look at ease, and as if she were not really in momentary terror of an attack upon her ankles and skirts.

"Halloa!"

"How are you? Still living in a shower of jewels?" /

"I *have* been, but it's clearing off! The combination bracelet finished the list. Now I'm beginning to live in fear of another burglary, on myself. It will be a relief to get the things distributed. Mother is to have the watch, Clemence the pendant, Lavender the brooch, and I am going to be greedy and keep the bracelet and necklace and ring for myself."

"What a miser!" cried Ralph, laughing. His grey eyes looked very handsome and agreeable lit up with the twinkling light of amusement, and Darsie's spirits rose still a degree higher as he whistled to the dogs and turned round with the evident intention of accompanying her home.

"We'll come along with you. It doesn't matter where we go so long as we have a run. Bound for the Manor, I suppose? How's the old lady? In a good humour, I should say. You look particularly full of beams this afternoon!"

"I am – brimming over! You see before you, kind sir, the touching spectacle of a young female who has not a single ungratified wish in the world, and is so happy that she doesn't know how to preserve a decent appearance of calm. It's the more extraordinary because she usually wants quite a lot."

Ralph's eyebrows went up in expressive disdain.

"Re-al-ly! You don't say so! Glad to hear it, I'm shaw! The kind donors would be much gratified to know of the magic effect of their gifts. I / wonder, under the circumstances, that you could bear to part from any of them!"

The words were spoken in his most drawling and superior voice, and brought the blood rushing into Darsie's cheeks. She stood still in the middle of the road, and glared at him with flashing eyes.

"Horrible boy! What a disagreeable mind you must have, to think such mean, contemptible thoughts! Bother the jewellery! It may go to Jericho for all I care. I'm happy for a very different reason. Aunt Maria has just promised to pay for me to go to Newnham, and that has been the dream of my life. There's nothing to sneer at, you see, though perhaps *you* can manage to be superior even about that!"

"Yes, easily. I hate blue-stockings," said Ralph calmly, but his eyes twinkled as he spoke, and in spite of herself Darsie was obliged to smile in response.

"And I hate narrow-minded, prejudiced young men! Oh dear! you've put me in a bad temper on this day of days, just when I felt that I could never be cross again. I'll forgive you only because it's impossible to go *on* being cross. I've just been to the post-office to telegraph the great news to my people at the seaside. They'll be wild with excitement, especially my chum who will be going up at the same time, Hannah Vernon – 'plain Hannah' we call her. Funny nickname, isn't it?" /

"Sounds ingratiating!" Voice and expression were alike so expressive that Darsie went off into a merry trill of laughter, as she hastened to take up the cudgels in plain Hannah's defence.

"She doesn't care a bit. Jokes about it with the rest. And she is so funnily ugly that it's really rather dear. *And* clever! She'll be a first-class girl, you'll see if she isn't. I shall be nowhere beside her, but I'm going to *grind*. Let me see: if we go up in three years' time, when we're eighteen, how long will you have left of your course?"

"Perhaps a year, perhaps two. Depends upon how soon I go up. It isn't as if I had to go in for a profession or anything of that kind. I shall spend my life looking after the property, and there's no particular need to swot for that."

"I hate loafers," said Darsie in her turn, then once more relented and said genially, "But I don't believe you mean half that you say. Anyway, I shall look forward to meeting you at Cambridge, and I hope you are prepared to be kind, and to be ready to return the good offices which I have been able to render to your respected family."

"I am. What do you want me to do?"

"To be nice to me at Cambridge! I shall be a shy, lone Fresher, and you can make things much livelier for me if you like. I want you to like! Dan Vernon will be there, too, but he's so / serious and clever that he won't be much good for the *fun* part. I want you to promise not to be superior and proud, but a real friend to take us about, and dance with us at the balls, and get up picnics on the river. I can manage the work part for myself, but I want some help for the fun!"

She expected an instant response, but Ralph was too cautious to be drawn into rash promises.

"Er – what exactly do you mean by 'we'?"

"Myself and my chum, of course – Hannah Vernon."

"Plain Hannah?"

"Plain Hannah!"

Ralph shook his handsome head.

"I make no promise as regards plain Hannah. I'm not particularly partial to plain Hannahs, but I'll do my level best for Darsie Garnett. Like to! You can count upon me to do my best to give you a. rattling good time."

Darsie regarded him doubtfully, reflected that it was wisdom to accept what one could get, and smiled a gracious approval.

"Thanks – so much! Then it's a promise?"

"Certainly. A promise!"

They laughed again. The dogs leaped in the air and barked with delight. Everything and every one seemed happy to-day. Darsie felt that if she lived to be a hundred she could never, by any possibility, reach a higher pinnacle of content. /

PART II // Chapter XVI

After Three Years

Is your trunk ready, Darsie? Are you ready to come down? Lunch is on the table and we're all waiting. Have you fitted everything in? Oh dear, oh dear, how bleak and bare the room does look! I shall never have the heart to enter it after you're gone."

Clemence Garnett, aged twenty years, gave a pitiful glance round the dismantled room, which a few hours before had been decorated with the many and varied objects which were Darsie's treasures. She looked at the wooden wardrobe, the doors of which swung wide, showing a row of empty pegs, at the scattering of paper and rejected ends of ribbon and lace which littered the floor, and finally back at the figure of Darsie herself, kneeling before the great black trunk, with her golden hair ruffling round a flushed, eager face.

"Sit on it, Clemence, like a lamb. It's *got* to meet, but it's inches apart still. Sit down with a flop, and be your heaviest, while I fight with the lock." /

"Better take something out. If you make it so full, it may burst half-way. How would you like that?"

"Not much; but better than leaving anything behind. It wouldn't dare to burst after costing so much money. There! It's done. You're a pretty substantial weight, my dear. Now then for lunch and a rest; I've had a terrific morning."

Darsie rose to her feet and stood for a moment before the mirror, putting a tidying touch to hair and dress. She was a tall, slim girl, nearly a head taller than the more substantial Clemence, and the easy grace which characterised her movements was the first thing which attracted an unaccustomed eye. Even Clemence, with perceptions dulled by custom, felt dimly that it was an agreeable thing to watch Darsie brush her hair and shake out her skirts, though in another person such acts would be prosaic and tiresome. The crisp hair needed nothing but a brush and a pat to settle itself into a becoming halo of waves, and the small face on the long white neck had a quaint, kitten-like charm. Clemence looked from the real Darsie to the reflected Darsie in the glass, and felt a sudden knife-like pang.

"Oh, how I *hate* you going! How dull it will be. Why *couldn't* you be content to stay at home instead of taking up this Newnham craze? I shall miss you hideously, Darsie!" /

Darsie smiled involuntarily, then nobly tried to look sad.

"I expect you will, but one grown-up at home is as much as we can afford, and there'll be lovely long vacs. You must think of those, and the letters, and coming up to see me sometimes, and term time will pass in a flash. I'll be back before you realise that I'm gone."

Clemence pouted in sulky denial.

"Nothing of the sort. It will seem an age. It's easy to talk! People who go away have all the fun and excitement and novelty; it's the poor stay-at-homes who are to be pitied. How would you like to be me, sitting down to-morrow morning to darn the socks?"

"Poor old Clem!" said Darsie lightly. A moment later, with relenting candour, she added: "You'll like it a lot better than being examined by a Cambridge coach! So don't growse, my dears; we've both got the work we like best. Come down to lunch, and let's see what mother has provided for my go-away meal!"

Darsie slid a hand through Clemence's arm as she spoke and the two sisters squeezed down the narrow staircase, glad in their English, undemonstrative fashion of the close contact which an inherent shyness would have forbidden except in this accidental fashion. Across the oil-clothed passage they went, into the red-walled dining-room, / where the other members of the family waited their arrival.

Mrs. Garnett smiled at the traveller with a tinge of wistfulness on her face; the four young people stared, with a curiosity oddly infused with respect. A girl who was on the eve of starting for college had soared high above the level of ordinary school. Lavender, at "nearly seventeen," wore her fair locks tied back with a broad black ribbons; her skirts reached to her ankles; she was thin and angular; her head was perpetually thrust forward, and a pair of spectacles were worn perpetually over the bridge of her pointed little nose. The description does not sound attractive, yet in some mysterious manner, and despite all drawbacks, Lavender *did* manage to be attractive, and had a select band of followers at school who practised stoops and poked-out heads out of sheer admiration of her defects.

Harry's voice was beginning to croak, which, taken together with a dawning passion for socks, ties, and brilliantine, was an unmistakable sign of growing up; Russell was preternaturally thin and looked all arms and legs; while Tim had forsaken knickers for full-fledged trousers, and resented any attempt at petting as an insufferable offence.

One and all were on their best company manners on the occasion of Darsie's last lunch, / and the most honeyed replies took the place of the usual somewhat stormy skirmish of wits; nevertheless, there was a universal feeling of relief when the meal was over, and a peal at the bell announced the arrival of the cab which was to convey Darsie and a girl companion on the first stage of their journey.

If anything could have added to Darsie's joy in the fulfilment of a lifelong ambition, it would have been the fact that Hannah Vernon was to be her companion at Newnham, as she had been through the earlier schooldays. All the Vernon family were dears of the first water, and might have been specially created to meet the needs of their neighbours, the Garnetts. It is true that the Vernons possessed the enviable advantage of a big grown-up brother, but when the Garnetts felt particularly tried on this score, they sought comfort from the reflection that a brother so solemn and scholarly, so reserved and unresponsive, hardly counted as a brother at all. Dan was already in the second year of his Cambridge course, and was expected to do great things before he left. So far as such a sober person could be made useful, Darsie Garnett intended to use him towards the furtherance of her own enjoyment of the new life.

For the rest, Vi, the eldest daughter of the Vernon household, was the sworn ally and confidante / of Clemence, and John, the younger son, was in himself such a tower of mischievous strength that the Garnett trio sat at his feet. Last, but certainly not least, came Hannah, and Hannah was – Darsie would have found it an almost impossible task to describe "plain Hannah" to an unfortunate who had not the honour of her acquaintance. Hannah was Hannah, a being distinct by herself – absolutely different from any one else. To begin with, she was extraordinarily plain; but, so far from grieving over the fact, Hannah wore it proudly as the foremost feather in her cap.

It was she herself who had originated and sanctioned the continued use of the sobriquet, which had its origin in a juvenile answer given by herself to a stranger who inquired her name.

Now Hannah was the only member of the family who was limited to one cognomen, so she answered unthinkingly, "Hannah; *plain* Hannah!" and instantly descrying the twinkling appreciation in that stranger's eyes, she twinkled herself, and henceforth led the adoption of the title. Long use had almost deadened its meaning in the ears of the family, but strangers still suffered at the hearing.

Plain Hannah's face peered cheerily out of the cab window, her little eyes twinkled merrily, her preposterous eyebrows arched in derision of the / melancholy group upon the doorsteps. No one dared shed a tear when she was so evidently on the watch for any sign of weakness, sentimental farewells were checked upon the speaker's lips, and the whole business of parting assumed a lighter, a more matter-of-fact air.

A second big box was hoisted on to the cab roof, a few kisses shamefacedly exchanged, and then the travellers were off, and nothing remained to the watchers but to trail drearily back into a house from which half the brightness seemed to have departed.

Well might Clemence say that the worst pain of a parting fell on those who were left behind! While the stay-at-homes struggled heavily through a long afternoon, in every moment of which the feeling of loss became even more acute, Darsie and plain Hannah were enjoying one of the most exciting experiences of their lives.

In spite of an almost lifelong interest in Cambridge, neither girl had as yet visited the town itself, so that each incident of the journey was full of interest and excitement. The station was disappointingly like other stations, and they had abundant opportunity of examining it at leisure, since the porters rushed in a body to attend to the male students[60] who had arrived at the same time, and who could be trusted to give larger tips than their female companions. The drive / through the streets also fell short of expectations; but, after all, Cambridge meant Newnham, and there could be no disappointment there!

Peered at through the cab window, the building appeared unexpectedly large and imposing. It gave one a thrill of importance to realise that for the next three years one would be part and parcel of its life, an inhabitant of its great halls.

The cabman descended from the box and rang a peal at the bell, and it came as something as a shock to see an ordinary-looking maid throw open the door, though what exactly they had imagined the girls would have found it difficult to say. The maid inquired their names, led them forward through a long corridor, and flung open the door of a sitting-room where a lady sat before a desk. It was a pretty, cheerful-looking apartment, full of flowers, books, pictures, and quaint old-world furniture, and the lady herself looked so much like other middle-aged ladies, that if you had not known it you would never have suspected her of being the Vice-President of a Women's College.[61]

She was kind and agreeable. She shook hands, and hoped you were well; hoped you had had a pleasant journey, hoped you would be happy in College, hoped you would like your room; but there was a certain mechanical quality in her voice which betrayed the fact that she had said the same thing over and over again on innumerable / occasions, would say it twenty times or more this very afternoon, and that your own personal arrival left her perfectly calm and cool.

The girls stuttered and stammered in response, felt vaguely crestfallen, and worried as to what they should do next, but the Vice herself was in no doubt. She "hoped they were ready for tea," and with a wave of the hand summoned the maid to lead them a stage forward on their journey.

The second stage deposited the new-comers in the dining-hall, where tea was already in progress, and about a dozen disconsolate-looking Freshers were munching at bread-and-butter and cake in a silence which could be felt. Apparently Darsie and Hannah were the only ones of the number lucky enough to have come up in pairs, but even their tried powers of speech were paralysed beneath the spell of that terrible silence, and still more so by the relentless scrutiny of those twelve pairs of eyes. And how those Freshers *did* stare! The whites of their eyes positively shone, as with one accord the pupils turned towards the opening door. They had been stared at themselves, had come through the ordeal of being the last arrival; now, with thanksgiving, they were revenging themselves upon fresh victims! Darsie felt a horrible certainty that she would drop her cup, and spill the tea over the floor; plain Hannah munched and munched, and looked plainer than ever, with / her shoulders half-way up to her ears and her chin burrowed in her necktie.

Presently the door opened again, and another Fresher entered, cast a frightened glance around, and subsided on to the nearest chair, while every eye turned to gaze upon her, in her turn. This programme was enacted several times over before Darsie and Hannah had finished tea, and were ready to be escorted to the upstairs apartments, which were to act as bedroom and study combined.[62]

Mercifully the rooms were close together, so that, leaving Darsie half-way along the corridor, the maid could point to a door near at hand, where she could join her friend when her inspection was complete. She entered with the feeling of one on the threshold of a new life, and stood gazing around in mingled disappointment and delight. The first impression was of bareness and severity, an effect caused by the absence of picture or ornament of any kind. A small white bed stood in one corner; a curtain draped another, acting as a substitute for a wardrobe; a very inadequate screen essayed unsuccessfully to conceal a wooden washstand, and a small square of glass discouraged vanity on the part of an occupant. So far, bad! but, on the other hand, the room contained inexpensive luxuries, in the shape of an old oak chest, a bureau, a standing bookcase, and a really comfortable wicker chair. / Darsie could hardly believe that these treasures were meant for her own use; it seemed more likely that they had belonged to a former student, who would presently demand their return. She was sorrowfully resigning herself to this contingency when the door burst open, and in rushed Hannah, aglow with excitement.

"I've got a chest, and a bookcase, and a bu –" Her eyes rounded with surprise. "I say! So have you – I thought I *was* swag! Do you suppose it's the usual thing?"

"Can't say. Topping for us if it is. But the screen's a wretch, and the walls will need a *lot* of covering. My few mites of pictures will go nowhere. There's not *too* much room for our clothes, either. We'd better unpack, I suppose, and get out things for dinner. What are you going to wear?"

"Oh, something – whatever comes handy," replied plain Hannah in her most casual manner.

The subject seemed to her of infinitesimal importance; but Darsie went through many agitations of mind before she decided on a high-necked summer frock, and then suffered still keener pangs because, on descending to Hall, several Freshers were discovered in full evening dress, and, in her imagination at least, eyed her lace yoke with disdain.

Dinner was almost as silent as tea – an ordeal / of curious, appraising eyes, as each Fresher continued to stare at every other Fresher, condemning her mentally for want of frankness and kindliness, while utterly neglecting to practise these virtues on her own account. Then one by one the girls slunk upstairs, tired, shy, and homesick, and crept gratefully into their narrow beds.

Sleep was long in coming to Darsie Garnett that night; she lay awake hour after hour, living over again in thought the events of the last three years.

First and foremost her thoughts went back to the old great-aunt to whose generosity she owed the present fulfilment of her ambition. Until Lady Hayes's death, a year ago, Darsie had spent the major part of her holidays at The Towers, and the friendship between the old woman and the girl had developed into a very real affection.

It had been a wonderful experience, Darsie reflected, to watch the gradual mellowing of character, the patient endurance of suffering, the peaceful death which was so truly a "falling asleep." Until that time Darsie had felt all a girl's natural shrinking from death, but the sight of Aunt Maria's peaceful face had dissipated that fear once for all. As she knelt by the bedside looking at the still, majestic features, she offered the most fervent prayer of her life – a prayer that she, too, might be enabled to "submit her way," and so in the end find peace in her soul! /

Her acquaintance with the Percival family had ripened into friendship, so that, though Noreen and Ida could never by any chance supplant the Vernon sisters, there were moments when she actually felt more at home with Ralph than with queer, silent Dan.

Ralph, at twenty-one, had outgrown many of his boyish failings – or rather, as Darsie shrewdly surmised, had attained the art of screening them from view. Instead of snubbing his sisters' friends and adopting airs of haughty superiority, he was now all deference and attention, transparently eager for her society. Dan, on the contrary, was absorbed in work; he had taken the Longs[63] in summer, so that Darsie had no chance of meeting him before starting on her annual visits to Lady Hayes. In the Easter vac. he had visited France and Germany to study languages, while at Christmas-times he was at once too shy and too busy to take part in the daily excursions indulged in by his brothers and sisters. He was doing brilliantly at College, and as a better preparation for his life's work had decided on a four-years course – taking the Tripos in two parts,[64] in both of which it was a foregone conclusion that he would take a first-class.

Ralph Percival was contentedly slacking it in preparation for a pass degree.[65] "What did it matter?" he demanded serenely. One came to / Cambridge, don't you know, because all one's people had been there, because it was the thing to do, and a rattling old place for sport and having a good time. He would be confoundedly sorry when it was over. Only wished he could slack it out for twice as long!

Darsie first frowned, and then smiled to herself in the dark as she recalled those utterances, and the actions fitly symbolized her sentiments towards the heir of the Percivals. Her head had no mercy for such an utter want of ambition and energy, but the heart plays often a bigger part than the head in an estimate of a fellow-creature, and Darsie's heart had a way of making excuses for the handsome truant, who smiled with such beguiling eyes, had such a pretty knack of compliment, and was – generally! – ready to play knight-errant in her service. She felt herself lucky in possessing so charming a friend to act the part of gallant, and to be at her service when she chose to call. And then quite suddenly she drew a sharp breath and said aloud in a trembling voice, "Oh, Aunt Maria, dear Aunt Maria!" and her pillow was wet with tears; for Aunt Maria was dead, had died too soon to hear of her grand-niece's experiences at Newnham, to which she had looked forward with such interest, but not before evoking a real love and gratitude in Darsie's heart. How thankful the girl was to remember / that she had been able to cheer the last year of that lonely life, to recall every loving word and action, every tiny scrap of self-denial on her own part which had repaid in some small way the great gift to herself. Thankful and grateful she would be to the end of her life, but she was not, and had not even pretended to be, *sorry* that Aunt Maria was dead!

"She was old, and she was lonely, and she was ill. I'm *glad,* not sorry," she had declared to the scandalised Lavender. "I'm glad she'll never come hobbling downstairs again, and sit all the long, long day in one chair, waiting for it to end. I'm *glad* she's forgotten all about her back, and her feet, and her head, and her joints, and all the thousand parts that ached, and could not rest. I'm *glad* she doesn't need any more spectacles, and sticks, and false teeth, nor to have people shouting into her ear to make her hear. I'm thankful! If I'd hated her I might have liked her to live on here, but I loved her, so I'm glad. She has gone somewhere else, where she is happy, and cheerful, and *whole,* and I hope her husband has met her, and that they are having a lovely, lovely time together...."

Darsie was glad, too, in quite an open, unconcealed fashion, when a legacy of a few thousand pounds lifted a little of the strain from her father's busy shoulders, made it possible to send Harry / and Russell to a good boarding-school, continue Clemence's beloved music lessons, and provide many needfuls for household use. It was not only pleasant but absolutely thrilling to know that as long as she herself lived she would, in addition, possess fifty pounds a year – practically a pound a week – of her very, very own, so that even when she grew too old to teach, she could retire to a tiny cottage in the country, and live the simple life. In the meantime, however, she was young, and life stretched ahead full of delicious possibilities and excitements.

Her great ambition had been achieved. She was a student at Cambridge; the historic colleges whose names had so long been familiar on her lips lay but a few streets away, while in her own college, close at hand, along the very same corridor, lay other girls with whom she must work, with whom she must play, whose lives must of a surety touch her own.

What would happen? How would she fare? When the last night of her three-years course arrived, and she lay as now in this narrow white bed, staring across the darkened room which had been her home, what would her dreams be then? What pictures would arise in the gallery of her mind? What faces smile at her out of the mist?

"Oh, God," sighed Darsie in a soft, involuntary appeal, "help me to be good!" /

Chapter XVII

The Auction

THE next day Darsie and Hannah were interviewed by their several coaches,[66] male and female, received instructions as to their future work, and had the excitement of witnessing the return of the second and third year girls, whose manner was strikingly different from that of the modest Freshers. Dinner that evening was more of an ordeal than ever, with a galaxy of such assured, not to say aggressive, young women, staring with all their eyes at their new companions, and, to judge from the expressions on their faces, forming the meanest opinion of their intelligence!

Hannah Vernon was of all the Freshers the least upset by their scrutiny, but then plain Hannah was proverbially thick-skinned about the opinion of others.

"Let 'em stare if it amuses 'em – *I* don't mind! Long time since I've been so much admired," she returned composedly to Darsie's indignant whisper. "Every dog has its day. Wait till it's *our* turn! I'll wear specs for that day – if I never do again, / and glare over them like our friend in green. I've been taking notes, and her glare is worth all the rest put together. I feel sure she sees into my pocket, and knows exactly how much there is in my purse. Perhaps she's jealous of you. You're the prettiest girl here – old or new!"

"Oh, am I? *Nice!*" cried Darsie, dimpling. She peered around the tables, examining the faces of the girls within sight with an appraising eye, compared them with the reflection which looked back at her out of her own mirror, and felt an agreeable sense of conviction. There was one slim, dark-eyed girl with a bright rose flush on her cheeks, as to whose claim she felt a moment's uncertainty, but when she turned her head – lo, a nose was revealed soaring so unbecomingly skyward that Darsie breathed again. Yes! she was the prettiest. Now if she could just manage to be the most popular also, and, not the cleverest, of course – that was *too* much to expect – but well in the front rank, how agreeable it would be, to be sure!

The dining-hall looked much more cheery tonight, when the long table was surrounded by over sixty students in their brightly coloured dresses; the buzz of conversation rose steadily throughout the meal, and by the time that coffee was served curiosity seemed satisfied, for the staring had come to an end. /

"I think you must be Dan Vernon's sister. May I introduce myself? I am Helen Ross." A tall girl, with brown hair brushed low over her ears, stood beside Hannah's chair, holding out her hand with an air of assurance which plainly intimated that the mention of her name was expected to arouse instant recognition. Hannah, who had never heard it before, and was not skilled in the art of pretence, stared back in blank surprise.

"Oh-h! Really? Yes, I'm Hannah Vernon. This is my friend Miss Garnett."

Helen Ross flicked her eyelashes at Darsie by way of a bow, but bestowed no spoken greeting.

"Rather beastly, the first day, isn't it?" she drawled, turning to Hannah once more. "Feel such a pelican in the wilderness,[67] wandering about, not knowing what to be after next. Make me useful, do! I'd like to be useful. Told your brother I'd show you the ropes. Did you get your milk last night? Half a pint each is your allowance. You get it from the pantry directly after dinner, and take it upstairs for cocoa. Have you discovered your gyp-room yet?"[68]

Hannah stolidly shook her head, whereupon Miss Ross proceeded to further explanations. The gyp-room was a species of pantry, one of which was to be found on each corridor, whence cups, saucers, and other utensils for the preparation of the famous ten o'clock "cocoas" could be obtained.[69] You / helped yourself, don't you know, and you took the things back when you had done with them, but you didn't wash them up. The gyp-room owned a presiding dignitary of its own who was known as the "gyp-woman," who obligingly performed that service. Then Miss Ross expressed a wish to see Hannah's room, and the three girls ascended the stairs together, and the two Freshers stood by meekly while the two-year girl indulged in candid criticism.

"Humph! Not so bad. Rather a barn at present, but it'll look all right when you've fixed it up. Always takes a few days to settle down, but one lives in one's room so much that it's worth taking pains. You can get no end into the coffin, that's one blessing!"

"Coffin!" Hannah and Darsie jerked at the ominous word, whereupon Miss Ross smiled with complacent superiority.

"Ah! of course, you don't know that name. The chest's the 'coffin,' and you keep hats in it, likewise odd boxes, and evening cloaks, and other perishable splendours. Every one calls them coffins, so you'll have to get used to it, I'm afraid; and the bureau's a 'burry,' and the screen's a 'farce,'[70] and a topply one at that. You'll have to buy another to take its place. They never *do* supply you with decent screens. By the way, there's an auction on to-night![71] Did any one / tell you? That's your chance of picking up the things you want. It's held in the Gym. at ten o'clock, and is not bad fun. I'll come along and take you, if you'd care to go."

"Thanks. Yes, I'd like to see everything that's going on. What sort of things are for sale?"

"All sorts of discards that have been left behind by other girls – screens, bedcovers, curtains, china flower-pots, chairs, kettles, pictures. Sometimes there's quite a fine show."

"Sounds attractive! And who is the auctioneer?"

"A second-year girl – the one who is credited with the greatest amount of wit."

There was a moment's silence while the two Freshers each mentally leaped a year ahead, and saw herself in this proud and enviable position.

"Who's the one to-night?"

"Margaret France." Miss Ross's lips curled expressively. "I hope you won't judge us by her standard. She's certainly not the one whom *I* should have chosen to fill the position!"

Silence again, while the Freshers reflected that they knew very well whom Miss Helen Ross would have chosen if she had had the chance, and were glad that she hadn't.

"Well, I'll call round about ten. Make up your fire, and be comfortable. You're allowed a scuttle / of coals a day, and let me warn you to *use* it! If it's not all burnt, keep a few lumps in a convenient cache – a box under the bed will do. It comes in handy for another day, and when it gets really cold you can stoke up at night and have a fire to dress by in the morning. The authorities don't approve of that – they say it's bad for the stoves. Personally I consider myself before any stoves."

She nodded casually and strode from the room, leaving the two friends divided between gratitude for her kindness and prejudice against her personality.

"Don't like her a bit, do you?"

"Humph. So-so! Means well, I think. Wonder how she knows Dan? He never mentioned her name."

"Not at *all* the sort of girl Dan would care for! Such a bumptious manner. A good many of them have, I observe. Fearfully self-possessed. Perhaps it's aspecial effort to impress the Freshers. She didn't take much notice of me, but I'm coming with you all the same to buy fixings for my room, and hear the second-year auctioneer. Call for me when you're ready, like a dear. I'm off now to read until ten o'clock."

Darsie shut herself in her room, and set to work at her burry with all the ardour of a beginner, so that the hour and a half passed like a flash, and it / seemed as if she had scarcely begun before Hannah's solid bang sounded at the door, and she went out into the corridor to follow Helen Ross to the Gym.

The auction had already begun, and the auctioneer, a fresh-looking girl with grey eyes planted extraordinarily far apart, was engaged in extolling the excellencies of an aged kettle to a laughing circle of girls. She wore a black dress cut square at the neck, and a rose-coloured ribbon twined round her head. She held out the kettle at the length of a bare white arm, and raised her clear voice in delightful imitation of the professional wheedle.

"Friends and Freshers! We now come to Lot Three, one of the most striking and interesting on the catalogue. A kettle, ladies, is always a useful article, but this is no ordinary kettle. We have it on unimpeachable authority that this kettle was the kettle in residence at the establishment of our late colleague Miss Constantia Lawson, the Senior Classic[72] of her year! The kettle of a Senior Classic, Freshers! The kettle which has ministered to her refreshment, which has been, in the language of the poem, the fount of her inspiration! What price shall I say, ladies, for the kettle of a Senior Classic? Sixpence! Did somebody say sixpence! *For the kettle of a Senior Classic!* Eightpence! Thank you, madam. For the kettle / of a – What advance on eightpence? Freshers would do well to consider this opportunity before it is too late. What an – an *inebriating* effect, if I may use the word without offence to the late lamented poet,[73] would be added to the cup that cheers by the thought that the same handle, the same spout, the same – er – er – furry deposit in the inside, have ministered to the refreshment of one of the master spirits of our day! Going at eightpence – eightpence-halfpenny – I thank you, madam! At tenpence! No advance on tenpence? Going – going – *gone!*"

The hammer descended with a rap, the auctioneer leaned back with an air of exhaustion, and handed the kettle to her clerk, in blue silk and crystal beads.

"Lady to the right. Tell the lady, Joshua, that the small hole in the bottom can easily be soldered by an obliging ironmonger, or, if she prefers, she can hang the kettle on the wall as an object of vertu!"[74]

Peals of laughter greeted this tragic disclosure. The lady to the right refused for some minutes to hand over her tenpence, but finally succumbed to the feeling of the meeting, when a crumpled cotton bed-cover was next produced for sale.

"Lot Four. Handsome Oriental bedspread – design of peacocks, vultures, and pear-trees, in gorgeous colourings. Encircling border on a background / of blizzard white, and corner pieces complete. Eight feet by three. Joshua! carry the bedspread round and allow the ladies to examine it for themselves. It is excessively hurtful to our feelings when purchasers imply that deception has been practised in order to induce them to purchase our goods. Show the ladies the spread! Pure cotton, ladies. Fast colours. Design by Alma Tadema,[75] in his happiest mood. You could not possibly purchase such a spread in any establishment, ladies, under the sum of two-and-six. Fine Oriental goods, warranted to impart an air of opulence to the humblest bedstead. Any Fresher wishing to give the last touch of costly elegance to her room should not neglect this opportunity. What am I to say, ladies, for this handsome spread? Sixpence again! Thank you, madam! Sixpences seem in the ascendant to-night. Let us hope the collections on Sunday next will benefit from the ensuing dearth. Ninepence! *At* nine-pence. Pardon, madam? The lady in the eyeglasses wishes to make a remark, Joshua. The lady in the eyeglasses remarks that one side of the spread has been torn. The lady is evidently unaware that that fact is a proof positive of the authenticity of the spread. No Eastern article, as all travellers are aware, is *ever* even at both sides."

Another burst of laughter greeted this point. The auctioneer showed her pretty white teeth in a / complacent smile, her wide grey eyes roved round the room, and met Darsie's eyes raised to her in beaming admiration.

"One-and-six did you say, madam?" she cried instantly. "Did I understand you to say one-and-six? The opportunity will never occur again. At one-and-six for the lady in violet. Take the name and address if you please, Joshua." And Darsie, with a shrug and a laugh, paid out her one-and-six, and received in return the blizzard-white cover, ornamented with a roughly mended tear all along one side.

" WHAT PRICE SHALL I SAY, LADIES, FOR THE KETTLE OF A
SENIOR CLASSIC? "

The next articles offered for sale were framed pictures of various sizes which had evidently not been considered worth the trouble of removing. Water-colour sketches by 'prentice hands, faded photographs, or pretty-pretty prints evidently torn from the pages of magazines. The auctioneer exerted all the blandishments to induce the Freshers to purchase these masterpieces, and deplored their scant response with pathetic reproaches.

"*No* bids for this tasty little picture? Ladies, ladies, this is a great mistake! In the midst of your arduous brain toil, what could be more soothing and refreshing than to gaze upon this charming pastoral scene? This azure earth, this verdant sky, this lovely maid who combined in her person all the simpering charms of youth, and never, for one / misguided moment, troubled her ochre head over the acquirement of that higher knowledge which, as we all know, is the proud prerogative of man! What price shall I say for 'The Maiden's Dream'?[76] *No* bids! Put it down if you please, Joshua. We have no art collectors with us to-night. Let me have the Botticelli for a change."[77]

The clerk in blue silk handed up another picture in a rickety Oxford frame, at which the auctioneer gazed rapturously for several moments before turning it towards her audience.

"Number Six on the catalogue. Genuine photograph of a Botticelli from the collection of Miss Eva Dalgleish. Attention, Freshers, if you please! This is an item of serious importance. The presence of a Botticelli bestows at once the air of culture and refinement without which no study is worthy of the name. A genuine photograph of a Botticelli, purchased by the owner in the Italian city of Florence, and borne home by her own fair hands, as the crack across the corner will give proof. In an Oxford frame[78] – a compliment to our sister University – glazed and complete, with hanging loops and fragment of wire. *What* offers for the Botticelli? Any Fresher who wishes to prove herself endowed with refined and artistic – One shilling? Thank you, madam. *And* sixpence! One and nine. One and nine for this genuine Botticelli. Ladies, ladies, this is a sad day for / Newnham. And nine – and nine. Going. Going – *gone!*"

It was Hannah who had testified to her own artistic qualities by purchasing this photograph. She tucked it proudly under her arm, and turned an envious eye on a brass flower-pot which was now engaging the auctioneer's attention. A simultaneous movement of the audience showed that this was an article on which many hopes had been set, and bidding promised to be brisk.

"Now, ladies, we come to one of the principal events of the evening, the bidding for this very rich and magnificent brass, hand-beaten, richly-chased, Oriental, ornamental flower-pot. We have several flower-pots in our catalogue, but none to be compared for one moment to the very superior article which you now see before you. It is safe to say that no student, even in her third year, can boast of a flower-pot to equal this lot in either quality or design. The possession of it will in itself ensure fame for its fortunate owner. Let me have a handsome bid, if you please, ladies, to start this valuable article. Half a crown!!! A lady, whose ignorance we can only deplore, offers me half a crown for a genuine antique brass! I am thankful that in such a large and enlightened audience such an error is not likely to be repeated. Three shillings. *Thank* you, madam. And six. Four shillings – four shillings. Freshers who / neglect to take advantage of this opportunity will be compelled to content themselves with one of these common china articles to my left. A flowerpot is a necessary article of furniture without which no room is complete. What is home without an aspidistra?[79] You laugh, ladies, but you can find no answer to that question. And six! Five shillings! The raw material for this masterpiece must have cost many times this sum. Five – five – no advance on five. The lady in green, Joshua. Take the lady's address!"

The auctioneer put up her hand to her head and patted the rose-coloured ribbon into place. Inspired by the laughing appreciation of her sallies, her cheeks had flushed to the same bright shade, and with her sparkling eyes and alert, graceful movements she made a delightful and attractive figure, at which the Freshers stared in undisguised delight.

"I adore her!" whispered Darsie in her friend's ear.

"Decent sort!" croaked Hannah the undemonstrative, and then by a common impulse their glance passed on to rest on Helen Ross's set, supercilious face.

"I loathe her," came the second whisper.

"Mean thing – jealousy!" croaked Hannah once more, and turned her attention to the business in hand. /

After the china flower-pots had been disposed of, a trio of basket-chairs gave an impetus to the bidding, as the truth of the auctioneer's words went home to every heart.

"'Three luxurious basket-chairs, cushioned complete in handsome cretonne,[80] stuffed pure wool. Condition – as new.' Ladies, in these basket-chairs you see not only elegant articles of furniture, but a solution of the dilemma which dogs every owner of a one-comfortable-chair study. One question haunts her waking and sleeping hours; one problem embitters the most social occasions – '*Shall I be comfortable or polite?*' To this question, in this college of Newnham, there can, ladies, be but one reply – and the wretched hostess sits on the coalbox and gives her visitor the chair. After long hours of mental toil, after the physical strain of the hockey-field,[81] a quiet hour is vouchsafed beside her own fireside, with the companionship of a beloved friend to soothe and cheer, and that hour, ladies – that precious hour – I say it with emotion almost too strong for words – that stolen hour of peace and rest must needs be passed – *on the coalbox!* Ladies, I need say no more. The remedy is in your own hands."

So on, and so on. After the chairs came curtains; after the curtains, bookcases, ornaments, and books. The auction flowed on, punctuated by explosions of laughter, until the last item on / the "catalogue" was reached, and the auction-eer was crimson with exhaustion.

Darsie and Hannah had amassed between them quite a stock of furnishings. A screen apiece, chairs, Oriental window-curtains in stripes of contrasting colours warm and comfortable to look upon, flower-pots, and odd pictures and ornaments. One felt a proprietor, indeed, as one looked over the spoils, and the inroads into capital had been agreeably small. Darsie was folding up her damaged "spread" when a voice spoke in her ear, and with a little jump of the heart she looked up to find Margaret France standing by her side.

"How do you do? I must thank you for your patronage. You chipped in nobly. Hope you'll like 'em, when you've got 'em. Just up, aren't you? What's your shop?"[82]

For a moment Darsie stared blankly, then a flash of intuition revealed the meaning of the word.

"Modern languages."

"Good! So'm I. And your friend?"

"Mathematics."

"Humph! Well, good luck! I'm off to bed. We shall meet on the Rialto!"

She smiled, nodded, and was gone. With a sudden realization of their own fatigue the Freshers turned to follow her example. Helen Ross joined them on their way along the corridors, and Darsie / could not resist expressing her appreciation of the auctioneer's wit.

"She was delicious. I *have* enjoyed it. She *is* amusing and clever."

"Think so?" said Helen coolly. "Really? Glad you were pleased. It's usually *far* better than that!"

With a curt good-night she turned into her own room, and the two friends made haste to follow her example.

The banked-up fires burned warm and red; the scattered oddments had been hidden from sight in the "coffin's" rapacious maw; photographs and knick-knacks gave a homy look to the rooms which had looked so bare and bleak twenty-four hours before. The Freshers tumbled into bed and fell happily asleep. /

Chapter XVIII

First Experiences

DURING the first month at Newnham Darsie and Hannah fell gradually and happily into the routine of college life. They grew to recognize their companions by name, and to place them according to their several "shops"; they entertained cocoa parties in their rooms; picked up slang terms, and talked condescendingly of "townees"; they paid up subscriptions to "Hall," "Games," "Flowers," and "Fic";[83] slept, played, and laughed and talked, and, above all, *worked,* with heart and mind, and with every day that passed were more convinced that to be a student at Cambridge was the most glorious fate that any girl could desire.

A week after the beginning of term Helen Ross, the fortunate possessor of a double room, gave a tea-party, with one of the younger Dons as chaperon,[84] to which Dan Vernon and a companion were invited. Ostensibly the party was given in Hannah's honour, but to her astonishment and dismay / Hannah's friend was not favoured with an invitation, and felt her first real twinge of loneliness in the knowledge that two old friends were making merry together but a few yards away, while she sat solitary and alone. What she had done to incur Helen Ross's dislike Darsie could not imagine, and, fortunately for herself, she was too large-hearted to suspect that it arose simply from an unattractive girl's jealousy of one whom all had combined to love and admire. Be that as it may, Darsie was left out of the tea-party, and her subsequent cross-questionings of Hannah were far from comforting.

"Had a good time?"

"Top hole."

"Nice people there?"

"Topping."[85]

"Good cakes?"

"Scrum!"[86]

"Dan ask for me?"

"No."

"Then he ought to have done!" Darsie told herself indignantly, and her thoughts flew off to Ralph Percival, wondering when she would see him next, and recalling with pleasure his promise to "see her through."

The approach of the Freshers' hockey match banished less important topics, for Hannah was on edge with anxiety to be at her best, and disport / herself sufficiently well to be included in after-team practices, while Darsie was scarcely less eager on her behalf.

When the afternoon arrived and the match began, the second and third year girls crowded to look on, while the Captain stood apart surrounded by a few satellites from the Committee, as truly the monarch of all she surveyed[87] as any king who ever graced a throne. The thoughts of each Fresher turned with an anguish of appeal towards this figure; a smile on her face raised them to the seventh heaven; a frown laid them in the dust! Extraordinary to think that two short years ago this oracle had been a Fresher like themselves! Inconceivable to imagine that in two years to come they themselves might occupy that same magnificent altitude!

The eyes of the Oracle fell upon Hannah and approved what she saw, and henceforth Hannah took part in team practices, and lorded it over Darsie, who in her turn affected a growing antagonism to the game.

"You can have too much of a good thing – even of games – and I seem to have *eaten* hockey every meal since I arrived!" she announced impatiently; and in truth, since an unwritten law forbade the discussion of "shop" at table, the conversation was largely limited to dissertations on this the most popular of games. /

On Sundays the two girls went together to King's College Chapel[88] and gazed with admiration at the vaulted stone roof, with its marvellous fan tracery; at its towering stained-glass windows, and the screen bearing the monogram of Anne Boleyn;[89] at the delicate carving of the stalls. It was so wonderfully different from the dreary town edifice in which they had been accustomed to worship, with its painted walls, heavy gallery, and wheezy organ played by an indifferent musician – so wonderfully, gloriously different that Darsie felt a pricking at the back of her eyes as though she were ready to cry for sheer pleasure and admiration. The music and the sermon seemed alike perfect, and Darsie ardently followed each stage of the service.

Some people are inclined to grow frivolous and forgetful when the world goes well with them and the desire of their hearts is accomplished; others are filled with a passion of gratitude and thanksgiving, and Darsie Garnett belonged to the latter category. Prosperity made her more humble, more kindly, more overflowing with love to God and man. A portrait of Lady Hayes stood on her study mantelpiece, and every morning and evening she bent her sunny head to kiss the stern old face. Dear old Aunt Maria! she had so loved being kissed – *really* kissed, as if one meant it. If in that higher life to which she had gone she / knew what was happening on earth, Darsie felt sure that she would like to know that her portrait was still cherished. Her thoughts hovered gratefully about the dead woman as she sat in this wonderful old church, and pictured with awe the succeeding generations who had worshipped within its walls. It was only when the sermon was at an end that, turning her head, Darsie met the gaze of a girl sitting a few seats away, and after a moment of bewilderment recognized the widely set eyes and curling lips of Margaret France.

In her dark hat and coat she looked less attractive than in evening dress, but the fact made no difference in the thrill of pleasure with which Darsie realized her presence. Some quality in this girl appealed to the deep places of her heart; she realized instinctively that if the attraction were mutual the tie between them would be close and firm, but it must be all or nothing – she could never dally with friendship with Margaret France!

Walking home slowly along Silver Street,[90] she found herself answering absently to Hannah's remarks, her whole attention riveted on watching the passers-by, wondering if by any possibility Margaret France would stop to speak to her once more, and her heart leaped with exultation as a footstep paused by her side, and the clear, crisp tones addressed her by name.

"Morning, Miss Garnett! Morning, Miss / Vernon! Ripping day, isn't it? Glad to see you in King's. Saw you long before you spotted me, and enjoyed your enjoyment. Never forgot *my* first services. Good to be there, isn't it?"

"Oh-h!" Darsie's deep-drawn breath of rapture was an eloquent response. "I *have* been happy! I've never in my life seen anything so wonderful before. It seems almost too good to be true that I can go there every Sunday for years to come. Cambridge is wonderful. I am more enchanted every day. Even to walk along the streets is a joy."

"Good!" cried Margaret heartily. "Drop in to five o'clock service sometimes when you're feeling tired, and tied up with your work. It's a grand soother. How goes the work so far? Enjoying the lectures? Finding the literature interesting?"

The two Modern Languages discussed work together eagerly, while mathematical Hannah marched on a few feet ahead. Darsie felt a pang of remorse, because she could not help wishing that she would *stay* ahead, and so give the chance of a prolonged *tête-à-tête* with Margaret France. The feeling of attraction was so strong now that they were face to face that it was only by an effort of will that she could resist slipping her hand through the black serge arm, but the expression of her face was eloquent, and Margaret / smiled back well pleased. When they parted a few minutes later to go to their different halls, the older girl said casually, but in a lowered voice which showed that the invitation was meant for Darsie alone –

"By the way, I'm at home for cocoa on Tuesday evenings at ten. Bring your milk, and come along, will you! I'd like to have you."

"Rather!" cried Darsie eloquently, and ran up to her room aglow with delight and pride, which grew still deeper at lunch when a casual reference to the invitation (it was really impossible to keep silent on so thrilling a point!) evoked a wide stare of surprise.

"To her Tuesdays! Are you sure? Nobody goes to those but her very boon companions. You *are* honoured!"

"Didn't ask *me,* I notice!" sniffed Hannah huffily. "No twin soul here. Recognized an affinity in you, I suppose."

"Well, *I* wasn't asked to play in team matches! Don't grudge me my little score!" returned Darsie, knowing well that an honour in sport was more to her companion than many cocoas. "Besides, you must remember you have Helen Ross!"

"Oh, ah, yes! Helen Ross dotes on me. Disinterested, of course. No connection with the brother over the way!" commented Hannah with / a grin. "By the way, I hear from Dan that your friend Ralph Percival is in trouble already, playing cards, getting into debt, and staying out after hours. Seems to be a poor-spirited sort of fellow from all accounts!"

"He saved my life, anyway, when I was a youngster, and very nearly drowned myself, paddling up a mill-stream. There's no want of spirit about Ralph. Life has been made too easy for him, that's the mischief!" said Darsie in her most elderly and judicial manner. "It's difficult to keep to the grind when you know that you will never need to work. He needs an object in life. Until he finds that, he will be content to drift."

"He'll drift into being sent down at this rate. That will be the end of him!" croaked Hannah gloomily; whereupon Darsie knitted her brows and collapsed into silence for the rest of the meal.

Poor, dear, handsome Ralph! At the bottom of her heart Darsie was hardly surprised to hear Hannah's report. The indifference with which he had entered upon his college life had not developed into any more earnest spirit, as had been abundantly proved by his conversation when the two had last met, during the long vacation, while the hesitating manner of his mother and sisters seemed to hint at a hidden anxiety. In the depths of her heart Darsie was feeling considerably / piqued by the fact that though she had now been over a month in Cambridge Ralph had shown no anxiety to meet her, or to fulfil his promise of "showing the ropes." Other girls had been invited to merry tea-parties in the different colleges, and almost daily she had expected such an invitation for herself, but neither of her two men friends had paid her this mark of attention; but for the fact of an occasional meeting in the streets they might as well have been at the other end of the land. Pride forbade her commenting on the fact even to Hannah; but inwardly she had determined to be very proud and haughty when the deferred meeting came about. Dan was too wrapped up in himself to care for outsiders; Ralph was a slacker – not worth a thought. Darsie dismissed them both with a shrug. Margaret France was worth a dozen men put together!

Ten o'clock on Tuesday evening seemed long in coming, but the moment that the clock pointed to the hour Darsie hastened to her new friend's study, and to her satisfaction found her still alone. The room looked delightfully cosy with pink shades over the lights, a clear blaze upon the grate, and Margaret herself, in a pink rest-gown curled up in a wicker-chair, was the very embodiment of ease. She did not rise as Darsie entered, but pointed to a chair close at hand, with an eagerness which was in itself the best welcome. /

"That's right. Come along! I'm glad you're the first. Sit down and look around. How do you like my den?"

Darsie stared to right and left with curious eyes, and came to the instant conclusion that Margaret's room was like herself. From floor to ceiling, from window to door, there was not one single article which did not give back a cheering impression. If the article were composed of metal, it shone and glittered until it could shine no farther; if of oak, every leaf and moulding spoke of elbow-grease, and clean, fresh-smelling polish; if it were a fabric of wool or cotton, it was invariably of some shade of rose, shedding, as it were, an aspect of summer in the midst of November gloom.

Over the fireplace was fastened a long brown-paper scroll, on which some words were painted in big ornamental letters. Darsie read them with a thrill of appreciation –

"Two men looked out through prison bars, One saw mud, the other stars!"[91]

The eyes of the two girls met, and lingered. Then Darsie spoke –

"That's your motto in life! You look out for stars –"

"Yes! So do you. That's why I wanted to be friends." /

"I wonder!" mused Darsie, and sat silent, gazing into the fire. "It is beautiful, and I understand the drift, but – would you mind paraphrasing it for my benefit?"

"It's so simple. There *is* mud, and there *are* stars. It's just a choice of where we choose to look."

"Yes – I see. But don't you think there are times – when one is awfully down on one's luck, for instance – when there's no one on earth so trying as the persistent optimist who *will* make the best of everything, and take a cheerful view! You want to murder him in cold blood. I do, at least. You feel ever so much more cheered by some one who acknowledges the mud, and says how horrid it is, and pities you for sticking so fast!"

Margaret's ringing laugh showed all her pretty white teeth. She rubbed her hands together in delighted appreciation.

"Oh, I know, I know! I want to kill them, too. Vision's not a mite of use without tact. But no bars can shut out the stars if we choose to let them shine."

Her own face was ashine as she spoke, but anything more unlike "goodiness," abhorred by every normal girl, it would be impossible to imagine.

"Tell me about your work – how do you get on with your coach?" she asked the next moment, / switching off to ordinary subjects in the most easy and natural of manners, and Darsie found herself laying bare all the little hitches and difficulties which must needs enter into even the most congenial course of study, and being alternately laughed at and consoled, and directed towards a solution by brisk, apt words.

"You're all right – you've got a head. You'll come through on top, if you'll be content to go slow. Want to take the Tripos first year, and honours at that – that's your style! Calm down, my dear, and be content to jog. It pays better in the end." She flashed a radiant smile at Darsie's reddening face, then jumped up to greet her other guests of the evening, three in number, who appeared at that moment, each carrying her own precious portion of milk.

One was "Economics" and owned so square a jaw that the line of it (there was no curve) seemed to run down straight with the ear; another was "Science" and wore spectacles; a third was "Modern Languages," like the host, but one and all shared an apparently unlimited appetite for Cocoa, Conversation, and Chelsea buns, the which they proceeded to enjoy to the full. "Modern Languages" being in the ascendant, indulged in a little "shop" as a preliminary, accompanied by the sighs, groans, and complaints incidental to the subject. /

"How's your drama getting on? Is it developing satisfactorily?" Student Number Two inquired of Darsie, in reference to the paper given out at the last lecture in Divinity Hall,[92] and Darsie shrugged with a plaintive air.

"I've been struggling to develop it, to *trace* its development, as he said; but the tracings are decidedly dim! I get on much better with a subject on which I can throw a little imagination. 'The growth of the novel,' for instance – I wove quite a fairy-tale out of that."

The girls smiled, but with a dubious air.

"Better be careful! That's a ruse which most of us have tried in our day, and come wearily back to sober fact. ... How do you like the Historical French Grammar?"

The Fresher made a gesture as if to tear her hair, whereupon the second-year girls groaned in chorus.

"Hopeless! Piteous! In last year's Tripos the paper was positively inhuman. The girls said it was impossible even to understand the questions, much less to answer them."

"Wicked! Waste of time, I call it. Most of us are training to teach, but it's not one in a hundred who will be called upon to teach *that* erudite horror."

Darsie looked at Margaret France as she spoke, and saw at once by the expression of her companions / that she had touched on a delicate subject. There was a moment's silence, then –

"I am not going to teach," said Margaret, smiling.

"Really! Then – What are you going to do?"

"Live at home."

A future profession[93] seemed so universal a prospect with the Newnham students that Margaret's reply amazed Darsie as much as it appeared to annoy her other hearers.

Economics sniffed, and muttered beneath her breath; Science stared fixedly at the ceiling through her glittering spectacles; Modern Languages groaned aloud.

"With your brain! With your spirit! After this training! Such wicked waste. ..."

Margaret laughed lightly.

"Oh, Darsie Garnett, how mean of you, when I feed you with my best Chelsea buns, to land me in this time-honoured discussion! I'm an only child, and my parents have been perfect bricks in giving me my wish and sparing me for three whole years! The least I can do is to go home and do a turn for them. I fail to see where the waste comes in!"

"All you have learned – all you have studied – all you have read –"

"Just so! I hope it will make me a more / interesting companion for them. And for myself! I've got to live with myself all the days of my life, remember, and I do *not* wish to be bored!"

"You have such power, such capacity! You might do some work for the world!"

"I intend to. What's the world made up of, after all, but a number of separate homes? As a matter of ordinary common sense isn't it best to work in one's *own* home, rather than in a strange one?"[94]

Margaret threw out her hands with a pretty appealing gesture, and her companions stared at her in silence, apparently too nonplussed to reply. Before they had time to rally to the attack, however, a startling interruption had occurred.

With a suddenness and violence which made the cocoa-drinkers jump in their seats the door burst open, and the figure of a girl in evening dress precipitated herself into their midst. Her light skirt was thrown over her shoulders, revealing an abbreviated white petticoat; her eyes were fixed with a deadly determination; regardless of the occupants of the room or of the articles of furniture scattered here and there, she flew at lightning speed to the window, closed it with a resounding bang, leaped like a cat at the ventilator overhead, banged that also, and with one bound was out of the room, the door making a third bang in her wake. /

Darsie gasped in dismay. She herself had been transfixed with astonishment, but her companions had displayed a marvellous self-possession. Margaret had wrapped her arms round the cocoa-table to protect it from upset, another girl had steadied the screen, a third had obligingly lifted her chair out of the way; but no sign of alarm or curiosity showed upon their faces, which fact did but heighten the mystery of the situation.

"Is she – is she *mad?*"

The second-year girls laughed in chorus. From afar could be heard a succession of bang, bang, bangs, as if in every study in the house the same performance was being enacted. Margaret nodded at the Fresher with kindly reassurance.

"Only the fire drill![95] They've had an alarm, and she's told to shut off draughts. Very good going! Not more than five or six seconds all told!"

"There isn't really –"

"Oh, dear, no. No such luck! Poor fun having a fire brigade, and no chance to show its mettle. But we live in hope. You ought to join. I can imagine you making a magnificent captain."

So here was another ambition. Darsie made a mental note to inquire into the workings of the fire brigade, and to offer her name as a recruit without delay. /

Chapter XIX

The Fancy Ball

It was somewhat of a shock to the Fresher contingency to receive one morning the intimation of a Costume Ball, to be held in Clough Hall[96] on the following night; but their protests met with scant sympathy from the elders.

When Darsie plaintively declared that she hadn't got a fancy dress, and would not have time to send home for it if she *had,* a third-year girl silenced her by a stern counter-question: "And where, pray, would be the fun if you *had,* and *could?* If at the cost of a postcard you could be fitted up as the Lady of the Lake in green draperies and water-lilies, it would no doubt be exceedingly becoming, but it would be no sport. No, young woman, you've got to contrive something out of nothing and an hour stolen from the night, and when you've done it you'll be in the mood to appreciate other people's contrivings into the bargain. Buck up! You're one of the dressy sort. We'll expect wonders from you." /

But when Darsie repaired to the seclusion of her study and set herself to the problem of evolving a fancy dress out of an ordinary college outfit, ideas were remarkably slow in coming. She looked questioningly at each piece of drapery in turns, wondered if she could be a ghost in curtains, a statue in sheets, an eastern houri in the cotton quilt, a Portia[97]

Black serge, grey tweed, violet ninon; two evening frocks, and the one white satin which was the *pièce de résistance* of the whole. A cloth coat, a mackintosh, an art serge cloak for evening wear – how *could* one manufacture a fancy dress from garments so ordinary as these?

In despair, Darsie betook herself to Margaret France's room and found that young woman seated before her dressing-table engaged in staring fixedly at her own reflection in the mirror. She betrayed no embarrassment at being discovered in so compromising a position, but smiled a broad smile of welcome out of the mirror, the while she continued to turn and to twist, and hold up a handglass to scrutinise more closely unknown aspects of face and head.

"I know what you've come for! I've had two Freshers already. Bowled over at the thought of inventing a costume – that's it, isn't it? / Oh, you'll rise to it yet. The only difficulty is to hit on an idea – the rest's as easy as pie. That's what I'm doing now – studying my phiz to see what it suggests. My nose, now! What d'you think of my nose? Seems to me that nose wasn't given me for nothing. *And* the width between the eyes! It's borne in upon me that I must be either a turnip lantern[98] or a Dutch doll. The doll would probably be the most becoming, so I'll plump for that. Don't breathe a word, for it must be a secret to the last. As for you – it would be easy to suggest a dozen pretty-pretties."

Margaret wheeled round in her chair, and sat nursing her knees, regarding Darsie with a twinkling eye. "Big eyes, long neck, neat little feet – you'd make an adorable Alice in Wonderland, with ankle-strap slippers, and a comb, and a dear little pinny over a blue frock! And your friend can be the Mad Hatter. Look well, wouldn't she, with a hat on one side? There are only the girls to see you, and the more comic you can make yourself the better they'll be pleased. You are about to be introduced to a new side of Newnham life, and will see how mad the students can be when they let themselves go. You'll laugh yourself ill before the evening's over. Well, think it over, and come back to me if you want any properties. My dress will be easy enough – braided hair, short white frock (butter-muslin / at a penny the yard), white stockings with sandals, another pair of stockings to cover my arms, chalked face and neck, with peaked eyebrows and neat little spots of red on the cheekbones and tip of the chin. If you feel inclined to be angelic, you might run up with your paint-box at the last minute, and dab on my joints."

"Joints!"

Darsie gaped in bewilderment, whereupon Margaret cried resentfully –

"Well, I must *have* joints, mustn't I? How do you expect me to move? A paint-box is invaluable on these occasions, as you'll find before you are through. Now, my love, I'll bid you a fond adieu, for work presses. By the by, one word in your ear! Don't ask a third-year girl to dance[99] with you if you value your nose!"

"What will happen to it if I do?"

"Snapped off! Never mind! look pretty and meek, and perhaps she'll ask *you*. Now be off – be off – I must to work!"

Darsie descended to Hannah's study and proposed the idea of the Mad Hatter, the which was instantly and scornfully declined. Hannah explained at length that though her head might be plain, it yet contained more brains than other heads she could mention, and that to play the part of idiot for a whole night long was a feat beyond the powers of a mathematical student / reading for honours. She then explained with a dignity which seemed somewhat misplaced that she had set her heart upon representing a pillar-box, and was even now on the point of sallying forth to purchase a trio of hat-boxes, which, being of fashionable dimensions, would comfortably encircle her body. Fastened together so as to form a tube, covered with red sateen, and supported by scarlet-stockinged legs, the effect would be pleasingly true to life.

"I'll have peep-holes for eyes, and the slit will outline my mouth. Between the dances I'll kneel down in a corner so that the box touches the ground, and I'll look so real, that I shall expect every one to drop in letters – *chocolate* letters, observe! You might buy some and set the example!"

For the next twenty-four hours an unusual air of excitement and bustle pervaded the college, and the conversation at mealtime consisted for the most part of fragmentary questions and answers bearing on the important subject of costumes in making.

"Lend me your boot brushes, like a lamb!"

"Got an old pair of brown stockings you can't wear again?"

"Be an angel and lend me your striped curtains just for the night!"

"Spare *just* ten minutes to sew up my back?" /

So on it went, and in truth it was a pleasant chance to hear the merry, inconsequent chatter; for, like every other class of the community, girl students have their besetting sins, and one of the most obvious of these is an air of assurance, of dogmatism, of final knowledge of life, against which there can be no appeal. Girls of nineteen and twenty will settle a dispute of ages with a casual word; students of economy will advance original schemes warranted to wipe the offence of poverty from the globe; science students with unlowered voices will indulge across the dinner-table in scathing criticisms on historic creeds which their fathers hold in reverence; and on each young face, on each young tongue, can be read the same story of certainty and self-esteem.

This state of mind is either sad, amusing, or exasperating, according to the mood of the hearer; but, whatever be his mood, he yet knows in his heart that it is a transitory phase, and an almost inevitable result of theoretical knowledge. A few years of personal grip with life and its problems will make short work of that over-confidence, and replace it with a gentler, sweeter touch.

But to-night was a night of frolic, and one would have to travel far indeed to find a more amusing spectacle than an impromptu costume dance in Clough Hall. Beauty is a secondary consideration, and the girl who has achieved the / oddest and most ludicrous appearance is the heroine of the hour.[100] Darsie Garnett made a fascinating Alice in Wonderland in her short blue frock, white pinny, and little ankle-strap slippers, her hair fastened back by an old-fashioned round comb, and eyebrows painted into an inquiring arch, but she received no attention in comparison with that lavished upon Hannah, when she dashed nimbly in at the door, and, kneeling down in a corner of the room, presented a really lifelike appearance of a pillar-box, a white label bearing the hours of "Chocolate deliveries" pasted conspicuously beneath the slit. Hannah's prophecies proved correct, for it became one of the amusements of the evening to feed that yawning cavity with chocolates and other dainties, so that more than one sweet tooth in the assembly made a note of the suggestion for a future day.

The Dutch Doll was another huge success; for so dolly and so beyond all things Dutch did she appear, standing within the doorway with jointed arms and rigid back, with dark hair plastered over the forehead in the well-known curve, and the three little spots of colour blazing out from the whitened background, that it was almost impossible to believe that she was living flesh and blood. Like a statue she stood until the laughter and applause had lasted for several minutes, and / then, stepping jerkily on one side, made way for a new and even more startling apparition.

Topsy,[101] by all that was wonderful and unexpected! A beaming, grinning little nigger girl, with tightly curled hair, rolling eyes, and white teeth showing to the gums. A short gown of brilliantly striped cotton reached to the knees, brown-stockinged arms and legs were matched by brown-painted face and neck; standing side by side with the Dutch Doll, the respective whiteness and brownness became accentuated to a positively dazzling extent, and the onlookers were jubilant with delight. The climax was reached when the two waltzed off together round the room, the doll sustaining a delightful stiffness and stoniness of mien, while Topsy's grin threatened to reach to her very ears.

Ordinary costumes fell somewhat flat after these triumphs, though to the Freshers there was a continuing joy in beholding dignified students in their third year pirouetting in childlike abandonment. There, for instance, was the cleverest girl in college, of whom it was accepted as a certainty that she would become a worldwide celebrity, an austere and remote personage who was seldom seen to smile; there she stood, the daintiest Christmas Cracker that one could wish to behold, in a sheath of shimmery pink, tied in the middle by a golden string, finished at either end with / a froth of frills, and ornamented front and back with immense bouquets of flowers. By an ingenious arrangement also, if you pulled a string in a certain way, a mysterious cracking sound was heard, and a motto made its appearance bearing an original couplet whose reference was strictly and delightfully local.

The run on these mottoes was great, and after their points were fully enjoyed, they were folded carefully away, to be kept as souvenirs of the great scholar of later years.

The evening was half over, and the girls had settled down to the dance, when suddenly, unexpectedly, the great excitement arrived. At a moment when the music had ceased, and the various couples were preparing for the usual promenade around the Hall, a loud roar was heard from without, and into the middle of the floor there trotted nothing more nor less than a tawny yellow lion, which, being confronted by a crowd of spectators, drew back as if in fear, and crouched in threatening manner. Its masked face showed a savage row of teeth; a mass of red hair, shortened by that mysterious process known as "back combing," produced a sufficiently convincing mane; a yellow skin hearthrug was wrapped round the body, while paint and wadding combined had contrived a wonderfully good imitation of claws. /

It was the colour of the hair alone which revealed the identity of the Lion to her companions. "It's that wretched little ginger Georgie!" "That little ginger beast!" went the cry from lip to lip. But, abuse her as they might, for the rest of the evening "Ginger Georgie" remained the centre of attraction, as she persistently ambled after Topsy, and gnawed at her brown feet, evidently recognising in her at once a compatriot and a tit-bit.

Well, well! *Il faut souffrire pour être – célèbre!*[102] When supper-time arrived, and the lion's mask was removed, behold a countenance so magenta with heat that compared with it even the Letter Box herself was pale. The two sufferers were waited upon with the most assiduous attention, as was indeed only fair. When one has voluntarily endured a condition of semi-suffocation throughout an evening's "pleasuring" for the unselfish reason of providing amusement for others, it's a poor thing if one cannot be assisted to lemonade in return.

The Lion sat up well into the night combing out her mane; the Letter Box had the first bad headache in her life, but both tumbled into bed at last, proud and happy in the remembrance of an historic success. /

Chapter XX

Undergraduate Friends

Hannah strolled into Darsie's study, open letter in hand.

"Here's games!" she announced. "An invitation from Mrs. Hoare for myself and friend – that's you – to go to tea on Sunday afternoon. That's because I'm Dan's sister, of course. He'll be there, too, I expect, and the handsome Percival, and lots more men. The question is, shall we go?"

Now Mrs. Hoare was the wife of the head of that well-known college of which Dan and Ralph were members, and the invitation was therefore the fulfil-ment of one of Darsie's dreams.

"Of course we'll go!" she cried ardently. "Sunday tea at a man's college is part of the Cambridge programme, and we want to see all that we can. Personally, I consider that they might have asked us before." She lay back in her seat, and stared dreamily at the wall, puckering her brow in thought, the while Hannah chuckled in the background. /

"I know what you are thinking about!"

"You don't!" cried Darsie, and blushed, a deep guilty blush.

"I *do!* Costume for Sunday, and the question of possibly squeezing out three or four shillings to buy an extra bit of frippery to add to your charms!"

"Boo!" cried Darsie impatiently; then with a sudden change of front: "And if I *was,* I was perfectly right! Newnham girls are not half careful enough about their appearance, and it tells against the cause. A perfect woman, nobly planned, ought to be as clever as she is – er – dainty, and as dainty as she is clever."

"Thank you for the concession! Very considerate of you, I'm sure. If you had stuck to 'beautiful,' I should have been hopelessly left out. Even 'dainty' is beyond me, I'm afraid; but I'll promise you to be neat and tidy, and saints can do no more – if they happen to have been born *plain* saints, that's to say!"

Hannah stood in front of the mirror, staring back at her flat, square face with an expression of serenely detached criticism.

"If you are the beauty of this college, I run a close race for the booby prize! Bit of a handicap that, if you care about popularity. This Sunday afternoon now! they'll all be buzzing round you like so many flies, while I do wallflower / in a corner. Nonsense to say that looks don't count! So far as I can see, the difference between your face and mine will probably make the difference in our lives. You'll marry a lord of high degree, and I'll school marm and be maiden aunt."

"Oh, Hannah!" Darsie was acutely discomfited by such words from Hannah's lips. True they were spoken in matter-of-fact tones, and without the suspicion of a whine, but as the first instance of anything approaching a lament, the occasion was historic. "Oh, Hannah, dear – it's only at first! After the first no one cares a rap *what* you look like, so long as you're nice."

"Fal-de-ral!" cried Hannah scornfully. "Of course they care! Any one would – should myself, but you needn't look so hang-dog, my dear. It's not *your* fault, and I am quite comfortable, thank you. If any man ever wants to marry me, I'll know jolly well that it's for myself, and that he really loves me through and through. There isn't any of the glamour business about this child to make him imagine that he cares, when it's only a passing phase. And if it's my lot to live alone, I'll back myself to be as happy as most wives I come across. It's my own big, splendid life, and I'm going to *make* it splendid, or know the reason why!" Hannah struck a dramatic gesture, danced a few fancy steps in an elephantine / manner, and stumped towards the door. "So be it, then! We accept with pleasure, and I'll leave you to trim your hat."

Whether or no any such embellishment did take place history sayeth not, but it is certain that Darsie Garnett made a very charming picture on the following Sunday afternoon, and that her dainty style of beauty showed to peculiar advantage against the oak panelling of the stately old room in which the head of – College and his gracious, fragile-looking wife dispensed tea to their guests.

The first few minutes after their arrival were rather an ordeal to the two Freshers, who had never before been present at such a gathering, and felt themselves the cynosure of every eye; but the kindness of host and hostess soon put them at their ease.

A fair sprinkling of college men were in the room, handing round tea and cakes to the guests. Dan Vernon greeted Darsie with an illuminating "Halloa!" and his sister with an even shorter grunt; but it was only when she was comfortably settled down to tea that Darsie caught sight of Ralph Percival's fair, close-clipped head at the far side of the table. He seemed in no hurry to speak to her – a fact duly scored against him in Miss Darsie's mind, and this indifference served to pique her into a more vivacious reception of the attentions of his companions. /

As Hannah had foretold, her pretty friend held quite a little court as one man after another strolled up to join the animated group around her chair. There were two other girls in that group, and a married woman with a strikingly sweet face, who had been introduced as the sister of the hostess. Mrs. Reeves, as she was called, appeared to be on intimate terms with the men, and her presence, instead of acting as a restraint, only added to their enjoyment. Darsie thought that she was a charming creature, was conscious that she herself was being scrutinized with special attention, and sincerely hoped that the verdict was favourable. It was a curious person who did not wish to stand well in Alicia Reeves's estimation!

Suddenly Ralph Percival edged in at the back of the group, and stationed himself by Darsie with an air of possession.

"Well, Miss Darsie Garnett, isn't it about time that you had some talk with me?"

"Quite time!" Darsie's tone was eloquent, and she looked Ralph in the face with a quiet steadiness, at which he had the grace to blush. He had been in no hurry to claim acquaintanceship until her social success was assured; she was fully aware of the fact, but her pique died a rapid death as she looked closely into the lad's face. Ralph at twenty-two was as handsome as in his boyhood, handsomer, indeed, but there were / other changes, which the girl's eyes were quick to read; for though we may keep silence with our tongue, the hand of Time imprints marks upon our features which are unfailing guides to our spiritual progress or decline.

For many months past Ralph Vernon had persistently allowed himself to fall short of his best, slacking in work, overstepping at play, abandoning "straightness" for a gathering mesh of deceit. Attached to his name was an unsavoury reputation of card-playing for high stakes, of drinking too much, although not to the extent of actual drunkenness; and the character had alienated from him the friendship of serious men, and evoked a disapproving aloofness in the manner of his instructors. At the moment when he most needed help those who were best fitted to give it sedulously avoided his company, and in this first moment of meeting Darsie was tempted to follow their example.

Horrid to look like that! At his age to own those lines, those reddened eyes, that dulled white skin! Up went the little head, the slender neck reared itself proudly, the red lips curled over small white teeth. Darsie intended to wither Ralph by the sight of such obvious distaste, but with the easy vanity of his nature he attributed her airs to girlish pique at his own neglect, and was correspondingly elated thereat. /

The little schoolgirl who had been his sister's friend had grown into a "stunning girl," with whom the men were evidently greatly impressed. Ralph decided that the hour had come to claim her as an old friend and take her under his wing. He sat himself down by her side and persistently monopolized her attention.

"College life evidently suits you, Darsie. You are looking rippingly well!"

"Am I? Sorry to be unable to return the compliment!"

"Oh!" Ralph moved impatiently. "Don't *you* begin that tune! It is dinned into my ears from morning till night. A fellow may swot himself into a rag, and not a word will be said, but if he oversteps an inch for his own amusement there's the dickens to pay. I said from the start that I intended to have a good rag. College is one of the best times in a man's life, and he's a fool if he doesn't make the most of his chance."

"It is also – incidentally – supposed to be a time for mental improvement," returned Darsie in sententious tones, which brought upon her an instant rebuke.

"Oh, for pity's sake don't come the Newnham swag over me! Can't stand those girls as a rule. Avoid 'em like poison. Take my advice as an old friend and avoid that style as you would / the plague. You're too jolly pretty to come the strong-minded female. Far better stick to your old style. Men like it a heap better."

"It is a matter of perfect indifference to me *what* men like!" declared Darsie, not, it is to be feared, with absolute veracity. "I am proud to be a Newnham-ite, and if the girls do have a few mannerisms, they count for precious little beside their virtues. They are up to work, and they *do* work with might and main, though there can be no place in the world where there is no fun. We are always having some prank or other – politicals,[103] and cocoa-parties and hockey matches, and dances –"

"What's the fun of dances with no men to dance with? Wait till May term, and see what a real ball is like. We'll have some river picnics, too, and breakfasts at the Orchard.[104] There's lots to be done in summer, but just now there's nothing on but teas. You must come to tea in my rooms. I've got a slap-up study." He turned towards Mrs. Reeves and addressed her with confident familiarity. "Mrs. Reeves will play chaperon, and I'll promise you the best cakes that Cambridge can produce."

"Oh, yes, I'll play chaperon." To Darsie's surprise the sweet-faced woman smiled back into Ralph's face with friendly eyes, not appearing even to notice the over-confidence of his manner. "Mr. / Percival gives charming parties, and I can answer for it that his boast as to the cakes is justified. I can never fathom where he gets them."

She turned to Darsie with a little gesture of confidence, and slightly lowered her voice. "I am known as 'the Professional Chaperon.'[105] I hope you will engage my services if you are in need of such a personage, but perhaps we ought to know one another a little better first. I should like so much to know you! Will you come to see me one afternoon next week when you are free, and feel inclined for a chat? I won't ask any one else, so that we can have a real cosy time."

Surprised and gratified, and more than a little flattered, Darsie mentioned her free hours, and received in return Mrs. Reeves's card bearing an address in Grange Road, then once more Ralph engrossed her attention.[106]

"I say! You might ask Ida up for a night or two, and bring her along. They'll let you have a friend now and then, and she'd like it all right. Awfully decent in writing to me, Ida is, and fights my battles at home. Sensible girl! Understand it's no good to jaw. I'd like to have Ida up for a bit."

"So would I. I'll ask her with pleasure." One of Ralph's best points had been his affection for his sisters, and the reminder thereof softened Darsie's heart. She smiled at him with recovered / friendliness. "I'll ask Ida, and you must ask Dan and Hannah Vernon, and make a nice family party. Do you see much of Dan? I don't expect *he* makes a rag of himself over amusement!"

Ralph shrugged carelessly. "I've no use for Vernon! Good head for routine work, but as a pal, dull as you make 'em! I'll ask him once as you make a point of it, but I don't fancy you'll want him twice. As for the sister – but perhaps I'd better not make any remarks?"

"Much better!" Darsie said frostily. "Your manners have not improved, Ralph. I think, if you please, that I would rather not talk to you any more for the present. Would you tell Dan Vernon that I want him to take your place?"

It was the first, the very first time in her life that Darsie had essayed the part of queening it over a member of the opposite sex, and the success of the venture was startling even to herself. Ralph flushed, flinched, rose without a word, and stalked across the room to summon Dan as required; and Dan came meekly forward, seated himself in the discarded chair, and faced her with an air of solemn expectation. His rugged face looked plain and roughly hewn in contrast with Ralph's classical features, but the dark eyes were eloquent as of yore, and the sight of the tilted chin brought back a score of old-time memories. Darsie looked at him with satisfaction, but with a disconcerting / blankness of mind as to what to say-first. From the other side of the room Ralph was looking on with cynical eyes; it was imperative that the silence should be broken at once.

"Dan, *please* say something! I wanted Ralph to go, so I asked for you. Do please find something to say."

Dan smiled broadly. Each time that she saw him smile Darsie wondered afresh how she could ever have thought him plain. His dark eyes glowed upon her with the look she liked best to see.

"What am I to say? It's good to see you here, Darsie. You are looking very – well! Everything going all right? Sure there's nothing I can do?"

"No." Darsie beamed happily. At that moment there seemed nothing left to wish. Dan's friendliness gave the finishing touch to her content, and the world was *couleur de rose*.[107] "I am loving it all more than I expected. The work's glorious, and the play's glorious, and I'm just absorbed in both. It's splendid, coming here to-day to see this lovely old house and meet you again. I thought you had forgotten all about me."

But Dan had drawn back into his shell, and refused to be cajoled. He glowered at the opposite wall for some minutes, then asked abruptly – /

"Why did you send off Percival?"

"Oh – !" Darsie hesitated, and then answered with discretion: "I had talked to him as much as I cared about for the moment, and I shall see him soon again.

He is going to get' up a tea-party for me, with that sweet Mrs. Reeves as chaperon. I told him to ask you and Hannah."

"You should not have done that!" Dan spoke with sharp displeasure. "I don't care to accept Percival's hospitality for myself, and certainly not for my sister. I shall tell Hannah to refuse."

Darsie glanced across to where Hannah sat, a typical plain Hannah at that moment, with feet planted well apart, and on her face the expression of dour determination which she adopted in moments of boredom; from her to Ralph Percival, standing in graceful pose, his fine, almost feminine, profile outlined clearly against the panelled wall, and, glancing, laughed softly to herself. It seemed so ridiculous to think of this girl needing protection from this man.

"I fancy Hannah is quite capable of looking after herself."

"I'm sure of it. She's a new-comer, however, and she doesn't get into Percival's set if I can help it."

"Dan! It can't be so bad if Mrs. Reeves is willing to go. She accepted in a minute. I heard her myself." /

"She goes everywhere, to the wildest fellows' rooms. She has her own ideas, no doubt, but I don't profess to understand them." He hesitated, puckering his brows, and looking at her with dark, questioning eyes. "I have no authority over you, Darsie, but I wish –"

"Ralph saved my life," interrupted Darsie simply.

Dan looked at her sharply, stared with scrutinizing attention at her face, but spoke no further word of protest. He evidently realized, as Darsie did herself, that it would be a mean act to reject the friendship of a man who had wrought so great a service.

Half an hour later the two girls slowly wended their way past the tower gateway of Trinity, past Caius, with its twinkling lights, stately King's, and modest Catherine's, to the homelike shelter of their own dear Newnham.[108]

"Well!" cried Hannah, breaking a long silence, "you had a big success and I had – *not!* But you're not a bit happier than I, that I can see. Men are poor, blind bats. I prefer my own sex; they are much more discriminating, and when they like you – they *like* you, and there's no more shilly-shally. Those men never know their own minds!" /

Chapter XXI

Mrs. Reeves Makes a Proposal

FOUR days later Darsie went by appointment to her *tête-à-tête* tea with the professional chaperon with a pleasurable expectation which was largely streaked with curiosity.

If physiognomy counted for anything, Mrs. Reeves must surely be a most sweet and noble character. Her grey eyes looked into yours with a straight, transparent gaze, her lips closed one upon another firmly enough to debar all trace of weakness, yet not so firmly as to hint at undue severity, her hair waved back from a broad white brow. It was, as Dan had said, difficult to understand how such a woman could be the willing companion of men whom even fellow-students were anxious to shun. Darsie wondered if the afternoon's conversation would throw any light on this knotty point.

She was shown, not into the drawing-room but into a cosy little den on the second floor, a sort of glorious edition of a college study, where Mrs. / Reeves sat reading by the fire, clad in a loose velvet gown of a curious reddish-brown, like the autumn tint of a leaf, which matched the high lights of her chestnut hair. Darsie watched her with fascinated attention as she presided over the tea-table, with lithe, graceful movements which made a poem out of the every-day proceeding, and Mrs. Reeves studied her in return, as she chatted lightly about a dozen casual subjects. Then the tea-things were carried away, and with the drawing nearer to the fire conversation took a more intimate turn.

"I hope your friend did not think me inhospitable for not including her in my invitation to-day, but when I want to get to know a girl I prefer to have her entirely to myself. Perhaps she will come another day, Vernon's sister ought to be worth knowing."

"You know Dan?" Darsie's smile was somewhat anxious, for Dan's own manner with respect to her hostess was still a disturbing element. "You know him well?"

"No," Mrs. Reeves smiled; "not well. But I like him well by repute! Vernon has no need of my services. He is strong enough to stand by himself."

"You mean tea-parties?" queried Darsie vaguely, whereat Mrs. Reeves subsided into a ripple of laughter. /

"No, I do *not* mean tea-parties – something very much wider. I don't fancy, however, that Vernon is sociably disposed, and the authorities here are not inclined to encourage meetings between the men and girl students. The head of his college is my brother-in-law, and one of your Dons is a very old friend, so I hear the question discussed from both sides, and then – like a wise woman – I gang my own gait! So long as men are men, and girls are girls, they are bound to attract each other; it's natural and right, and when they are bound to meet in any case, it is my little hobby to help them to do so under the best conditions. I flatter myself I am quite an expert in the art of being just chaperon enough, and not too chaperon, and I never refuse to act if I can possibly contrive to do so."

"No! Dan said –" began Darsie involuntarily, and then stopped short with a furious blush. Mrs. Reeves, however, did not share her discomfiture; she laughed, and said shrewdly –

"Oh, I have observed his disapproving eye. I can guess what he said. Many people feel the same, who judge only from the surface, and don't take the trouble to realize my motives. One doesn't explain such things to the world in general, but I want *you* to understand. If one man less admirable than another; if his friends and his entertainments are inclined to become rowdy / and discreditable, does he need help *less,* or more? Vernon and other men of his kind consider that they do their duty by leaving such a man severely alone. I find mine in being with him – just – as – much – as ever I can!" She emphasized the words by a series of taps with the poker on the top of an obstinate coal, given in the most delightfully schoolgirlish manner. "I chaperon his parties; I talk to him and his friends; I make myself so agreeable that they love to have me, and want to have me again. I try with every power I possess to encourage all that is good, and kind, and honest, and cheering in themselves and their conversation, and deftly, delicately, invisibly, as it were, to fight against everything that is mean and unworthy. It's difficult, Darsie! – I may call you Darsie, mayn't I? it's such a beguiling little name! – one of the most difficult feats a woman could set herself to accomplish, and though I've had a fair measure of success, it's only a measure. It's such a great big work. Think of all that it means, that it *may* mean to England, if we can keep these men from drifting, and give them a pull-up in time! I am constantly looking, looking out for fellow-workers. That's why I invited you here to-day – to ask *you* to be on my side!"

"I!" Darsie's gasp of amazement sounded throughout the room. "Il Oh, you can't mean / it! What could I do? I can do nothing – I'm only a girl!"

"Only a girl! But, dear child, that's your finest qualification! You can do more than I can ever accomplish, just because you *are* a girl, and will be admitted to an intimacy which is impossible for me. Besides, Darsie, you are a particularly pretty and attractive girl into the bargain; you know that, don't you? You *ought* to know it, and be very, very thankful for a great weapon given into your hands. If you will join the ranks with me, and act as my curate, you will immensely increase my power for good."

"But I can't! I can't! I'd love to if I could, but you don't know how impossible it is. I couldn't preach to save my life."

"I'm thankful to hear it. I don't want you to preach. You'd soon lose your influence if you did. It's a case of *being,* Darsie, rather than doing; being your tru-est, sweetest, highest self when you are with these men, so that they may feel your influence through all the fun and banter. Lots of fun, please; you can't have too much of that; a dull girl is soon left to herself. People in general don't half realize the influence of just right *thinking* – the atmosphere which surrounds a person who is mentally fighting for good. The sunbeams fall on the dark earth and soak up the poisoned waters, and so may our thoughts – our / prayers," She was silent for a few moments, her hand resting lightly on Darsie's knees. "There is a girl in your house – Margaret France – I expect you know her! She has been one of my best helpers these last years. Wherever Margaret is there is fun and laughter; she is just brimfull of it, but – can you imagine any one going to Margaret with an unworthy thought, an unworthy cause? I want you to follow in her steps!" She paused again for a long minute, then said slowly and emphatically –

"Ralph Percival needs help, Darsie! He has not fallen very low as yet, but he is drifting. He is in a bad set, and, like too many of our richer men, he lacks purpose. They come up here because their fathers have been before them, and it is the correct thing to do. There is no real reason why they should work, or take a high place, but there seems to themselves every reason why they should have a good time. Parents sometimes seem to hold more or less the same opinion; at others they seem distressed, but powerless. College authorities are regarded as natural enemies; religious influences for the time beat on closed doors; now, Darsie, here comes the chance for 'only a girl!' A man like Ralph Percival, at this stage of his life, will be more influenced by a girl like you than by any power on earth. It's a law of Nature and of God, and / if every girl realized it, it would be a blessed thing for the race. I once heard a preacher say that so long as one dealt with general principles, and talked broadly of the human race, there was very little done. We have to fine it down to *my next-door neighbour* before we really set to work. Fine down what I have said to Ralph Percival, Darsie, and help me with him! He's drifting. He needs you. Help me to pull him back!"

Darsie nodded dumbly. Mrs. Reeves thought the expression on her downcast face touchingly sweet and earnest, but even she missed the clue to the girl's inmost thought.

Years ago she herself had been drifting, drifting towards death, and Ralph had stepped forward to save her; now, in an allegorical sense, the positions were reversed, and she was summoned to the rescue. There was no refusing a duty so obvious. Heavy and onerous as the responsibility might be, it had been placed in her hands. Darsie braced herself to the burden. /

Chapter XXII

Christmas Day

It was Christmas Day; fifteen eventful months had passed by since Darsie Garnett and Hannah Vernon had made their appearance in Clough in the character of modest and diffident Freshers. Now, advanced to the dignity of second-year girls, they patronized new-comers with the best, and talked, thought, and behaved as though, deprived of their valuable support, the historical centre of Cambridge must swiftly crumble to the dust.

The little air of assurance and self-esteem which seems inseparable from a feminine student had laid its hand on Darsie's beauty, robbing it of the old shy grace, and on each fresh return to the old home Clemence and Lavender eloquently described themselves as "squelched flat" by the dignified young woman who sailed about with her head in the air, and delivered an ultimatum on every subject as it arose, with an air of "My opinion is final. Let no dog bark!"[109]

These mannerisms, however, were only, after / all, a veneer; and when two or three days of merry, rollicking family life had passed by, the old Darsie made her appearance once more, forgot to be learned and superior, forbore to refer to college and college ways in every second or third sentence, and showed a reviving interest in family affairs.

Clemence was fatter than ever, a subject of intense mortification to herself, though at each fresh meeting she confided in whispered asides that she had "lost five pounds – ten pounds," as the case might be. No one believed in these diminutions, but if one happened to be amiably disposed, one murmured vaguely, and affected conviction; and if one were not, one openly jeered and scoffed!

Lavender was sentimental and wrote poetry in which "pale roses died, in the garden wide, and the wind blew drear, o'er the stricken mere." She had advanced to the dignity of long skirts, and dressed her hair – badly! – in the latest eccentricity of fashion.

Vi Vernon, on the contrary, had developed into a most elegant person, quite an accomplished woman of the world, darkly suspected of "going to be engaged "to a young lawyer with a dark moustache, who had lately developed a suspicious fondness for her father's company.

It really gave one quite a shock to realize *how* / grown-up the old companions had become even the brothers Harry and Russell were transformed into tall striplings who bought newspapers on their own account, and preferred, actually *preferred,* to be clean rather than dirty! It was a positive relief to listen to Tim's loud voice, look at his grimy paws, and reflect that one member of the family was still in the enjoyment of youth!

As usual, the postman's arrival was the first excitement of Christmas morning. He brought with him an armful of letters and parcels, and Darsie was quick to spy Ralph Percival's handwriting upon one of the smallest and most attractive-looking of the packets.

The colour came into her cheeks as she looked, but after holding the parcel uncertainly for a moment, she laid it down again, and proceeded to open other letters and boxes, leaving this particular one to the last. An onlooker would have been puzzled to decide whether it was more dread or expectation which prompted this decision; and perhaps Darsie herself could hardly have answered the question. The table was soon spread with envelopes and wrappings of paper which had enclosed souvenirs from college friends, and the more costly offerings from Mrs. Percival and her girls, inscribed with the orthodox words of greeting. Darsie ranged them in order, and then, still hesitating, turned to the last packet of all. /

Inside was a note folded so as to act as additional wrapper for a small white box. Ralph's writing, large and well-formed like himself, filled the half-sheet.

"DEAR DARSIE, – I hope you will accept the enclosed trifle which has been made for you, from my own design. You will understand its meaning! I am more than ever in need of pulling up! Don't fail a fellow, Darsie!

"Yours,

"RALPH B. PERCIVAL."

Inside the box lay a small bu beautifully modelled anchor brooch, with a fine golden rope twined round the stock. Darsie looked at it with the same mingling of joy and pain which seemed inseparable from each stage of her friendship with this attractive but irresponsible young man.

It was just like Ralph to have thought of this pretty and graceful way of expressing his sentiments, and it was not in girl nature to resist a glow of gratified vanity; but as she turned the golden anchor in her hands and realized the significance of the symbol, an old impatience stirred in Darsie's heart. A man who trusted to another for anchorage in life, and who was ever in danger of breaking loose and drifting on to the rocks, was not the strong knight of a young girl's dreams. There were moments when the protecting tenderness / which had prompted the last year's efforts gave place to sudden intolerance and resentment.

Inspired by Mrs. Reeves's words in her first term at college, Darsie had set gallantly to the task of influencing Ralph Percival for good, and preventing his further deterioration. At first it had appeared a forlorn hope; and she would have despaired many a time if it had not been for the encouragement which she received from Mrs. Reeves and her "curate," Margaret France. Then gradually and surely her influence had begun to make itself felt. It could not truthfully be said that she had so inspired Ralph that he had turned over a new leaf, and abandoned bad practices from a desire for the right itself. If the truth must be told, desire for his pretty mentor's approbation and praise had been a far stronger factor in the improvement which seemed to have been effected.

Ralph was emotional, and as his interest in Darsie deepened into the sentimental attachment which seemed a natural development of their intimacy, he grew increasingly anxious to stand well in her estimation. During the May term there had been teas in the college gardens, breakfast parties at the Orchard, picnics on the river, which had afforded opportunities of *tête-à-tête* conversations when, amidst the flowers and the sunshine, it had been quite an agreeable sensation to lament over one's weaknesses and shortcomings, / and to receive in return the wisest of counsels from Darsie's pretty lips.

"To please *you,* Darsie!... I'm hanged if I care what other people think, but if *you* ask me –" The promises gained were all couched in this personal vein. "If you chuck me, Darsie, I shan't worry any more." This was the threat held out for the future. Unsatisfactory, if you will, yet the fact remained that for the first part of the last term Ralph *had* appeared to show greater interest in work than he had before manifested, and had been involved in a minimum of scrapes.

There were moments when, remembering these facts, Darsie felt proudly that she had not lived in vain; moments when Ralph's dependence on herself and graceful acknowledgments of her help seemed the chief interest in life. But there were also other moments when the bond between them weighed heavy as a chain. In less than two years the training days would be over, Ralph would be a man, and she herself a woman on the threshold of life. Would she be expected to play the part of permanent anchor, and, if so, could she, should she undertake the task?

For the last few weeks of the term Darsie had been so absorbed in her own surroundings that she had had no time or thought to bestow on outside interests, and Mrs. Reeves being abroad, no college news came to her ears from that source. / Now since the beginning of the holidays Ralph's name had hardly been mentioned, since family interests were predominant, and Darsie had learned from experience that the subject of "Percival" was calculated to send Dan Vernon into his most taciturn mood.

On this Christmas morning, however, Darsie was in a mood of somewhat reckless gaiety; let the future take care of itself. For to-day, at least, she was young and happy and free; the Vernon family was coming over in bulk to spend the evening, when the presence of one of Dan's chums would supply an agreeable element of novelty to the occasion. Not one single gloomy thought must be allowed to cloud the sunshine of this Christmas Day!

Dinner was served at seven o'clock, and was truly a festive occasion. The dining-room table being unequal to the task of providing accommodation for sixteen people, the schoolroom table had to be used as a supplement. It was a good inch higher than the other, and supplied with a preponderance of legs, but these small drawbacks could not weigh against the magnificent effect of the combined length, covered, as it was, with fruit, flowers, and a plethora of bright red bonbons and crackers. The girls wore their prettiest evening frocks; the turkey, the goose, the plum-pudding, and the mince-pies were all paragons / of their kind, while dessert was enlivened by the discovery of small surprise presents cunningly hidden away within hollowed oranges, apples, and nuts. Silver thimbles, pocket-calendars, stamp-cases, sleeve-links, and miniature brooches, made their appearance with such extraordinary unexpectedness that Darsie finally declared she was afraid to venture to eat even a grape, lest she might swallow a diamond alive!

When the hilarious meal had come to an end, the company adjourned into a drawing-room illumined by firelight only, but such firelight! For over a week those logs had been stacked by the kitchen grate so that they might become "as dry as tinder."

Placed in the big grate, they sent up a leaping, crackling flame which was in itself an embodiment of cheer, and when the sixteen chairs were filled and ranged in a circle round the blaze, there was a Christmas picture complete, and as goodly and cheery a picture as one need wish to see. A basket of fir-cones stood at either side of the grate, and the order of proceedings was that each guest in turn should drop a cone into the heart of the fire, and relate an amusing story or coincidence the while it burned. Results proved that the amount of time so consumed varied so strangely that suggestions of foul play were made by more than one raconteur. /

"It's not fair! Some one has got at these cones! Some of them have been soaked to make them damp! –"

Be that as it may, no one could possibly have foretold who would happen to hit on this particular cone, so that the charge of injustice fell swiftly to the ground.

Mrs. Garnett opened the ball with a coincidence taken from her own life, the cone burning bright and blue the while.

"When I was a girl of twenty, living at home with my father and mother, I had a curiously distinct dream one night about a certain Mr. Dalrymple. We knew no one of that name, but in my dream he appeared to be a lifelong friend. He was a clergyman, about sixty years of age – not handsome, but with a kind, clever face. He had grey hair, and heavy black eyebrows almost meeting over his nose. I was particularly interested in his appearance, because – this is the exciting part! – in my dream I was engaged to him, and we were going to be married the following month.... Next morning, when I awoke, the impression left was unusually distinct, and at breakfast I made them all laugh over my matrimonial plans. My sisters called me 'Mrs. Dalrymple' for several days, and then the joke faded away, and was replaced by something newer and more exciting. Two years passed by, and / then, in the summer holidays, I went to Scotland to pay a visit. A slight accident on the line delayed me at a small station for a couple of hours, and I strolled through the village to pass the time by seeing what could be seen. It was a dull little place, and the principal street was empty of every one but a few children until, when I reached the end, a man in a black coat came suddenly out of a house and walked towards me. He was tall and elderly and thin, his hair was grey, his eyebrows were dark and met in a peak over his nose. My heart gave a great big jump, for it was the face of the man I had seen in my dream – the man who was to have been my husband! You can imagine my surprise! It was many, many months since I had given a thought to the silly old dream, but at the first glance at that face the memory of it came back as clear and distinct as on the morning after it had happened. I walked towards him quite dazed with surprise, and then another extraordinary thing happened! He was evidently short-sighted, and could not distinguish figures at a distance, but presently, as we drew nearer together, he in his turn started violently, stared in my face as if he could hardly believe his eyes, and then rushed forward and seized me by the hand. 'I *am* glad to see you – I *am* glad! This *is* a pleasure! When did you come?' Poor old man! My blank face showed him his mistake, / and he dropped my hand and began to mumble out apologies. 'I've made a mistake. I thought you were – I thought you were – ' He frowned, evidently searched in vain for a clue, and added feebly, 'I thought I knew you. *Your face is so familiar!*' It was all over in a minute. He took off his hat, and hurried on overcome with embarrassment, and I turned mechanically in the direction of the church. It was closed, but by the gate stood a board bearing the hours of services, and beneath them the name of the minister of the parish. I read it with a thrill. The name was '*The Rev. John Dalrymple*'!"

Mrs. Garnett lay back in her chair with the contented air of a *raconteuse*[110] who has deftly led up to a *dénouement,* and her audience gasped in mingled surprise and curiosity.

"How *thrilling!* How weird!"

"What an extraordinary thing! Go on! Go on! And what happened next?"

Mrs. Garnett chuckled contentedly.

"I met your father, married him, and lived happily ever after! As for Mr. Dalrymple, I never met him again nor heard his name mentioned. The sequel is not at all exciting, but it was certainly an extraordinary coincidence, and caused me much agitation at the time. I have timed myself very well – my cone has just burned out. Who's turn comes next?" /

There followed a somewhat lengthened pause while every one nudged a next-door neighbour, and disdained responsibility on his own account. Then Mr. Vernon stepped into the breach.

"I heard a curious thing the other day. A friend of mine was taken suddenly ill on a hillside in Switzerland, was carried into a châlet and most kindly tended by the good woman. When, at the end of several hours, he was well enough to leave, he wished to make her a present of money. She refused to take it, but said that she had a daughter in service in England, and that it would be a real pleasure to her, if, upon his return, my friend would write to the girl telling her of his visit to the old home. He asked for the address, and was told, 'Mary Smith, care of Mr. Spencer, The Towers, Chestone.' He read it, looked the old woman in the face and said, "*I* am Mr. Spencer! *I* live at The Towers, Chestone; and my children's nurse is called Mary Smith!' There! I can vouch for the absolute truth of that coincidence, and I think you will find it hard to beat."

"And what did he say to the nurse?" asked literal Clemence, to the delight of her brothers and sisters, whose imaginary dialogues between master and maid filled the next few minutes with amusement.

Dan's friend hailed from Oxford, and gave a / highly coloured account of a practical joke in several stages, which he had played on an irritating acquaintance. The elder members of the party listened with awe, if without approval, but Tim showed repeated signs of restlessness, and in a final outburst corrected the narrator on an all-important point.

"That's the way they had it in *Britain's Boys!*"[111] he declared, whereupon the Oxford man hid his head under an antimacassar, and exclaimed tragically that all was discovered!

"Now it's Darsie's turn! Tell us a story, Darsie – an adventure, your own adventure when you went out in that punt, and the mill began working –"

"Why should I tell what you know by heart already? You'd only be bored."

"Oh, but you never tell a story twice over in the same way," persisted Clemence with doubtful flattery. "And Mr. Leslie has never heard it. I'm sure he'd be interested. It really *was* an adventure. So romantic, too. Ralph Percival is *so* good-looking!"

"I fail to see what his looks have to do with it," said Darsie in her most Newnham manner. "Strong arms were more to the purpose, and those he certainly does possess."

"Strong arms – stout heart!" murmured Lavender in sentimental aside. "Well, then, tell about / the treasure-hunt in the Percivals' garden – and how you – you know! Go on – that's another *real* adventure."

"All Miss Darsie's adventures seem to have been in connection with the Percival family!" remarked the Oxford man at this point.

Darsie flushed with annoyance, and retired determinedly into her shell. She was seated almost in the centre of the circle, between her father and John Vernon, and the leaping light of the fire showed up her face and figure in varying shades of colour. Now she was a rose-maiden, dress, hair, and face glowing in a warm pink hue; anon, the rose changed into a faint metallic blue, which gave a ghostlike effect to the slim form; again, she was all white – a dazzling, unbroken white, in which the little oval face assumed an air of childlike fragility and pathos. As she sat with her hands folded on her knee, and her head resting against the dark cushions of her chair, more than one of the company watched her with admiration; but Darsie was too much occupied with her own thoughts to be conscious of their scrutiny.

As each story-teller began his narrative, she cast a momentary glance in his direction, and then turned back to fire-gazing once more. Once or twice she cast a curious glance towards the far corner where Dan Vernon was seated, but he had drawn his chair so far back that nothing / could be distinguished but the white blur of shirt-front. Darsie wondered if Dan were uninterested, bored, asleep – yet as her eyes questioned the darkness she had the strangest impression of meeting other eyes – dark, intent eyes, which stared, and stared –

Vi Vernon was telling "a *most interesting* coincidence," her opening sentence – "It was told to me by a friend – a lawyer" – causing surreptitious smiles and nudges among her younger hearers. "There was a girl in his office – a typewriting girl. All the money had been lost –"

"Whose money? The lawyer's or the office's?"

"Neither! Don't be silly. The girl's father's, of course."

"You never told us that she had a father!"

"Russell, if you interrupt every minute, I won't play. Of course he'd lost it, or the girl wouldn't have been a typist. Any one would know that! Ed – the lawyer did sea-sort of business – what do you call it? – marine things – and the girl typed them. Years before a brother had disappeared –"

"The lawyer's brother?"

"No! I'm sorry I began. You are so disagreeable. The *girl's* uncle, of course, and they often wanted to find him, because he was rich, and might have helped them now they were poor. One day, when she was typing out one of the depositions –" /

"Ha!" The unusual word evoked unanimous comment. "'De-positions' – if you please! How legal we are becoming, to be sure!"

Vi flushed, and hurried on breathlessly –

"She came across the name of John H. Rose, and she wondered if the H. meant Hesselwhaite, for that was her uncle's second name, and she looked it up in the big document, and it *was* him, and he was on the west coast of South America, and they wrote to him, and he left them a lot of money, and they lived happy ever after."

Polite murmurs of astonishment from the elders, unconcealed sniggerings from the juniors, greeted the conclusion of this thrilling tale, and then once more Darsie was called upon for her contribution, and this time consented without demur.

"Very well! I've thought of a story. It's about a managing clerk who was sent to Madrid on business for his firm. I didn't know him myself, so don't ask questions! While he was in Madrid he went to the opera one night, and sat in a box. Just opposite was another box, in which sat a beauteous Spanish maid. He looked at her, and she looked at him. They kept looking and looking. At last he thought that she smiled, and waved her fan as if beckoning him to come and speak to her. So in the first interval the eager youth made his way along the richly carpeted corridors; but just as he reached the door / of the box it opened, and a man came out and put a letter into his hand. It was written in Spanish, which the youth did not understand; but, being filled with a frenzy of curiosity to know what the fair one had to say, he decided to run to his hotel, and get the manager to translate it without delay. Well, he went; but as soon as the manager had read the note he started violently, and said in a manner of the utmost concern: 'I exceedingly regret, sir, to appear inhospitable or inconsiderate, but I find it my painful duty to ask you to leave my hotel within an hour.' The clerk protested, questioned, raged, and stormed, but all in vain. The manager refused even to refer to the letter; he simply insisted that he could entertain him no longer in the hotel, and added darkly: 'It would be well for the Señor to take the first train out of Spain.'

"Alarmed by this mysterious warning, the unhappy youth accordingly shook off the dust from his feet and returned to London, where he confided his woes to his beloved and generous employer. The employer was a Spanish merchant and understood the language, so he naturally offered to solve the mystery. No sooner, however, had his eye scanned the brief lines, than a cloud shadowed *his* expressive countenance, and he addressed himself to the youth more in sorrow than in anger. 'It grieves me to the heart, Mr. – er – *Bumpas*,' / he said, 'to sever our connection after your faithful service to the firm; but, after the perusal of this note, I have unfortunately no choice. If you will apply to the cashier he will hand you a cheque equal to six months' salary; but I must ask you to understand that when you leave my office this morning it is for the last time!'"

A rustle of excitement from the audience, a momentary glimpse of Dan's face in the flickering light, testified to the interest of this extraordinary history.

Darsie bent forward to encourage her fir-cone with a pat from the poker, and continued dramatically –

"Bewildered, broken-hearted, almost demented, the unfortunate youth betook him to an uncle in America (all uncles seem to live in America), who received him with consideration, listened to his sad tale, and bade him be of good cheer. 'By a strange coincidence' (coincidence again!), 'said the worthy man,' there sups with me to-night a learned professor of languages, resident at our local college. He, without doubt, will make plain the mysterious contents of the fatal note!' Punctual to his hour the professor arrived, and the harassed youth hailed with joy the end of his long suspense. Whatever might be the purport of the words written in that fatal paper, the knowledge thereof could not be worse than the fate which had dogged / his footsteps ever since that tragic night when he had first cast eyes on the baleful beauty of the Spanish maid. Yet might it not be that once again the sight of these words would send him wandering homeless o'er the world – that the stream of his uncle's benevolence might be suddenly damned by a force mysterious as inexorable?

"Trembling with emotion, the young man thrust his hand into his pocket to bring forth this mystic note –"

Darsie paused dramatically.

"And – and – and then –?"

"He discovered that it was not there! In the course of his long wanderings it had unfortunately been mislaid."

The clamour of indignation which followed this *dénouement* can be better imagined than described; but the example having been set, wonderful how many stories of the same baffling character were revived by the different members of the company during the remainder of the firelight *séance*. So wild and exaggerated did the narratives become, indeed, that the meeting broke up in confusion, and took refuge in those admittedly uproarious Christmas games which survived from the happy nursery days, when "to make as much noise as we like" seemed the climax of enjoyment.

And so ended Christmas Day for the joint ranks of the Vernons and Garnetts. /

Chapter XXIII

The Melodrama

ON Boxing Day, Lavender excused herself from joining a rinking party,[112] and lay curled up on a sofa reading a Christmas number.

The following morning she stayed in bed to breakfast, and complained of a swollen face. On the third day, the sight of the huge cheeks and doubled chin sent the family flying for the doctor, and the tragic verdict of "mumps" was whispered from mouth to mouth.

Mumps in the Christmas holidays! Isolation for the victim for days, even weeks; the risk of infection for others; the terrible, unthinkable possibility of "missing a term"! Mrs. Vernon came nobly to the rescue, and invited Darsie to spend the remainder of the holidays under her roof, since, with a Tripos in prospect, every precaution must be taken against infection.[113] For the rest, Lavender's own little eyrie was situated at the end of a long top passage, and might have been originally designed for a sanatorium; and there, in solitary state, the poor mumpy poetess bewailed / her fate, and besought the compassion of her companions. Letters were not forbidden, and she therefore found a sad satisfaction in pouring out her woes on paper, as a result of which occupation the following poetical effusion presently found its way to the schoolroom party –

> "All gay and fair the scene appeared:
>   I was a gladsome maid;
> When the dire hand of circumstance
>   Upon my life was laid.
> Upon the eve of festal day
>   The first dread symptoms fell;
> And those who should have sympathised,
> Whose tender words I would have prized,
> Did sneer, and jeer, and with loud cries,
> Ascribe the reason to mince-pies!
>
> What time I woke the third day morn,
> By mirror was the sad truth borne;
> Not alone exile, grief, and pain
> Must fill my cup – but also *shame!*
> Gone is my youthful glee and grace,
> I have an elephantine face;
> My cheeks are gross, which were so thin;
> I have a loathsome pendant chin.
> All who behold me smile aside,
> And their derision barely hide.
> Oh, cruel fate! instead of tears,
> In my sad plight I get but jeers.

Friends, comrades, readers of this ditty,
If heart ye have, on me have pity.
Go not unthinking on your way,
Content to sing, content to play,
While I and mumps sit here alone
In an unending, drear 'At home.'
Put wits to work, think out some way
To cheer the captive's lonely day, /
Forget yourself, and think of me,
And doubly blessed you shall be.
For since the days of earliest youth
You have been brought up on this truth –
To help the ailing by your side
Is the true work of Christmas-tide!"

To disregard so touching an appeal being plainly an impossibility, an impromptu committee meeting was held in the Vernons' study, when the idea of an open-air melodrama was proposed, and carried with acclamation. A melodrama acted in the back garden, underneath Lavender's window, opened out prospects of amusement for the actors as well as the audience, and a rainy afternoon was passed in the merriest fashion discussing the plot, characters, and costume.

Darsie sat on the hearthrug, and prodded the fire vigorously to mark each point scored. Vi wrote from dictation at the centre table. Dan sat chuckling in his own particular chair, and allowed himself to be cast as hero with lamblike calm, and plain Hannah affected dire displeasure at being passed over for the part of beauteous maid. It was like the dear old days when they had all been young – *really* young – in pinafores and pigtails, with no dread of coming Tripos, no agitation about youthful lawyers to chase away sleep at night!

Looking back through the years, that hour stood out in remembrance as one most happily typical of the dear home life. /

The programme was delicious. Vi discovered a great sheet of white paper, left over from the parcel wrappings of the week before; Dan printed the words in his most dashing fashion; John nailed it on the lid of a packing-chest, and the whole party escorted it round the terrace to the Garnett dwelling, and waited in the street beneath until it was conveyed upstairs, and Lavender, discreetly swathed in a shawl, appeared at her lighted window and waved a towel in triumph.

This was the programme –

On Wednesday Afternoon Next
(*Weather permitting*)
In Aid of the Fund for Sick and Suffering Spinsters
A First Performance
will be given
of
The Blood-Curdling and Hair-Raising Melodrama
entitled
THE BLUE CABBAGE
by
ALLTHELOTOFUS.
Dramatis Personæ.

Efflorescence (A Guileless Maid)	Miss Darsie Garnett.
Meretricia (1st Villainess)	Mr. Harry Garnett.
Mycrobe (2nd Villainess)	Mr. Russell Garnett.
Elijah B. Higgins (Hero)	Mr. Dan Vernon.
Sigismund La Bas (A False Caitiff)	Mr. Percy Lister.
D. Spenser (Certificated Poisonmonger)	Mr. John Vernon.
Endeavora (A Well-Meaner)	Miss Clemence Garnett
The Greek Chorus	Miss Hannah Vernon.

N.B. – There is no Cabbage! /

Imagine the feelings of a solitary invalid on receipt of such a programme as the above – a programme of an entertainment organised, composed, and designed wholly and solely for her own amusement! Lavender's mumps were at a painful stage – so sore, so stiff, so heavy, that she felt all face, had no spirit to read, craved for companionship, and yet shrank sensitively from observing eyes. Let those jeer who may, it *is* an abominable thing to feel a martyr, and look a clown, and poor Lavender's sensitive nature suffered acutely from the position. Then oh! it was good to feel that to-morrow something exciting was going to happen – that she would be amused, cheered, comforted; that her dear companions would be near her, so near that once again she would feel one of the merry throng.

If only it were fine! Really and truly Lavender felt that she could not support the blow if it were wet. Mumps seem to sap the constitution of moral force; if she could not see the melodrama, she would weep like a child!

It *was* fine, however. The very elements conspired in her behalf, and produced a still, unshiny day, when the pageant of the melodrama appeared to the best advantage, and the voices rose clear and distinct to that upper window, before which Lavender stood, a muffled figure, in a fur coat and cap, and a great wool shawl swathed round / face and neck after the fashion of an English veil.

The melodrama proved even more thrilling than had been expected. On his, or her, first appearance on the scene, each character advanced to a spot directly in front of the upstairs window, and obligingly related the salient points of his life, character, and ambitions, together with a candid exposition of his intentions towards the other members of the cast; the while Hannah, as Greek Chorus, interposed moral remarks and reflections on the same. After an indulgent hearing of these confessions, it would appear that two ambitions were common to the actors – either they wished to elope with the hero or heroine, or to poison the False Caitiff, and the Villainess Number One or Two, or such a contingent of these worthies as excluded themselves.

The Well-Meaner assiduously endeavoured to foil these intents, and received the scant amount of encouragement which falls to well-meaning interference in real life; the Certified Poison-monger presided over three tin pails of liquids, labelled respectively, "Lingering," "Sudden," and "A highly superior article in writhes and coils. As patronised by the Empress of China," and the demand for these wares was naturally brisk in so quarrelsome a company: the False Caitiff chose a sudden death for his rival, the Hero; Meretricia, / the first Villainess, poisoned the Caitiff by a more lingering means; Villainess Number Two, under the false impression that the Hero had given his heart to Meretricia, poisoned that good lady, sparing no money on the deed, whereby Russell was afforded an admirable opportunity of exhibiting his wriggling powers. The guileless maid poisoned herself with the dregs in her lover's glass; and the Poisonmonger, fatigued with the rush of Christmas business, fainted away, and, being revived by potions from his own pails, survived only long enough to administer a forcible dose in revenge. The Well-Meaner's fate differed from that of her companions in that she was insidiously poisoned by each actor in turn, so that, figuratively speaking, the curtain descended upon a row of corpses, in the midst of which the Greek Chorus intoned exemplary precepts and advice.

Hannah, as Greek chorus, was by common consent pronounced the star of the company, her interpolated reflections being so droll and to the point that even the lingering victims found themselves overcome with laughter.

As for the audience, her joy, though great, was not unmixed with pain. As the melodrama approached its critical point the actors could see her at her window, holding up her mumps with either hand, and the piteous plea – "Don't make / me laugh! Don't make me laugh!" floated down on the wintry air.

Next day Lavender was worse, and melodramas were banned as a means of recreations; but she sent a touching message of thanks to the troupe, in which she declared that "the joy outweighed the pain," so that, all things considered, "The Blue Cabbage" was voted a great success. /

Chapter XXIV

Dan and Darsie

No sooner did the news of Lavender's illness, and Darsie's consequent absence from home, reach the Percival household than three separate letters were dispatched, insisting that at least a part of the remaining holidays should be spent at the Manor.

Pray why, the girls demanded, should Hannah Vernon be allowed to engross Darsie, when she enjoyed her society practically the whole year round? It was unjust, mean, contemptible. They were so dull and sad this Christmas-time. Wouldn't Darsie come?

Pray why, inquired Ralph ingenuously, did Darsie not come when she had the chance? She knew that he would be glad to see her. It was quite horribly dull. The parents were absurdly humped [114] –

Mrs. Percival's words were few but disturbing: "I want to consult with you about Ralph. You have more influence over him than any one else. Do come, dear child, if you possibly can."

In face of the last letter it was impossible to / say no. Darsie was not sure that she wanted to say no; on the other hand, she was aggravatingly uncertain if she wanted to say yes. At college and at home alike the atmosphere was at once austere and bracing; it would be agreeable to live for a time in the lap of luxury – to be regarded as a miracle of cleverness and beauty, which treatment was invariably bestowed upon her during her visits to The Manor. She would enjoy staying with the Percivals, but she would be sad to miss the cosy hours when Dan and his friend, Percy Lister, joined the little party in the old study, and they all talked together round the fire.

What talks they had; what themes they discussed! What animated discussions sprang from a casual word, and were pursued with a go and a spirit which seem to exist only on such informal occasions. Sometimes they laughed and quipped, and beheld everything from the comic point of view; anon, a sudden spirit of earnestness would pass from one to the other, and as the fading light hid their faces from view, tongues were set free, so that they talked of the things which mattered, the towering realities which lay at the heart of life! During these discussions Dan invariably seated himself in the darkest corner, and Darsie, looking across, had again and again the impression of deep eyes staring – staring!

Vi Vernon considered the Percivals "grasping / creatures," and didn't care who knew it; Hannah was placidly unconcerned; Dan made no remark; Percy Lister was leaving himself, and considered that things "fitted in well." Altogether, in comparison with the enthusiasm of the invitation, the opposition was blightingly resigned. Darsie tossed her head, packed her boxes, and prepared to depart a whole three days sooner than she had originally intended.

On the afternoon before her departure a party was made up for the rink, but at the last moment Darsie excused herself, and declared a wish to stay at home. There were several pieces of sewing and mending which were necessary, there was a letter to be written to Margaret France, and a farewell ode to cheer poor Lavender. A gas fire in her bedroom allowed her to perform these tasks in solitude, but as soon as they were satisfactorily accomplished she made her way downstairs to the study, prepared to enjoy an hour over an interesting book.

The gas was unlit, the usual large fire blazed in the grate; an arm-chair was drawn up to the side, and within it sat Dan, head leaning on hand, in an attitude which spoke of weariness and dejection.

He raised his eyes and looked at her, and Darsie shut the door and came forward eagerly.

"Dan! Back again so soon? Is anything wrong?" /

"No!"

"But you look strange. You – you didn't hurt yourself at the rink?"

"No."

"Quite, quite sure?"

"Quite."

Darsie subsided on to her favourite seat – the hearthrug – with a little sigh of relief.

"That's all right. You're very monosyllabic, Dan. Shall I disturb you if I sit here for a time?"

"No."

"A hundred thanks! You are *too* gracious. I can be quiet if you like. I like staring into the fire and dreaming myself."

Dan did not answer. Darsie peered at him, moving her little head from side to side so as to get the clearest view. He looked very large – a great shapeless mass of dark in the old red chair.

She liked the bigness of him, felt the old satisfaction at sight of the strong, rugged face, the old craving for confidence and approval. Strange how different one felt in company with different people. *Tête-à-tête* with Ralph Percival, Darsie felt a giant of strength and resource – assured, self-confident, a bulwark against which others might lean. With Dan, well, with Dan she was just a slip of a girl, conscious of nothing so much as her own weaknesses, mental and physical her / difficult gropings, compared with his clear vision; her tiny hands and wrists, compared with his big sinewy paw; her slim form, compared to the bulk of the square-cut shoulders. Never – Darsie realized it with a smile – never did she feel so humble and diffident as when in Dan's society; yet, strangely enough, the sensation was far from disagreeable.

"Dan!"

"Darsie!"

"Is anything the matter? Between you and me! You don't happen to be snar-key, do you, about anything I've done?"

"Why should you think I am 'snarkey'?"

"Because – you *are!* You're not a bit sociable and friendly – even *your* sort of sociability. I'm a guest in your mother's house if I'm nothing else and it's your duty to be civil."

"Haven't I always been civil to you, Darsie?"

Darsie drew a quick breath of impatience and, seizing upon the poker, beat at the unoffending coal as the best method of letting off steam.

"You are so painfully literal. I can *feel* what other people are thinking, how-ever much they try to disguise it."

"How do *I* feel, for example?"

Darsie turned her head and stared curiously into Dan's face. The hand on which it leaned shielded it somewhat from view, but, even so, there was / some-thing in the intent gaze which filled her with a strange new discomfort. She turned back to her poking once more.

"I think – there's something that I don't understand – I think – there's some-thing you disapprove! I'm a very good girl, and I work very hard, and I'm fond of my friends, and I expect them to be fond of me in return. I don't *like* you to disapprove, Dan!"

"I can't help it, Darsie. I've hated that friendship from the beginning, and I hate it more with every month that passes."

"Oh! *that* old story." Darsie's voice took a tone of impatience; for it was annoying to find that Dan was harking back on the well-known subject of dis-pute. "Well, I'm sorry to distress you, but I am conceited enough to believe that I have taken no harm from my friendship with Ralph Percival, and that he has reaped some little good from mine. While that state of thing continues, I shall certainly refuse to give him up – even to please you!"

There was silence for several moments, then Dan said slowly –

"If I agreed with your conclusions, I should not try to persuade you, Darsie; but I do not, and my opportunities of judging are better than yours." /

"You are unfair, Dan. It is a pity to allow yourself to be so prejudiced that you can't give a fair judgment. I should have imagined that even you would be forced to admit that Ralph had done better this term."

Dan did not speak. He turned his head and looked Darsie full in the eyes, and there was in his look a puzzled, questioning air, which she found it difficult to understand. When he spoke again, it was not to reply in any direct way to her accusation, but to ask a question on his own account.

"Darsie, do you mind telling me – is your position entirely disinterested? Do you look upon the fellow merely as a man to be helped, or do you care for him for his own personal sake?"

Darsie deliberated. The firelight played on her downcast face, on the long white throat rising from the low collar of her white blouse, on the little hands clenched round the steel poker. Before her mind's eye arose the memory of handsome, melancholy eyes; imagination conjured back the sound of impassioned appeals. Her expression softened, her voice took a deeper note.

"He needs me, Dan!"

That was her answer. Dan nodded in silence, accepting it as sufficient. He rose from his chair, and paced up and down the room, hands thrust deep into his trouser pockets, head held back with / the characteristic forward tilt of the chin. Darsie, watching him, thought involuntarily of a caged animal striving restlessly against the bars. Her heart gave a little throb of relief when he spoke again in his own natural voice.

"All right, Darsie. Good luck to your efforts! I appreciate your intentions, and am only sorry that I can't agree. According to my belief no one can help a man who refuses to help himself. We've got to fight our own battles, and to bear our own burdens! If some one steps forward and offers to undertake for us, we may imagine for a time that we are set free, but it's a mistake! Sooner or later the time comes when we're bound to fight it out alone, and it doesn't get easier for being deferred. Everything that is worth learning in life we have to worry out for ourselves!"

Darsie drew a long, trembling sigh. How puzzling life was, when the two people on whose judgment you most relied delivered themselves of directly opposing verdicts! Mrs. Reeves believed that her help was all-important to Ralph's progress; Dan insisted that her efforts were in vain.

Was he right? Was he wrong? Could she honestly assure herself that Ralph was stronger, more self-reliant, more able to stand alone without the stimulus of constant support and encouragement? Instinctively Darsie's hand went up to touch the little golden brooch which fastened the / lace collar of her blouse. If the anchor were withdrawn, would Ralph drift once more towards the rocks? The answer was difficult. She pondered it aloud, speaking in low, anxious tones, with lengthened pauses between the words.

"We're both right, Dan. We've both got hold of *bits* of the truth! In the end we must win through for ourselves, but surely, in preparation for the battle, we can give each other *some* help. Some natures seem made to stand, and others to lean. A prop is not of much account, but it may serve to keep a plant straight while it is gathering strength. The big oaks need no props; they are so strong that they can't understand; they have no pity for weakness."

Dan stopped short in his pacings.

"That meant for me, Darsie?"

"Humph! Just as you please! Oaks are nice things – big, and strong, and restful, but just a little bit inclined to grow – *gnarled!*"

Dan vouchsafed no reply, and Darsie sat, hands clasped round knees, staring into the fire for five long, silent minutes. She was hoping that Dan would never grow "gnarled" towards herself, longing for him to speak and promise that he would not, but he still remained silent, and presently the door burst open, the rinking party appeared on the threshold, and the opportunity for quiet conclave was over. /

Chapter XXV

New Year's Eve

SEATED alone in the train, *en route* for her visit to the Percivals, Darsie had time to think in a more quiet and undisturbed fashion than had been possible in the past bustling days, and a disagreeable feeling of apprehension arose in her mind as she recalled the wording of the three invitations. In each was present the same note of depression, the same hint of trouble in connection with the son of the house. Could anything have happened of which she was unaware? No letter from The Manor had reached her for some weeks past, but letters were proverbially scarce at Christmas-time, so that it would be foolish to argue ill from that fact alone. Darsie braced herself physically and mentally, squared her shoulders, and resolutely dismissed gloomy thoughts.

Noreen and Ralph met her at the station, looking reassuringly cheerful and at ease; a magnificent new motor stood in waiting outside, with a cart for the luggage. Inside the beautiful old house / the atmosphere was warmed by hot pipes, and scented with the fragrance of hothouse plants, banked together in every corner. It was not the usual case of being warm and cosy inside a room, and miserably chilled every time one crossed a passage or ascended the stairs. Mrs. Percival and the girls were marvels of elegance in Parisian gowns, Ralph looked his handsomest in knickerbocker suit and gaiters, and the servants moved noiselessly to and fro, performing their tasks with machine-like accuracy.

Extraordinary how complete a change of scene may take place between lunch and tea! How swiftly a new atmosphere makes the old unreal!

As Darsie sat drinking her tea in the old wainscoted hall, it seemed impossible to realize that such things as poverty and struggle were in existence; even the shabby bustle and squeeze of her own dear home became incredible in the face of this spacious, well-ordered calm!

Mrs. Percival made no attempt at private conversation, and showed no trace of "ulterior motive" in manner or conversation, which was a huge relief to Darsie's mind. She was not in a mood for serious conversation; what she wanted was the usual Percival offering of praise, admiration, and petting, and this was bestowed upon her with even more than the usual generosity. The grey-whiskered old Squire kissed her on both / cheeks; the girls assured her that she was prettier than ever, and greeted her feeblest sallies with bursts of delighted laughter. Ralph gazed at her with adoring eyes; it was all, as Darsie had been wont to remark, most grateful and comforting!

The first evening passed pleasantly enough, though there was a noticeable effort on the part of each member of the family to keep the conversation from touching upon the subject of Ralph's affairs. Any reference to Cambridge was taboo, as Darsie swiftly discovered, but there were many points of interest left, which were both pleasant and amusing to discuss.

The next morning – the last morning of the year – broke fine and bright, and the view seen through the long windows of the dining-room was almost as beautiful as in summer itself. The park showed the same stretch of velvet green, a belt of evergreens and tall Scotch firs filled up the far distance, while the leafless boughs of elms and beeches made a lacelike tracery against the sky. To the right the old cedar stood calm and unmoved, as it had stood while generations of Percivals had lived, and loved, and sorrowed, and died.

When breakfast was over – and breakfast in the country is a meal which pursues a calm and leisurely course – the four young people strolled into the porch to discuss the programme for the day. /

"Darsie is nerving herself to look at the horses' tails!" said Ida laughingly. It was a Percival peculiarity, agreeable or irritating according to the mood of the hearer, that they never by any chance forgot a remark, but continually resurrected it in conversation for years to come. Never a morning had Darsie spent at the Manor that she had not been reminded of scathing comments on the habit of daily visits to kennels and stables, as delivered by herself on the occasion of her first visit. To-day, however, she had only time to grimace a reply, before Ida continued cheerfully –

"You won't be asked, my dear! We have something far more important on hand. You have walked right into the jaws of the tenants' annual New Year's treat, and will have to tire your hands decorating all the morning, and your gums smiling all the evening. It's an all-day-and-night business, and we get home at cock-crow in a state of collapse –"

"It's held in the village hall," Noreen took up the tale, slipping unconsciously into what Darsie called her "squire's-eldest-daughter-manner."

"Quite a nice building. We make it look festive with wreaths and bunting. They think so much of decorations!" ("They" in Percival parlance alluded to the various tenants on the estate.) "We try to think of something novel each year as a surprise. They like surprises. We've arranged / with half a dozen girls to be there to help. Quite nice girls, daughters of the principal farmers. You must be *quite* sweet to them, Darsie, please! It is our principal meeting of the year, and we make a point of being friendly."

"Must I really?" Darsie assumed an expression of dejection. "What a disappointment! It's so seldom I get an opportunity of being proud and grand. What's the good of staying at a Manor House, and driving down with 'the family,' if I have to be meek and friendly like any one else? Couldn't you introduce me as the Lady Claire, and let me put on airs for a treat? It would act as a contrast to your 'friendly ways,' and make them all the more appreciated."

The girls laughed as in duty bound, and declared that it *would* be sport, and wondered if they dared, but Ralph sharply called them to order.

"Rot! As if everybody in this neighbourhood didn't know Darsie by heart! Put on your hats, and don't talk rubbish. It will take us all our time to get through with the hall before lunch."

Town-bred Darsie privately hoped that the motor would appear to carry the helpers to the hall three miles away, but the Percivals themselves never seemed to dream of such a possibility. In short skirts and thick boots they plodded cheerfully across boggy meadows and muddy lanes, / climbed half a dozen stiles, and arrived at last in the High Street of the little village, close to the entrance of the unpretentious wooden building which called itself the Village Hall.

Darsie thought that she had never beheld an interior which seemed so thoroughly to need, and at the same time to defy, decoration! Whitewashed walls, well splashed by damp; a double row of pegs all round the walls at a level of some five or six feet from the ground; wooden forms, and a small square platform, made up a whole which was bare and ugly to a degree.

A group of five or six girls stood beside a pile of evergreens; a youth in shirt-sleeves was in process of unpacking crumpled flags and flattened Japanese lanterns from an old tin box; two ladders stood against the walls.

The entrance of "the family" was marked by a general movement among the little company, and Darsie watched the greetings which ensued with twinkling amusement.

Noreen and Ida were *so* pleasant, *so* full of gratitude for the presence of each individual helper, *so* anxious to be assured that they could *really* spare the time. Ralph was so laboriously polite, while the girls themselves, pleasant, kindly, and well-educated, were either happily unaware of the thinly disguised patronage, or had the good manners to conceal their knowledge. / There was no doubt which side appeared to best advantage in the interview!

"The first thing we must do is to decide upon a scheme of decoration," Ida declared. "Darsie, suggest something! You have never done it before, so your ideas ought to be novel. What can we do to make the hall look pretty and cheerful?"

"Rebuild it!" was Darsie's instant and daring reply, whereat the farmers' daughters laughed *en masse,* and the Percivals looked haughtily displeased.

"Father built it!"

"Awfully good of him! *And* wicked of his architect. I shan't employ him to build *my* house!"

"I think," said Noreen loftily, "that we had better confine ourselves to discovering the scheme of decoration. It is too late to interfere with the structure of the hall. We generally make wreaths and fasten them to the gas brackets, and drape the platform with flags."

"Then we may take it as settled that we *won't* do that to-day. What happens to the pegs?"

"They hang their things on them, of course – hats, and coats, and mufflers –"

"That *must* be decorative! How would it be to make them leave their wrappings at the entrance to-night, or put them under their own chairs, / and to arrange a broad band of holly round the room so as to hide the pegs from view? It would be so easy to tie on the branches, and it would have quite a fine frieze effect."

"'Mrs. Dick,[115] you are invaluable!'" quoted Ralph gaily. "It's a ripping idea. Let's set to at once, and try the effect."

No sooner said than done; the little band of workers spread themselves over the room, and began the task of trying prickly holly branches to the line of pegs in such fashion as to form a band about two feet deep, entirely round the room. Berries being unusually plentiful that year, the effect was all the more cheery, and with the disappearance of the utilitarian pegs the hall at once assumed an improved aspect. A second committee meeting hit on the happy idea of transforming the platform into a miniature bower, by means of green baize and miniature fir-trees, plentifully sprinkled with glittering white powder. The flags were relegated to the entrance-hall. The Japanese lanterns, instead of hanging on strings, were so grouped as to form a wonderfully lifelike pagoda in a corner of the hall, where – if mischievously disposed – they might burn at their ease without endangering life or property. The ironwork of the gas-brackets was tightly swathed with red paper, and the bare jets fitted with paper shades to match. From an artistic point of view / Darsie strongly opposed the hanging of the time-worn mottoes, "A Hearty Welcome to All," "A Happy New Year," and the like, but the Squire's daughters insisted that they liked to see them, and the farmers' daughters confirming this theory, up they went, above the evergreen frieze, the white cotton letters standing out conspicuously from their turkey-red background.

It was one o'clock before the work was finished, and a tired and distinctly grubby quartette started out on their three-mile return walk across the fields. Certainly country-bred folk were regardless of fatigue! "If I owned a motor I should *use* it!" Darsie said to herself with a distinct air of grievance as she climbed to her own room after lunch, and laid herself wearily on her couch, the while the Percival trio trotted gaily forth for "just a round" over their private golf-links.

The evening programme was to begin with a concert, alternate items of which were to be given by the villagers and members of the surrounding "families."

At ten o'clock refreshments were to be served, in adjoining classrooms, and during the progress of the informal supper chairs and forms were to be lifted away, and the room cleared for an informal dance, to be concluded by a general joining of hands and singing of "Auld Lang Syne" as the clock struck twelve. /

The Percival ladies and their guests from the surrounding houses made elaborate toilettes for the occasion. The villagers were resplendent in Sunday blacks, "best frocks" and bead chains, the small girls and boys appearing respectively in white muslins and velveteen Lord Fauntleroy suits; the Squire opened proceedings with expressions of good wishes, interspersed with nervous coughs, and Noreen and Ida led off the musical proceedings with a lengthy classical duet, to which the audience listened with politely concealed boredom.

To Darsie's mind, the entire programme as supplied by "the families" was dull to extinction, but to one possessing even her own slight knowledge of the village, the contributions of its worthies were brimful of interest and surprise.

The red-faced butcher, who, on ordinary occasions, appeared to have no mind above chops and steaks, was discovered to possess a tenor voice infinitely superior in tone to that of his patron, the Hon. Ivor Bruce, while his wife achieved a tricky accompaniment with a minimum of mistakes; the sandy-haired assistant at the grocer's shop supplied a flute obbligato, and the fishmonger and the young lady from the stationer's repository assured each other ardently that their true loves owned their hearts; two school-children with corkscrew curls held a heated argument – in rhyme – on the benefits of temperance; and, most surprising and thrilling / of all, Mr. Jevons, the butler from The Manor, so far descended from his pedestal as to volunteer "a comic item" in the shape of a recitation, bearing chiefly, it would appear, on the execution of a pig. The last remnant of stiffness vanished before this inspiring theme, and the audience roared applause as one man, whereupon Mr. Jevons bashfully hid his face, and skipped – literally skipped – from the platform.

"Who'd have thought it! Butlers are human beings, after all!" gasped Darsie, wiping tears of merriment from her eyes. "Ralph, do you suppose Jevons will dance with me to-night? I *should* be proud!"

"Certainly not. He has one square dance with the mater, and that finishes it. You must dance with me instead. It's ages since we've had a hop together – or a talk. I'm longing to have a talk, but I don't want the others to see us at it, or they'd think I was priming you in my own defence, and the mater wants to have the first innings herself. We'll manage it somehow in the interval between the dances, and I know you'll turn out trumps, as usual, Darsie, and take my part."

Ralph spoke with cheerful confidence, and Darsie listened with a sinking heart. The merry interlude of supper was robbed of its zest, as she cudgelled her brains to imagine what she was about to hear. Ralph was evidently in trouble / of some sort, and his parents for once inclined to take a serious stand. Yet anything more gay and debonair than the manner with which the culprit handed round refreshments and waited on his father's guests it would be impossible to imagine.

Darsie watched him across the room, and noted that wherever he passed faces brightened. As he cracked jokes with the apple-cheeked farmers, waited assiduously on their buxom wives, and made pretty speeches to the girls, no onlooker could fail to be conscious of the fact that, in the estimation of the tenants, "Master Ralph" was as a young prince who could do no wrong.

For reasons of his own, Ralph was tonight bent on ingratiating himself to the full. For the first half-hour of the dance he led out one village belle after another, and it was not until waltz number five had appeared on the board that he returned to Darsie's side.

"At last I've a moment to myself! My last partner weighed a ton, at least, and I'm fagged out. Got a scarf you can put round you if we go and sit out?"

Darsie nodded, showing a wisp of gauze, and, laying her hand on Ralph's arm, passed with him out of the main room into the flag-decked entrance. For the moment it was empty, the dancers having made *en masse* in the direction of the refreshment-tables. Ralph looked quickly from side to side, / and, finding himself unobserved, took a key from his pocket and opened a small door leading into the patch of garden at the back of the hall. The moonlight showed a wooden bench fitted into a recess in the wall. Ralph flicked a handkerchief over its surface, and motioned Darsie towards a seat.

"It's clean enough. I gave it a rub this morning. You won't be cold?"

"Oh, no; not a bit." Darsie wrapped the wisp of gauze round her shoulders, and prepared to risk pneumonia with as little thought as ninety-nine girls out of a hundred would do in a similar case. The hour had come when she was to be told the nature of Ralph's trouble; she would not dream of losing the opportunity for so slight a consideration as a chill!

Ralph seated himself by her side, rested an elbow on his knees, the thumb and first finger of the uplifted hand supporting his chin. His eyes searched Darsie's face with anxious scrutiny.

"You didn't hear anything about me before you left Newnham?"

"Hear what? No! What was there to hear?"

Ralph averted his eyes, and looked across the patch of garden. The moonlight shining on his face gave it an appearance of pallor and strain.

"Dan Vernon said nothing?"

"No!" Darsie recalled Dan's keen glance of / scrutiny, the silence which had greeted her own remarks, and realized the reason which lay behind. "Dan is not the sort to repeat disagreeable gossip."

"It's not gossip this time; worse luck, it's solid, abominable fact. You'll be disappointed, Darsie. I'm sorry! I *have* tried. Beastly bad luck being caught just at the end. I was sent down, Darsie! It was just at the end of the term, so they sent me down for the last week. A week is neither here nor there, but the parents took it hard. I'm afraid you, too –"

Yes! Darsie "took it hard." One look at her face proved as much, and among many contending feelings, disappointment was predominant – bitter, intense, most humiliating disappointment.

"Oh, Ralph! What for? I hoped, I thought – you *promised* me to be careful!"

"And so I was, Darsie! Give you my word, I was. For the first half of the term I never got anything worse than three penny fines. It isn't a deadly thing to stay out after ten. And I was so jolly careful – never was so careful in my life. But just the night when it was most important I must needs be caught. You can't expect a fellow to get away from a big evening before twelve. But that's what it ended in – a big jaw, throwing up all my past misdeeds, and being sent down. Now you can slang away." /

But Darsie made no attempt to "slang." With every word that had been uttered her feelings of helplessness had increased. Ralph had apparently made little difference in his ways; he had only been more careful not to be found out! At the very moment when she had been congratulating herself, and boasting of the good results of her friendship, this crowning disgrace had fallen upon him. No wonder Dan had been silent; no wonder that he had looked upon her with that long, questioning gaze! The thought of Dan was singularly comforting at this moment – strong, silent, loyal Dan, going forth valiantly to the battle of life. Darsie's little face took on a pinched look; she shivered, and drew the thin scarf more tightly round her. Her silence, the suffering written on her face, hit Ralph more hardly than any anger; for the first time something deeper than embarrass-ment showed itself in face and voice.

"For pity's sake, Darsie, speak! Say something! Don't sit there and look at me like that."

"But, Ralph, what is there to say?" Darsie threw out her arms with a gesture of hopelessness. "I've talked so often, been so eloquent, believed so much! If this is the outcome, what more can be said?"

"I *have* tried! I *did* want to please you!"

"By not being found out! It's not much comfort, Ralph, to feel that I've encouraged you in / deception. And all those nights when you stayed out late, were you betting as usual – getting into debt?"

Ralph frowned.

"I've been beastly unlucky, never knew such a persistent run. That's the dick-ens of it, Darsie. I haven't dared to tell the Governor yet, but I positively must get hold of the money before the tenth. I'm bound to pay up by then. It's a debt of honour."

Darsie's red lip curled over that word. She sat stiff and straight in her seat, not deigning a reply. Ralph appeared to struggle with himself for several moments, before he said urgently –

"The mater is going to talk to you. She knows that you have more influence with me than any one else. It's true, Darsie, whatever you may think – I should have drifted a lot deeper but for you. When she does, do your best for a fellow! They'll be down on me for not having told about this debt. The Governor asked if there was anything else, but upon my word I hadn't the courage to own up at that moment."

Still Darsie did not reply. She was wondering drearily what she could find to say when the dreaded interview came about; shrinking from the thought of adding to the mother's pain, feeling a paralyzing sense of defeat; yet, at this very moment of humiliation, a ray of light illumined the darkness and showed the reason of her failure. / Dan was right! no one could truly help a man without first implanting in his heart the wish to help himself! She had been content to bribe Ralph, as a spoiled child is bribed to be good; had felt a glow of gratified vanity in the knowledge that her own favour was the prize to be won. If the foundations of her buildings were unstable, what wonder that the edifice had fallen to the ground? The thought softened her heart towards the handsome culprit by her side, and when she spoke at last it was in blame of herself rather than of him.

"I'm sorry, too, Ralph. I might have helped you better. I rushed in where angels fear to tread. I gave you a wrong motive. It should have been more than a question of pleasing me – more even than pleasing your parents. . . . Oh, Ralph, dear, you know – you know there is something higher than that! ... Is religion nothing to you, Ralph? Don't you feel that in wasting your life you are offending against God – against Christ! Can't you try again with *that* motive to help you? ... I can't make light of things to your people, but I can take part of the blame on myself. If it is true that I have any influence over you, I have thrown it away. . . ."

Ralph laid his hand over the gloved fingers clasped together on Darsie's knee.

"Don't say that! Don't think that, Darsie. / I may be a rotter, but I'd have been a hundred times worse if it hadn't been for you. And don't exaggerate the position: it's a pity to do that. Every man isn't born a Dan Vernon. Most fellows only reach that stage of sobriety when they are middle-aged. It would be a pretty dull world if no one kicked over the traces now and then in their youth. What have I done, after all? Slacked my work, helped myself to a bit more play and come down on the Governor for an extra cheque now and again. Lots of fellows come a worse cropper than that –"

Darsie wondered if a "worse cropper" might not possibly be a less serious ill than persistent slacking and irresponsibility; but now that the bad news was out, Ralph was fast regaining his composure.

"I'll turn out all right yet, Darsie, you'll see. The tenants like me. I'll settle down and make a first-rate squire when my time comes. And I'll make up to you then for all this worry and bother." For a moment his voice was significantly tender, then the recollection of his present difficulty swept over him once more, and he added hastily: "You'll – you'll break it to the mater, won't you? About that money, I mean. She'll take it best from you –"

Darsie rose from her seat, and stood before him, tall and white in the moonlight. /

"No!" she said clearly. "I will not. You must make your own confession. Things have been made easy for you all your life, Ralph. Now you must fight for yourself."

* * * * *

Ralph bore no malice; even his momentary irritation at finding himself, as he considered, "left in the lurch," lasted but a few moments after his return to the hall. Darsie would rather have had it last a little longer. To see an unclouded face, to catch the echo of merry laughter within ten minutes of a humiliating confession, seemed but another instance of instability of character. It seemed literally impossible for Ralph to feel deeply on any subject for more than a few moments at a time; nevertheless, such was the charm of his personality that she felt both pleased and flattered when twelve o'clock approached and he came smilingly forward to lead her to her place in the great ring encircling the whole room. "I must have you and mother – one on either side," he said, and as they crossed the floor together Darsie was conscious that every eye in the room followed them with a smiling significance. The young Squire, and the pretty young lady who was his sister's friend – a nice pair they made, to be sure! Every brain was busy with dreams of the future, weaving romantic plans, seeing in / imagination other scenes like the present, with Darsie in the place of hostess. She knew it, divined instinctively that Ralph knew it too, felt the recognition of it in the grip of Noreen's hand, in the tender pathos of Mrs. Percival's smile. And once again Darsie wondered, and doubted, and feared and felt the weight of invisible chains.

There are moments, however, when doubts and fears are apt to be swept away in a rush of overwhelming emotions, and one of those is surely the beginning of a new year. To be young and pretty; to be by general acceptance the queen of the evening – no normal girl could help being carried away by such circumstances as these! When the last chime of the twelve rang slowly out, and the audience with one accord burst into the strains of "Auld Lang Syne,"[116] Darsie's eyes shone with excitement, and she returned with unction the pressure of Ralph's fingers.

"Then here's a hand, my trusty friend,
And gie's a hand o' thine!"

The volume of sound swelled and sank, here and there a voice took a husky tone; here and there an eye grew dim, but these belonged as a rule to the patriarchs among the guests, for whom the past was full of tender memories, for whom but a few more New Years could dawn. Perhaps this might be the last, the very last, they / would live to see. The young folks shed no tears; they were not unconscious of the prevailing emotion, but with them it found vent in a tingling expectation. Life lay ahead. Life was to come. What would life bring?

When the song ceased, and the linked circle broke up into separate groups, Darsie, glancing up into Ralph's face, was surprised to see it white and tense. She smiled, half amused, half sad, bracing herself to hear some emotional protest or vow for the future; but Ralph spake no word. Instead, he led her to a seat, bowed formally before her, and, still with that white, fixed look, marched straight across the room to his father.

Darsie's pulse quickened, her little teeth clenched on her lower lip, she pressed her hands against her knee the while she watched the eloquent scene. Father and son faced each other; handsome man, handsome youth, strangely alike despite the quarter of a century between their respective ages; the Squire's face, at first all genial welcome and unconcern, showing rapidly a pained gravity. Ralph was speaking rapidly, with an occasional eloquent gesture of the arm, obviously recounting some facts of pressing importance to himself and his hearer, as obviously pleading a cause. With a thrill of excitement Darsie leaped to the true explanation of the situation. Fresh from the singing of the New Year / song, Ralph had not paused to consider conventions, but then and there had hastened to make his confession in his father's ears.

"Governor! I'm sorry! I was a coward, and wouldn't own up. I've been playing the fool again, and have lost more money. I owe over fifty pounds, and it has to be paid up by the tenth of this month."

The Squire looked his son full in the face.

"Is that all the truth, Ralph, or only a part?" he asked quietly. "Let me hear the whole please, now that we are about it."

"That is the whole, sir. There's nothing more to be told."

"The money shall be paid, but you must do something for me in return. We can't talk here. Come to my study when we get home!"

The Squire laid his hand on his son's shoulder with a momentary pressure as he turned aside to attend to his guests, but Ralph looked crestfallen and discomfited. It was one thing to blurt out a disagreeable confession on the impulse of a moment, and another and very different one to discuss it in cold blood in the privacy of a study. In the middle of the night, too! Ralph shivered at the thought. Why on earth couldn't the Governor be sensible, and wait till next morning? The money would be paid – that was the main point – all the rest could wait. /

Chapter XXVI

At the Orchard

RALPH percival spent a long hour alone with his father in the chill dawn of that New Year's morn, and during its passing heard more stern home-truths than he had ever before listened to from those indulgent lips. The Squire had not insisted on any arduous work on his son's part: in his heart he shared Ralph's theory that a man whose life is to be spent looking after his own land has no need of much scholarly lore. He must be straight and manly, intelligent enough to understand and move with the movements of the day, but not so intelligent as to grow discontented with a circle of admirable, but somewhat humdrum, neighbours. He must be possessed of courteous and agreeable manners, able on occasion to take the chair at a meeting, possibly even on a Bench, with credit to himself and his family.

A 'Varsity education was obviously the best means of developing such qualities, but who was / going to bother his head as to the question of honours or no honours? There was no reason why the boy should slave as if he had his living to make by sheer brain effort. The Squire was prepared to show the utmost leniency towards Ralph's scholastic efforts, but that he should have persistently broken the rules, ignored warnings, incurred gambling debts, and, crowning indignity of all, that he should have been sent down, even for the last week of the term – that stabbed the honest old countryman to his heart.

He said very little on the subject of his own feelings; such men are not given to talk of themselves, but the tone of his voice was eloquent, and Ralph winced before it. It was a new experience for the spoilt son and heir to hear any accents but those of love and appreciation from a member of his own family, and the experience was unexpectedly bitter. Who could have believed that the Governor would cut up so rough – could deliver himself of such sledge-hammer judgments? The card debts would be paid, there was no question of that – every debt should be paid – and Ralph should return to college with a clean sheet so far as money was concerned, and with his handsome allowance undiminished – *for the present*. He himself must decide what would happen in the future. The Squire asked for no promises; he had had experience of the uselessness of promises (the / listener winced again at the significance of those words); but Ralph must understand that any debts would be subtracted from his own future allowance. He must also understand that he was expected to take his pass the following May. There had been too much shirking and running loose – now he must work for a change. For his parents' sake, his sisters' sake, he must make amends for the pain and shame of the last weeks.

It was a painful scene for both father and son, but the charm of manner which was the great secret of Ralph's popularity did not forsake him, even in this hour of humiliation. He made an ideal penitent – abashed, yet manly, subdued and silenced, yet when the right moment came ready with a few apt, quietly spoken words.

"Thank you, sir. You are always generous. I've made a beastly poor return. I hope this year may end better than it has begun."

Poor Ralph! How little he guessed at that moment all that the year held in store! How little the father dreamed of the altered conditions with which he would face another New Year's Day! But so long as they both lived it was good to remember that the interview had ended peacefully and with a renewed sense of harmony, with a firm hand-grip and an affectionate glance.

Ralph took his candle from a table in the hall and made his way quietly up the oak staircase, / and his father stood below and watched him go, while his heart waxed tender within him.

His son – his only son! He would give his heart's blood for the lad. Had he been just, wise, prudent, in the words which he had said? Had he been stern enough? – too stern? He was in a thousand minds about his own conduct, but in only one as regards Ralph's. The boy had taken his dressing like a man. How handsome he had looked as he stood to listen, not flinching or hanging his head as an ordinary culprit would have done, but drawn to his full height, with straight, fearless gaze. With what a frank air he had held out his hand for that farewell grasp! Bless the boy! his heart was in the right place. He would settle down, and make a fine man yet. Patience! Patience!

And so when the family met again for a late breakfast that New Year's morning there was no shadow visible on the horizon, and throughout the remainder of Darsie's visit every day seemed given up to enjoyment, and brought with it some fresh festivity.

Contrary to her expectation, the subject of Ralph's troubles was avoided rather than sought, and it was only on the eve of her departure to Newnham that mother and sisters broke the silence to urge in each case the same request –

"See as much of Ralph as you can during these / next six months! Have a little talk with Ralph now and again! Show an interest in his work. Let him see that you care. We must all do our best to encourage him to work!"

By all the members of the family it was taken for granted that Darsie's interest in Ralph's future was equal to, if not greater than, their own; they made no secret of their belief that her influence had the more weight. If Darsie had known a passing temptation to abandon her efforts, it would have been impossible to do so in the face of such unanimous appeals.

Well, it was good to be back in Newnham once more, to get to work again after the lazy weeks, to wake up one's brains with tussles over Anglo-Saxon texts, to wrestle with philology, instead of browsing over novels and magazine tales. The Divinity Schools[117] were stuffy as ever, the men on one side shutting up the windows with their usual persistence, while the girls on theirs frowned and fumed; but the Chaucer lectures were full of interest, and coaching assumed a keener interest as spring advanced and the prospect of "Mays" drew near.[118] Last year both Darsie and Hannah had gained second-class honours; this year they had determined to gain firsts, or perish in the attempt. With a second and a first record for Mays there was a possibility – a dazzling possibility – of firsts in the final Tripos. When one / thought of that it seemed impossible to work too hard, to put too much energy into one's studies. But the happy blending of work and play which characterises Newnham life prevented industry from being carried to an exaggerated extent. The hour's informal dancing after dinner on Wednesday and Saturday evenings seemed to quicken circulation and brain alike, and the great Shakespeare Ball was a distinct fillip, although – or was it *because?* – it involved some slackness for the preparation of costumes.

The short Easter vac. served but as a breathing-space, and then another May term began with an unparalleled succession of fine and sunny days. Everything seemed early this spring; trees and shrubs rushed into leaf, a wealth of blossom gave a fairy-like beauty to the old-world gardens, and in every youth and maid the spirit of the spring awoke also, and called to them to come out to play. This was the season for picnics, for walks along the fields by the riverside, for boating, for bathing, for garden teas, for breakfast parties at the Orchard, amidst the pink and white wonder of the apple-blossom.

Darsie Garnett was fired with a desire to give an Orchard party on her own account, the guests to be Hannah, Margaret France, her special Fresher adorer (Marian White by name), Ralph Percival, Dan Vernon, two agreeable Classics from King's; / Mrs. Reeves to play chaperon – just a cheery little party of nine. What could you wish for more?

Margaret, preternaturally solemn, opined that *ten* would be a more desirable number. "Poor Mrs. Reeves! What has *she* done? Why not ask some one to play about with *her?* I can't bear to see a Lonely at a picnic or to be interrupted myself!"

"It *might* be judicious to invite Minerva!"[119] agreed Darsie, twinkling, and alluding to the Don who enjoyed the privilege of Mrs. Reeves's special friendship. "Two chaperons! What a character for propriety I shall gain, to be sure! They little know."

"They know perfectly well, but they are human creatures after all. They've been young themselves, and they enjoy the Orchard! Set to work at once, my dear, and get out your invitations. This weather can't possibly last, and it's going to break my heart if it is wet."

But there was no sign of rain on that exquisite morning when at the striking of six o'clock Darsie leaped out of bed, and thrust her ruffled golden head out of the opened window. A few feathery white, clouds served but to intensify the blueness of the sky; the air was soft and sweet, the garden beneath was already bathed in sunlight. Darsie gave a little caper of delight. Sunshine, a picnic, a pretty frock and hat waiting to be worn, and one's / very best friends to admire the result – what healthy girl of twenty could fail to be happy under such circumstances as these?

She sang as she dressed; she made little fancy steps, and three separate pirouettes which would have delighted the heart of a terpsichorean mistress.[120] One pirouette greeted the effect of the white dress; the second, that of the wide straw hat, with its appropriate garland of blossom; the third was partly in celebration of the combined effect, and partly out of sheer inability to keep still.

Her toilette completed, Darsie repaired to Hannah's room and surprised that tasteless young woman engaged in putting the final touches to her own costume, in the shape of an abomination designated "a neck arrangement," composed of the cheapest of machine lace and papery satin ribbon. Hannah jumped with dismay as a hand descended suddenly over her shoulder, and tore this treasure from her grasp.

"No!" cried Darsie firmly. "You are my childhood's friend, and I love you dearly, but wear lace frills with a linen collar at my Orchard party *you – shall not!* Miserable woman! Will you never learn how to dress?"

"I paid eleven-three for it, near the end of a term. Thought I *would* please you this time! Hate the tickling stuff myself. Some people are / never satisfied," grumbled Hannah, rummaging in her tie-box, but it never occurred to her to dispute the decree. On questions of toilette Darsie's word was absolute.

The two girls descended the stairs together, and found the other three members of the party awaiting them at the door, Margaret and the little Fresher abeam with smiles, and even Minerva herself looking quite young and skittish. At moments like these it dawned upon the student mind that even a don herself could occasionally enjoy a mixture of play with her work.

At the river Mrs. Reeves and the four men came forward to meet the Newnham party, the canaders[121] were ranged ready for the embarkment, and Darsie felt the honours of her position press heavily, as the other members of the party stood silently waiting for her to apportion the crews. The worst of it was that one felt obliged to take the least desirable place oneself. Considered as a don, Minerva had many points, but when bound for a river picnic one did not exactly hanker after her society. Still, there it was. Every position has its drawbacks. The row up the river on that exquisite morning was a joy independent of society, and when the Orchard itself was reached it was undeniably agreeable to sit at the head of the table, and play the gracious hostess to one's guests. /

Orchard appetites are proverbial, but this particular party claimed to have broken all previous records. Soon there was hardly a fragment of food left on a plate. The pile of banana-skins was positively startling to behold; tea and coffee pots were drained, and drained again; requests for milk and more milk threatened the supply of later guests, and the birds in the trees overhead chattered not a whit more gaily than the company around the board.

"Shop"[122] was sternly forbidden as a subject of conversation, and the remotest reference thereto was instantly booed into silence, for behind all the lightsomeness of demeanour a weight of anxiety lay on each heart. The critical time was approaching when the result of the year's work would be put to the test. The two classics, as sons of a poor clergyman, were acutely conscious of all that was involved by a first or second class. Ralph Percival was realising painfully the difficulty of making up for years of slacking, or even of keeping up a spurt beyond a few days at a time; the little Fresher trembled at the thought of her first Mays; even Margaret France herself showed signs of nerves before the ordeal of the Tripos, and on one tragic occasion had even been discovered weeping hysterically upon her bed.

"C-c-couldn't remember a context," was her hiccoughing explanation of the breakdown, and / henceforth Darsie had taken her in hand, fagged for her, petted her, scolded her, put her to bed, and ruthlessly carried off notebooks to her own study, to frustrate disastrous attempts at midnight toil.

As for Dan, he was a giant among pigmies. Examinations had no terrors for him; his place was assured. When strangers visited Cambridge, their sons and brothers pointed out his big, lumbering form in the streets, and bade them remember Vernon – Vernon would arrive! Darsie was conscious that his presence lent distinction to her party, for Dan but seldom appeared in the social world.

And he was behaving so well, too! taking part in the conversation, even telling stories and capping anecdotes of his own accord, and behaving quite amiably to Ralph. Darsie beamed approval on him from the end of the table, and deliberately singled him out as her companion for the after-breakfast stroll.

"Come down to the river, Dan! There's a tree with the most convenient forked branch where one can sit hidden by the leaves and watch the canaders come up. Last year I heard some quite thrilling fragments of conversation."

"I'll be wary of that tree," said Dan solemnly, but he helped Darsie to her eyrie, and swung himself up beside her with an alacrity which showed / that the suggestion fell in well with his own wishes, and there they sat like birds in a nest, smiling at each other with bright, friendly glances.

"Isn't this fine? No one saw us come, did they? They'll think we're lost. I'm tired of being polite. Thank you for coming to my party, Dan, and for being so jolly."

"Thank you for asking me and for looking so – ripping!" Dan cast an appreciative glance at the white dress and blossom-wreathed hat. "Glad to see you're not knocking yourself up with too much work."

Darsie bent her head with a dubious air.

She wished to look well, but, on the other hand, a little sympathy would not have been unwelcome. "I'm excited this morning, and that gives me a colour," she explained. "If you could see me at the end of the day – I'm so weak in my mediæval French Grammar. It haunts me at night –"

"Stop!" cried Dan warningly. "Don't let it haunt you here, at any rate – it would be a crime among this blossom. Tell me a story as you used to do in the old schoolroom days. I haven't heard you tell a story since that Christmas night when we all sat round the fire and burnt fir-cones, and the light shone on your face. You wore a white dress then. You looked *all* white." /

"And you sat in the corner and glowered – I could see nothing, but I *felt* eyes. That will be one of the times we shall remember, Dan, when we look back on our young days – all together, and so happy and free. I had a melancholy turn during that cone-burning, one of the shadows that fall upon one causelessly in the midst of the sunshine, but that was only a bit of the happiness, after all. It's rather wonderful to be twenty, Dan, and never to have known a real big sorrow! Most of the girls here have come through something, some of them a great deal. I feel such a babe beside them. It isn't good for one, I suppose, to have things *too* smooth."

"I hope they'll continue smooth for a long time to come. You're too young for troubles, Darsie," said Dan hastily. He sat silent for a few moments, his chin poking forward, his thin, expressive lips twitching as if struggling with difficult speech. A canader came gliding slowly by, the man and girl occupants chatting gaily together, unconscious of the watchers in the tree on the bank. Their words fell absently on Darsie's ear, she was waiting for what Dan had to say.

"When they *do* come, you know you can depend on me. I'm not much of a hand at social life, so it's best to keep out of the way and let other fellows chip in who can make a better show, / but if there's anything useful to be done, you might give me a turn. We're very old friends."

Darsie gave him an affectionate glance. "Indeed I will. I should feel you a tower of strength. Thank you, dear Oak-tree."

"Thank you, Apple-blossom!" returned Dan quite gallantly, if you please, and with a laugh which followed the passing seriousness vanished.

For the next half-hour they laughed and sparred, capped stories, and made merry, more like a couple of happy children than hard-worked students on the verge of examinations; and then, alas! it was time to return to work, and, sliding down from their perch, Dan and Darsie walked forward to assemble the scattered members of the party. /

Chapter XXVII

Disaster

CAMBRIDGE May week is a function so well known, and so often described, that it would be superfluous to enter in detail into its various happenings.[123] In their first year Darsie and Hannah had taken little part in the festivities, but upon their second anniversary they looked forward to a welcome spell of gaiety. Not only were the Percivals coming up for the whole week, but Mr. and Mrs. Vernon and

Vi were also to be installed in rooms, and the Newnham students had received permission to attend the two principal balls, being housed for the nights by their own party. Throughout Newnham the subject of frocks became, indeed, generally intermingled with the day's work. Cardboard boxes arrived from home, cloaks and scarves were unearthed from the recesses of "coffins," and placed to air before opened windows; "burries" were strewn with ribbons, laces, and scraps of tinsel, instead of the usual notebooks; third-year girls, reviving slowly from the strain of the Tripos, consented / languidly to have their hats re-trimmed by second-year admirers, and so, despite themselves, were drawn into the maelstrom. One enterprising Fresher offered items of her wardrobe on hire, by the hour, day, or week, and reaped thereby quite a goodly sum towards her summer holiday. A blue-silk parasol, in particular, was in universal request, and appeared with *éclat* and in different hands at every outdoor function of the week.

In after-years Darsie Garnett looked back upon the day of that year on which the Masonic Ball[124] was held with feelings of tender recollection, as a piece of her girlhood which was altogether bright and unclouded. She met the Percival party at one o'clock, and went with them to lunch in Ralph's rooms, where two other men had been invited to make the party complete. There was hardly room to stir in the overcrowded little study, but the crush seemed but to add to the general hilarity.

Ralph made the gayest and most genial of hosts, and the luncheon provided for his guests was a typical specimen of the daring hospitality of his kind! Iced soup, lobster mayonnaise, salmon and green peas, veal cutlets and mushrooms, trifle, strawberries and cream, and strong coffee, were pressed in turns upon the guests, who – be it acknowledged at once – ate, drank, enjoyed, and went forth in peace. Later in the afternoon the little party strolled down to the river, and in / the evening there was fresh feasting, leading up to the culminating excitement of all – the ball itself.

Beside the Percivals' Parisian creations, Darsie's simple dress made but a poor show, but then Darsie's dresses were wont to take a secondary place, and to appear but as a background to her fresh young beauty, instead of – as is too often the case – a dress *par excellence,* with a girl tightly laced inside. When she made her appearance in the sitting-room of the lodgings, the verdict on her appearance was universally approving –

"You look a *lamb!*" gushed Ida enthusiastically.

"How do you manage it, dear? You *always* seem to hit the right thing!" exclaimed Mrs. Percival in plaintive amaze; and as he helped her on with her cloak, Ralph murmured significantly –

"As if it mattered what *you* wore! No one will notice the frock."

At the ball there was an appalling plethora of girls; wallflowers sat waiting round the walls, and waited in vain. Darsie felt sorry for them, tragically sorry;

but the sight of their fixed smiles could not but heighten the sense of her own good luck in having the chance of more partners than she could accept. Ralph showed at his best that evening, evincing as much care for his sisters' enjoyment as for that of their friend. Not until the three programmes were filled to the last extra[125] / did he rest from his efforts, and think of his own pleasure. It is true that his pleasure consisted chiefly in dancing with Darsie, and their steps went so well together that she was ready to give him the numbers for which he asked. As for Dan Vernon, he did not dance, but out of some mistaken sense of duty, felt it his duty to put in an appearance and *glower.*

"See old Vernon, glowering over there?" inquired Ralph, laughing, as he whirled Darsie lightly by to the strains of an inspiriting two-step, and for a moment a cloud shadowed the gaiety of her spirits. Dan ought either to dance or stay away! She didn't *like* to see him looking glum!

The dancing was carried on until four in the morning, when in the chill grey light the company were ranged in rows, and photographed, apparently to provide a demonstration of how elderly and plain even the youngest of the number could look under such inauspicious circumstances.

The three girls had breakfast in bed the next morning, somewhere about twelve o'clock – a delightful occasion when all three talked at the same time, relating thrilling experiences of the night before, comparing notes, admiring, quizzing, shaking with laughter over a dozen innocent drolleries. These after-conferences are perhaps the best part of the festivities of our youth; and Noreen, Ida, and Darsie began that fine June / day as gaily, as happily, as unconscious of coming ill as any three girls in the land.

Ralph had been anxious that his people should again lunch in his rooms, but Mrs. Percival had prudently decided in favour of a simple meal at home, and it was approaching tea-time when the party sallied forth to witness the day's "bumping" on the river.[126] The elders were frankly tired after their late hours, but the three girls looked fresh as flowers in their dainty white frocks, and enjoyed to the full the kaleidoscopic beauty of the scene.

The two Percivals' interest in the bumping was of the slightest description – Ralph was not taking part this afternoon, and with Ralph began and ended their concern. They stood on the crowded bank, rather hot, rather bored, amusing themselves by scanning the people near at hand. The Vernon party were but a few yards away, and Hannah attracted special attention.

"She *is* plain!" exclaimed Noreen; whereat Darsie snapped her up in double-quick time.

"Of *course* she is plain! She wouldn't dream of being anything else!"

Beloved plain Hannah! No features, however classic, could be as eloquent as hers in her old friend's eyes. Darsie tossed her head, and looked flusty and annoyed, whereat Noreen feebly apologised, emphasising her offence by blundering explanations, and Ralph grew restless and impatient. /

"I say! This is getting slow. Come along, girls; let's take the ferry and cross to the other side. It's not half bad fun to see all the shows. It will be a change, anyhow, and you can come back when you're tired."

"I'll stay with mother," Noreen decided dutifully. Ida surveyed the crowd on the opposite bank with the dubious air of one who has lived all her life within her own gates. "I don't *think* I care to go into that crush."

"Oh, come along, Darsie. Thank goodness you're not so squeamish. Let's get out of this." Ralph pushed impatiently forward, and Mrs. Percival turned to Darsie, with raised eyebrows, and said urgently –

"Do go, dear! Ralph will take care of you. We will wait for you here."

Darsie smiled assent, the thought passing lightly through her mind that Mrs. Percival looked particularly sweet and gracious when she smiled. She never dreamt that that particular smile, that little glance of appeal, were to remain with her all heir life, to be her comfort in a bitter grief.

They passed the spot where Hannah and Dan were standing with their friends, and acting on a sudden impulse, Darsie turned her head, with a few laughing words of explanation: "We're going to look at the Punch and Judies!"

There was no definite response, but Hannah's / exclamation had an envious tone which made Ralph quicken his footsteps. It was rare good luck to get Darsie to himself for an hour; he certainly did not wish to be saddled with plain Hannah as an unwelcome third.

The ferry-boat was on the point of starting, its flat surfaces crowded with pleasure-seekers. Ralph and Darsie had to run the last few yards in order to secure a bare space for standing. Ralph took the outside with the nonchalance of the true boating-man, who would almost as soon fall in the water as not. Darsie, standing close by his side, glanced from one to the other of her companions, her never-failing interest in *people* discovering a story in each new group.

They had reached the middle of the stream, when a movement of the deck upset her balance, and sent her swaying against Ralph's arm. She looked up with a laughing apology, and was startled by the sight of his face. So far was he from sharing her amusement, that never in the course of their acquaintance had she seen him so pale, so set. He seized the hand she had laid on his arm, and held it in a vice-like grip, as he bent to look at the deck. At that moment Darsie stumbled afresh, and felt the lapping of water against her thinly clad feet. She exclaimed loudly, but her voice was drowned in the chorus of cries, questions, and appeals which arose from every side. /

How swiftly, with what incredible, paralyzing speed a scene may change, and seeming security give way to panic fear! Darsie, turning her head to look at the crowd of faces which towered so strangely above her, met but one expression in every eye – breathless, agonizing dread.

Looking back upon the scene in after-life, it seemed the nightmare of a moment; then the grip upon her arm tightened, she felt herself being pushed past Ralph towards the edge of the boat, heard his voice speaking to her in crisp, firm tones which she had heard in dreams, but never, never from his living lips.

"Darsie! She's turning turtle![127] There's no danger, darling, if you jump clear. The water's not deep. Some one will come. I'm going to throw you in. Strike out for your life!"

She was lifted like a doll in his strong arms; her wild eyes, searching his, met a cheery smile in response, she felt herself swayed to and fro, realized with a shudder the parting from the firm grasp – fell, splashed, felt the water close over her head.

When she rose to the surface the water near her seemed full of struggling forms; she caught a terrified glimpse of a perpendicular deck, of passengers falling like flies from their perch, and with the instinct of despair struck out in the opposite direction.

Like most Newnham girls, she was a fair / swimmer – happy hours spent in the swimming-tent[128] had ensured so much; but it was her first experience of fighting the water in all the crippling fineries of race-week attire. Her shoes, her skirts, the floating ends of sash and scarf all held her down; her soaking hat flopped over her eyes, her very gloves seemed to lessen the force of her stroke; but breathless and spent as she was, she could not pause while from behind arose that dread, continued cry. Ralph had told her to strike out, that there was no danger if only she kept clear.

"All right, Darsie – all right! Keep calm – keep calm! I'm coming! I've got you! Leave yourself to me."

It was Dan's voice speaking in her ear, clear and distinct in the midst of the clamour; she felt herself seized in scientific fashion – in the way at which she herself had played at rescuing her companions from imaginary death – and, relinquishing all effort, was towed numbly to the shore.

It seemed as if hundreds of people were waiting to rescue her; hundreds of arms stretched out in welcome; hundreds of eyes grew suddenly moist with tears. She was tired, and wet, and dazed, but she could stand on her own feet, had no need of helping arms. Dan took her hand in his and ran swiftly across the grass to the nearest tent, / where already preparations were in train for the restoration of the unfortunates.

Darsie was the first of the crew to reach this shelter, and Mrs. Percival and the girls awaited her tearfully on the threshold. She awoke to fuller consciousness at sight of their faces, smiled in reassurement, and murmured disjointed phrases.

"I'M GOING TO THROW YOU IN—STRIKE OUT FOR
YOUR LIFE!"

"Quite all right – only wet! Ralph saved me! A second time! So calm and brave!"

"Yes, dear child; yes! Take off that wet hat!" replied Mrs. Percival urgently, the girl's praise of her son adding to her tender solicitude, and she hovered around with tender touches, the while from around rose a ceaseless string of suggestions.

"Brandy! Hot tea!" "She ought to change at once!" "My house is just at hand – do come to my house!" "My motor is waiting outside! Let me drive you home!"

So on, and so on, innate kindliness of heart bubbling to the surface as it invariably does in moments of disaster. As each unfortunate entered the tent the same programme was enacted, the same kind offices volunteered. "My house is close at hand – do come to my house!" "My motor is waiting – do let me drive you back!" Each victim of the immersion wore at first the same dazed, helpless expression, but the presence of their companions, the kindly voices speaking in / their ear, the hot, reviving draughts soon brought about a change of mood, so that they began to smile, to exchange remarks, to congratulate themselves on escape. Darsie, with characteristic elasticity, was one of the first to regain composure, and the Percivals hung delightedly on her description of Ralph's composure and resource.

"I was terrified. It was a dreadful sensation to feel the deck sinking beneath your feet on one side, and to see it gradually rising above you on the other. And all the bewildered, terrified faces! Ralph never turned a hair. He told me that there was no danger so long as I kept clear of the boat; he lifted me up in his arms as if I had been a doll."

The colour mounted to Darsie's white cheeks as she spoke, and a thrill of emotion tingled her blood. The first time she hears herself addressed as "darling" in a man's deep voice is one that a girl cannot lightly forget. She turned her head over her shoulder so as to be able to see the entrance into the tent.

"Where *is* Ralph?"

"He will be here presently. None of the men have come in yet. Ralph will be so useful. He is as much at home in the water as on land. He will be busy helping the others."

Mrs. Percival spoke with happy assurance; nevertheless, she left Darsie's side and edged her / way through the crowd towards the open doorway, through which she ought now to be able to see her son's return. As she was within a few yards of the entrance it was suddenly blocked by a group of men – hatless, dripping, dishevelled, but in demeanour composed and cheery, as if what had happened had been quite an enjoyable experience.

The foremost of the group greeted their friends with smiles and waving of hands.

"Hullo! Hullo! Here we are! How are you feeling? All serene now? Every one comfortably on shore? Got any tea left?"

"Is my son with you? Have you seen my son – Ralph Percival?"

Mrs. Percival spoke in a high, clear voice, at the sound of which a young undergrad. wheeled round quickly towards his companions.

"By Jove – yes! He was on board. I thought we were all here. Where's Percival?"

He dashed out of the tent, stood looking blankly around, turned a blanched face towards the tent.

Then from an inner corner of the tent another voice questioned sharply: "Mary! Where's Mary – Mary Everard? She was with us – standing quite near. *Mary's not here!*"

No one answered. There was a breathless silence, while each man and woman in that crowded tent was subtly, overpoweringly conscious of a new presence filling the atmosphere around – the presence of *Fear!* Heavy as a palpable presence / it pressed upon them; it lapped them round; the fumes of it mounted to their brains.

Months before, Darsie had listened while a woman who had been near San Francisco at the time of the earthquake and fire[129] endeavoured to describe what was in truth indescribable, how the very air itself was at that time charged with a poignancy of agony – an impalpable spiritual agony, apart from such physical cause as heat and fire, an agony which arose from the grief of thousands of tortured hearts.

She had listened – interested, curious, pleased to nestle in her easy-chair, and ponder over a novel thought; but at this terrible moment she had no need to ponder; realization came sharp and sure. Tragedy was in the air; she inhaled it with every breath, tasted it, felt its heavy hand.

With one accord the occupants of the tent streamed across the lawns towards the waterside, where even now an informal inquiry was taking place. The officials in charge of the ferry-boat were defending themselves against their accusers. Overcrowded? The ferry-boat had been as crowded on two previous days, and all had gone well. It was impossible to account for the accident. Since no further harm than a few minutes' ducking had happened to the passengers, the greater loss was on their own side.

To these officials, protesting, excusing, arrived / in a mass a body of white-faced men and women, demanding with one voice their lost – a young man, an undergraduate; tall, fair, in a white flannel suit; last seen standing on the side of the boat helping to lower the women into the water; a young girl, in a boating-dress of blue and white. They were not among the rescued. They had not been seen since the moment of the accident.

Where were they?

As Darsie stood, ghastly and shuddering, by the water brink, she was subconsciously aware of a strong arm in hers. Subconsciously also she was aware that the arm belonged to Dan Vernon, but she had no time for look or word; her whole being was strung to one agonizing thought. Mr. Percival supported his half-fainting wife; the two sisters clung together; the relations of Mary Everard paced wildly to and fro. On shore all was tumult and confusion, on the river sunbeams sparkled, the stream was quiet and undisturbed.

"Percival was like a fish: Percival could have kept afloat for hours."

A voice separated itself from the confused babel, and struck on Darsie's ear, but even as her heart leaped upward another voice spoke. "It is not a case of swimming. If he were not quick enough in getting away – if he were caught beneath-penned!"

The strong arm gripped her more firmly still, / steadied her trembling. A fierce voice issued an order for "Silence! Silence!"

Margaret France came up with beautiful soft eyes and a beautiful soft voice. She spoke wise, tender words. You were to come away – it was better so. It would add to your friends' distress if you were ill. You were wet, cold. You were to be sensible and come home.

Darsie looked at her thoughtfully for a long moment. She was thinking that she loved Margaret France, that she had taken a fancy to her the first evening at Newnham. How droll and witty she had been as an auctioneer! Of the purport of her present words she had no comprehension. She sighed and turned her face to the river.

"Leave her to me," said Dan's voice quietly. "I will take care of her."

* * * * *

They found them at sundown; the two young, fair bodies – the tall, pale lad, the slim, dark maid – two cold effigies of youth, and health, and joy. On Ralph's forehead was a deep red mark, the mark of the blow which had given him a prey to the waters; but Mary's brown locks floated round a sweet, untroubled face.

They bore them to the mortuary, and those who loved them sat and wept alone. Darsie spent the / two following days with the stricken family, who found their one comfort in listening again and again to the story of Ralph's brave end. Weak and unstable in life, in death he had shown a gallant front, and more than one of the unfortunate crew came forward to testify to his courageous and self-less efforts on their behalf.

Mr. Percival went about with a set face and shoulders bowed like those of an old man. The girls wept helplessly from morn till night; Mrs. Percival lost in one night all lingering trace of youth; she kept up bravely before her husband and daughters, but alone with Darsie her anguish found vent.

"My son, my son! He was so good to me – so loving and kind. His faults were the faults of youth, and, oh, Darsie, *my* faults also! We blamed him for faults which we had not tried to check. If he had lived and had been obliged to face life for himself he would have risen to it, as he rose to that last great chance. It takes a brave man to face death calmly. He was not weak or selfish then – my Ralph!

No one dared call him weak. Thank God! We were with him to the end, we were happy together, and you were with him too. That is what he would have wished. He loved you, Darsie. If he had lived, he would have wished you for his wife."

"Yes!" sighed Darsie, and laid her head gently / on the other's knee. In the silence which followed she was acutely aware of the unspoken question which filled the air, acutely distressed that she could not give the stricken mother the assurance for which she craved.

In Ralph's lifetime his friendship had brought Darsie as much pain as joy, and, though death had wiped away all but tender recollections, even in this hour of grief and shock she did not delude herself that she sorrowed for him with the deepest sorrow of all. The anxious, pitiful affection which she had felt for the man who leaned so heavily upon her was more that of a sister than a wife.

Darsie stretched out her hand, found the chilly one of the poor mother, and leaning her soft cheek over it, pressed it tenderly with her lips.

"You must let me be your third daughter! We can talk about him together. I can tell you about this last year – every little tiny thing that he said and did. You'll never be anxious about him any more, dear, never afraid! You will always be proud of your hero boy."

Mrs. Percival sighed. She was in too sensitive a mood not to realize the meaning of the girl's lack of response, but the first pang of disappointment was followed by a thought full of comfort to the sore mother-heart.

"I loved him best. He was mine to the end! No one loved him like his mother!" /

Chapter XXVIII

Brighter Days

Six months passed by – months of grief and pain, and bitter, unavailing regret; of work and play, of long summer days, and wintry fog and cold; of reviving happiness also, since, thank God! joy returns like the spring, bringing back hope and joy to a darkened world. There was a place in Darsie's heart which would ever be consecrated to the memory of Ralph; but it was not a foremost place – that most crushing of sorrows had been spared her; and when one not yet twenty-one is living the healthiest and most congenial of lives, and is above all elevated to the proud position of third-year girl, it would be as unnatural as wrong to dwell continually upon a past grief.

At first Darsie felt shocked and ashamed when the old gay mood swept her off her balance, and she found herself dancing, singing, and making merry as of yore, but her two mentors, Mrs. Reeves and Hannah Vernon, united to combat this impression. /

"To bear a sorrow *cheerfully* is the only resignation worthy of the name!" This was the older woman's verdict; the younger preached the same precept in student vernacular –

"Why grizzle when you want to smile? Pray, what good can you do yourself, or any one else' by going about with a face like a fiddle? Remember Margaret France, and don't block up the window to shut out the stars! Let them twinkle for all they are worth, the blessed little things. They are *tired* of hiding behind the clouds. You have a duty to the living as well as to the dead; remember that!"

Yes, it was true. Looking back over the last eight months Darsie realized what a debt of gratitude she owed to relations and friends alike for their tenderness and forbearance. It had been hard on the home party to have the summer holidays clouded by the presence of a mourner who shuddered at the sight of water, collapsed into tears at unexpected moments, and lived in a condition of supersensitiveness, ready as it seemed to be hurt by the most innocent word; yet how gentle and patient they had been, every single one of them, down to Tim himself!

Mother and father, of course, had been angels; one took it for granted that they would be, but who could have believed in such consideration from the boys and girls. Dear old Clemence! What a / comfort she had been! Darsie had often been inclined to think that, for sheer rest and soothing, no one could compete with a plump, practical, matter-of-fact sister, who had no thought for "ifs" or "whys," but was full of care to ensure your present physical well-being. Then, if for a moment Clemence seemed to fall short, there was Lavender, ready to pour out floods of sympathy, to mingle her tears with yours, and listen to endless reminiscences. As for the boys, Harry and Russell forbore to tease, affected blindness to reddened eyes, and said, "Buck up, old girl!" with real heartiness of feeling, while Tim was assiduous in the offer of sticky sweets.

The Vernons, lucky creatures! went off *en masse* to Switzerland for July and August. Darsie morbidly told herself that they were anxious to avoid the depression of her own presence during the chief holiday of the year. She was, as she expressed it, "too proud to say so," but the inward soreness made her so cold and abrupt in manner that her friends had good cause to reverse the accusation.

With regard to Dan Vernon in especial there was a soreness at Darsie's heart. During the first days after the tragic happening Dan had been a tower of strength, always at hand to comfort, support, and take every difficulty upon his own shoulders. To outward appearance Darsie had / appeared oblivious of his presence, but subconsciously she had leaned on his strength with a profound relief. It was hard to have Dan withdraw into his shell just as she was beginning to long for his presence; but he *had* withdrawn, and like most naturally shy and reticent people, withdrawn farther than ever, as if in reaction from his unusual demonstration.

In hall itself the absence of Margaret France made a big blank. Having passed her tripos with a first class, Margaret had placidly returned home to help her mother in the house, and take part in an ordinary social life. "What a waste!" cried her Newnham acquaintances, but Margaret's friends, remembering her own words on the subject, believed that she had chosen the better part.

With October came the return to Newnham, and for the first few weeks an access of grief and depression. It was hard to fall into the old life shorn of its greatest interest, to be reminded of Ralph at every turn, to see his friends pass by, laughing and gay, while his place was blank.

Then it was that Darsie discovered the real tenderness of heart which lies beneath the somewhat callous exterior of the college girl. Freshers, second-year girls, even austere thirds themselves, combined to surround her with an atmosphere of kindness and consideration. No *word* of sympathy was ever spoken, but almost every hour / of the day brought with it some fresh deed of comfort and cheer. Offerings of flowers, tendered by a friend, or laid anonymously on "burry" or coffin; bags of fruit and cake, invitations galore, surprise visits to her own study, each in turn bringing a gleam of brightness to the day. Plain Hannah, too, dear old plain Hannah! In the midst of her grief Darsie was filled with amusement at Hannah's unique fashion of showing her sympathy. Hot water evidently commended itself to her mind as the ideal medium, for at a dozen hours of the day and night the door of Darsie's study would open and Hannah would appear on the threshold, steaming can in hand. Early morning, eleven o'clock, before lunch, before tea, before dinner, before cocoa, before bed, Hannah and her can never failed to appear. For the first half of the Michaelmas term Darsie might literally have been described as never out of hot water.

And now it was the Lent term; eight months had passed by since the date of Ralph's death, and it surely behoved Darsie to rise above her depression, and to throw herself once more into the full, happy life of the house.[130] She was thankful to do it, thankful to welcome dawnings of the old zest, to feel her feet involuntarily quicken to a dance, to discover herself singing as she moved to and fro. The winter had passed; / spring was in the air. It seemed right that it should be in her heart also.

As usual in the Lent term, hockey was the one absorbing subject outside "shop," and Hannah Vernon, now advanced to the lofty position of captain, had special reasons for welcoming her friend's reviving spirits.

One chilly day in February she entered Darsie's study with a somewhat unusual request.

"The girls are getting restive, and think that it's quite time we had another fancy match. They want me to arrange one on the spot. It's so blighting to be told that one is so clever, and looked to for inspiration. Every idea forsakes one on the instant. You've been hibernating for an age, you ought to have lots stored up!"

"I haven't – I've grown hideously dull. What did we have last?"

"Thicks against Thins! Never shall I forget it! To play forward padded with three separate cushions, and with shawls wound round your limbs, is the sort of thing one rises to *once* in a lifetime, but never twice. I made an adorable fat woman! The Thins had no spirit left in them when they beheld my bulk. I vote that we don't have anything that involves padding this time. One never knows one's luck."

"No-o! I think we might hit on something more subtle," Darsie ruminated, with her eyes on / the ceiling. Her reputation of being the Newnham belle remained unchallenged after two separate incursions of Freshers.

As she sat before a "burry," clad in a blue, pinafore-like garment, from which emerged white silk sleeves to match the collar and yoke, her hand absently turning over a pile of notebooks, bound in green and blue and rose, she made a striking contrast to Hannah Vernon in a cinnamon coat and skirt, built for wear by a cheap tailor on the principle of "there or thereabouts." Even the notebooks reflected the personality of their owners, for the one which Hannah carried was of the shiny black persuasion which seemed to proclaim that, being made for good solid work, it disdained the affectation of beauty. Plain Hannah's little eyes twinkled affectionately at her old friend. She detached a pencil from a chain which dangled by her side, and said tentatively –

"Subtle – yes! Good biz! Let's have a Subtler by all means."

"I – was thinking – we might have something touching upon future possibilities. I've not quite got it yet, but something about brides and spinsters. Future brides – budding brides – beautiful brides."

"Easy enough to have adjectives for the brides. Where do the spinsters come in?"

"Oh, one would have to infer – subtly, of course – that they *would* be spinsters! That would be / adjective enough. Embryo spinsters – preparatory spinsters – p-p-probable spinsters. I have it! I have it! 'Possible Brides against Probable Spinsters!'"

"Ha!" ejaculated Hannah, and drew her forefinger slowly down her nose. "*Good!* Top hole. Amusin', but – injudicious? Shouldn't mind one rap myself; lead off the Probables with a cheer. But, I fear me, there'd be brickbats floating in the air. How much would you take in coin of the realm to go up to Vera Ruskin and invite her to play for the spinsters? Personally I'd rather be excused."

"I'd volunteer as a start! Love to do it!"

"Ye-es! Just so. Noble of you, no doubt; but unconvincing," returned Hannah dryly. "No! It's a fine suggestion in theory, but in practice I'm afraid it won't work. I don't want to imperil my popularity for good. Think of something a trifle less searching! Er – er – Slackers against – against what? Slackers against Swotters! How would that do for a change?"

Darsie curled her little nose.

"Dull! No scope. How would you dress?"

"Oh-h! The Swotters might have bandages round their heads, and study notebooks between play. The Slackers would just – could just –"

"Just so! 'Could just'! Too feeble, my dear! It won't do. What about worth and charm? / Might make up something out of that. Worth – solid worth, genuine worth –"

"Moral worth!"

"That's it! Moral Worth against Charm, personal charm! That'll do it. That'll do it! *Moral Worth against Personal Charm.* Nobody can be offended at being asked to represent Moral Worth."

"They will, though! The female heart is desperately wicked," returned Hannah shrewdly. "But if they do it's their own look-out. We'll preserve a high and lofty tone, and be *surprised!* Thanks awfully, old girl. It's an adorable idea. What price the Moral Worth costume – eh, what?"

The Hockey captain went off chuckling, and excitement ran high in the hockey world when the thrilling announcement was posted that afternoon. "For which side shall I be asked to play?" Forwards, Backs, and Goals alike agitated themselves over these questions, and, sad to relate, Hannah proved a true prophet, for while an invitation from the 'Personal Charm' captain aroused smiles of delight, the implication of 'Moral Worth' was but coldly received.

Darsie Garnett herself was conscious of an electric shock of the most unpleasant nature when, but half an hour after the posting of the notice, the "Moral Worths" invited her to join their ranks! With all the determination in the world, she found it impossible to repress a start of surprise, and / was acutely conscious of smothered giggles of amusement from those around. She accepted, of course, with protestations of delight, and ten minutes later found balm in the shape of an invitation from the rival team. The "Personal Charms" deplored Darsie's loss, but considered it a masterpiece of diplomacy on the part of the "Moral Worth" captain to have headed her team with the name of the Newnham Belle. "No one could be snarkey after that!"

The two teams held committee meetings on the subject of costumes, which were kept a dead secret until the hour for the match had arrived, when a large body of spectators awaited their arrival on the ground, with expectations pleasantly excited. The "Personal Charms" appeared first, marching in pairs with heads erect, and stamped on each face that brilliant, unalterable, toothy smile affected by actresses of inferior rank. Each head was frizzed and tousled to about twice its natural size, and crowned by an enormous topknot of blue ribbon. White blouses and skirts, blue belts, ties, and hose completed an attractive costume, and as a finishing touch, the handle of the hockey-stick was embellished with a second huge blue bow.

From a spectacular point of view the "Personal Charms" were certainly an unusually attractive spectacle, but as regards popularity with the / "field," they fell far behind the rival team. The "Moral Worths" allowed a judicious time to

elapse after the appearance of the "Personal Charms," and then, just as the spectators were beginning to wax impatient, excitement was aroused by the appearance
of a white banner, borne proudly aloft in the arms of two brawny Forwards.
Printed on the banner were two lines of poetry, which at nearer view proved to
be a highly appropriate adaptation –

"Be good, sweet maid,
And let who will be charming!"[131]

Certainly the "Moral Worths" had been at pains to disguise any charm they
possessed! Even Darsie herself looked plain with her hair dragged back into a
tight little knot, her grey flannel shirt padded into the similitude of stooping
shoulders, her skirt turned carefully back to front. With lumping gait and heavy
footsteps the team marched round the field, and drew up beside the beaming
"Personal Charms," who despite the blasts of easterly wind through summer
muslin blouses, continued to smile, and smile, and smile.

Throughout the heated game which followed the "Moral Worths" were distinctly the favourite team; nevertheless, it is the deplorable truth that the "Personal
Charms" won at a canter, despite the handicap of their beribboned sticks. /

When, tired and muddy, Darsie reached her study again, it was to find a postcard from Lavender which a kindly Fresher had laid upon her "burry." It bore but
a few words written in large characters, and plentifully underlined –

"*Which team were You asked to play for?*"

What a glow of satisfaction it gave one to be able to reply, truthfully and
accurately, with one short, illuminating – "*Both!*"

Among the other joys of the last terms, one shone out pre-eminent in Darsie
Garnett's estimation. She was Prime Minister![132] It seemed almost too splendid
to be true! She, who three years before had made her first appearance at Political
as the bashful representative of Bootle-cum-Linacre, to have advanced to this
dizzy height of power! To be captain of the Hockey Club paled into insignificance before this crowning honour, but as Hannah was "Speaker," Darsie was
unable to crow as loudly as she would have done if her friend's place had been
below the gangway.

Political was held in College Hall on Monday evenings at eight o'clock, and
in old-fashioned style the members were divided into three parties, Conservatives, Liberals, and Unionists, whose seats were so arranged as to form three sides
of a square.

Viewed from afar there was a strong element of humour about this mock
Parliament. Prophetic / it might be, but it was distinctly droll to hear Honoura-
ble Members addressed as "Madam," while some of the statutes embodied in the
Constitution-book were quite deliciously unexpected, the special one, which
ran, "*Members occupying the front benches are requested not to darn stockings during Political,*" being a constant source of delight to parents and friends.

Darsie was a Liberal. Members of the Opposition accused her openly of Socialism. *What! shall we sacrifice our brother man for the sake of the demon gold?* she would declaim with waving hands and cheeks aflame, whereat the Liberals would cheer as one girl, and even the Conservatives themselves be moved to admiration.

Debates relating to Education, Suffrage, and the House of Lords were held during the winter months, but the crowning excitement followed a daring Bill introduced by the Liberal party for the abolishment of the Unionists *in toto,* on the ground that, being neither fish, flesh, nor good red herring, they acted but as a drag on the wheels of progress. The benches were crowded to their fullest capacity on the occasion of this historic debate; even the Dons themselves came in to listen, and the whips flew round the corridors, giving no quarter to the few skulkers discovered at work in their studies, until they also were forced into the breach. As a result, the Unionist party, / supported by Moderates on both sides, achieved a brilliant and decisive victory.

So much for Political, but the Prime Minister occupied another proud position, for Margaret France's prophecy had been fulfilled, and Darsie was now captain of the Clough Fire Brigade. Beneath her were two lieutenants, and two companies, each seven girls strong, and the duty of choosing times of the utmost inconvenience and unpreparedness for drill alarms rested entirely at her discretion. When the fire-bell rang, every member of the brigade must leave whatever she happened to be about, and dash pell-mell to the assembling-ground on an upper story. There the force ranked up in order, the captain explained the locality and nature of the supposed conflagration, and each "man" received "his" own instruction – one to shut windows and ventilators, and so diminish draughts, another to uncoil the hose, a third to affix the nozzle, and so on. The work was accomplished, examined by the authorities, and the "men" were back on the top landing, ranked up in their original order, in an incredibly short space of time, when the captain gave a sharp criticism of the performance, followed by a few questions to test the general knowledge of the staff: Where was Mary Murray's study? What was its aspect? What was the nearest water supply? &c. /

One excuse for non-attendance, and one only, was allowed to pass muster – a member who chanced to be in a hot bath what time the bell rang forth the alarm might lie at ease and smile at the scurry without, health and the risk of chill being considered before imaginary dangers. If, however, the bath were *cold,* out she must get, dash into the coat and skirt which, for members of the fire brigade, supplanted the ordinary dressing-gown, and take her place with the rest.

Nor – with Darsie Garnett as captain – was it any use to attempt deception, as a tired little Fresher discovered to her cost, when she naughtily turned a warm stream into her cold bath and refused to budge. No sooner were lightning-like instructions rapped out upstairs than down flew the irate captain, rapped at the door, demanded admission, and – in the absence of steam upon the wall – sentenced the cringing truant to a month's suspension of privileges.

Nor was Darsie's own position free from anxiety, for once in a term it was the prerogative of the brigade to surprise the captain, and woe befall her prestige if, on that occasion, she were found wanting! Coat, skirt, and slippers lay nightly on a chair by her bedside, together with the inevitable pile of notebooks, and she felt a burden off her mind when the alarm had come and gone.

Deep, deep down in the recesses of Darsie's / mind there slumbered a fell ambition. If there could be a *real* fire before her term of office expired! Not a serious one, of course – nothing to imperil the safety of the dear old house, but just sufficient to cause a *real* alarm, and give the brigade an opportunity of demonstrating its powers! It was almost too aggravating to be borne to hear one morning that a second-year girl had indulged in a study fire, and had extinguished it of her own accord. Extinguished by private effort, when a captain, two lieutenants, and fourteen "men" were languishing for an opportunity to exhibit their powers! The captain spoke sternly to the second-year girl, and rebuked her.

"How," she demanded, "can you *expect* a reliable force, if precious opportunities are to be wasted like this? Curtains ablaze, and the bed-clothes singeing. We may wait for *years* for another such opportunity!"

"But where do *I* come in?" cried the second-year girl. "I gave ten and sixpence for that quilt. And a jug of water standing close at hand! It was only human nature –"

"I hope," returned the captain of the Fire Brigade icily – "I *hope* that is not the spirit in which you propose to go through life. It's a poor thing if you cannot sacrifice a ten-and-sixpenny quilt in the interest of the public good." And she stalked majestically from the room. /

Chapter XXIX

Tripos Week

THE Tripos week! Every third-year girl felt as if life and death trembled in the balance during those eventful days. They woke on the Monday morning with much the same feeling as that of a patient who expects to have an arm amputated at eleven, and is morally convinced that she will sink beneath the strain, and when at seven o'clock a second-year friend crept into the study, tray in hand, and administered sympathising cups of tea, the final touch was given to the illusion.

Darsie quailed before the prospect of those three-hour papers. Experience had proved that she was not at her best in examinations; imaginative people rarely are, since at the critical moment the brain is apt to wander off on dire excursions into the future, envisaging the horrors of failing, instead of buckling to work in order to ensure success. Historical French Grammar in especial loomed like a pall, and she entered the Mission / Room at St. Columba's[133] with the operation-like feeling developed to its acutest point.

For several minutes after taking the first paper in her hand Darsie found it impossible to decipher the words. The type danced mistily before her eyes; and when at last letters shaped themselves out of the confusion, the last state was worse than the first, for she. was convinced – drearily, hopelessly convinced – that she could not answer a single question out of the number.

She laid down the paper, and steadied herself resolutely. All over the room other girls were sitting on hard, uncomfortable chairs before tables like her own, some motionless and stunned-looking like herself, some already setting briskly to work. On the walls, among a number of quotations, "*Help one another!*" stared her in the face with tragic significance, and again: "How far high failure over-leaps the bounds of low successes."[134] *Failure!* She lifted the paper again, and decided with a glimmer of hope that she could answer at least *one* question, set to work, and scribbled for life until the last moment of the prescribed three hours!

What exhaustion! What collapse! Positively one's legs wobbled beneath one as one trailed wearily Newnhamwards. What a comfort to be fussed over and petted, treated as distinguished invalids whom the College was privileged to tend! / The Tripos girls "sat at High"[135] at the head of the room, surrounded by attentive Dons, with the V.C. herself smiling encouragement, and urging them to second helpings of chicken (chicken!!). By the time that it was necessary to start forth for the afternoon's ordeal they felt mentally and physically braced, and the operation feeling lessened sensibly.

At the afternoon's ordeal, however, the weariness and depression grew more acute than ever, and on the walk home the comparing of answers had anything but a cheering effect. No girl was satisfied; each was morally convinced that her companions had done better than herself. Where she had failed to answer a question, a reminder of the solution filled her with despair. Of course! It was as simple as A B C. She had known it off by heart. Nothing short of softening of the brain could explain such idiotic forgetfulness.

It was a kindly custom which separated the sufferers on their return to Col-lege, each one being carried off by her special second-year adorer to a cheery little tea-party, for which the most congenial spirits and the most delectable fare were provided. Here the tired senior was soothed and fed, and her self-esteem revived by an attitude of reverence on the part of the audience. The second-year girls shuddered over the papers; were convinced that never, no never, could they face / the like, and suggested that it would be a saving of time to go down at once.

Later on that first evening, when Marian White appeared to put her invalid to bed, she bore in her hand a letter from Margaret France, which Darsie hailed with a cry of joy.

"Ah! I *thought* she would write to me. I wondered that I didn't have a letter this morning, but she was right as usual. She knew I should need it more to-night!"

Margaret's letter was short and to the point –

"DEAREST DARSIE – A year ago you were cheering me! How I wish I could do the same for you in your need, but as I can't be present in the flesh, here comes a little line to greet you, old dear, and to tell you to be of good cheer. You are very tired, and very discouraged, and very blue. I *know!* Every one is. It's part of the game. Do you remember what a stern mentor I had, and how she bullied me, and packed me to bed, and took away my books? Oh, the good old times! The good old times, how happy we were – how I think of them now, and long to be back! But the best part remains, for I have still my friend, and you and I, Darsie, 'belong' for our lives.

"Cheer up, old dear! *You've done a lot better than you think!*

"MARGARET". /

"What's the matter now?" asked the second-year girl sharply, spying two big tears course slowly down her patient's cheeks, and Darsie returned a stammering reply –

"I've had such a ch-ch-cheering letter!"

"Have you indeed! The less of *that* sort of cheering you get this week, the better for you!" snapped Marian once more. She was jealous of Margaret France, as she was jealous of every girl in the College for whom Darsie Garnett showed a preference, and she strongly resented any interference with her own prerogative. "Hurry into your dressing-gown, please, and I'll brush your hair," she said now in her most dictatorial tones. "I'm a pro. at brushing hair – a hair-dresser taught me how to do it. You hold the brush at the side to begin with, and work gradually round to the flat. I let a Fresher brush mine one night when I'd a headache, and she began in the middle of my cheek. There's been a coldness between us ever since. There! isn't that good? Gets right into the roots, doesn't it, and tingles them up! Nothing so soothing as a smooth, hard brush."

Darsie shut her eyes and purred like a sleek, lazy little cat.

"De-lic-ious! Lovely! You *do* brush well! I could sit here for hours."

"You won't get a chance. Ten minutes at / most, and then off you go, and not a peep at another book till to-morrow morning."

"Marian – *really* – I *must!* Just for ten minutes, to revive my memory."

"–I'll tell you a story!" said Marian quietly – "a *true* story from my own experience. It was when I was at school and going in for the Cambridge Senior,[136] the last week, when we were having the exams. We had *slaved* all the term, and were at the last gasp. The head girl was one Annie Macdiarmid, a marvel of a creature, the most all-round scholar I've ever met. She was invariably first in everything, and I usually came in a bad third. Well, we'd had an arithmetic exam, one day, pretty stiff, but not more so than usual, and on this particular morning at eleven o'clock we were waiting to hear the result. The Mathematic Master was a lamb – so keen, and humorous, and just – a *rageur*[137] at times, but that was only to be expected. He came into the room, papers in hand, his mouth screwed up, and his eyebrows nearly hidden under his hair. We knew at a glance that something awful had happened. He cleared his throat several times, and began to read aloud the arithmetic results. 'Total, a hundred. Bessie Smith, eighty-seven.' There was a rustle of surprise. Not Annie Macdiarmid? Just Bessie – an ordinary sort of creature, who wasn't going in for the Local at all. 'Mary Ross, / eighty-two. Stella Bruce, seventy-four.' Where did *I* come in? I'd never been lower than that. 'Kate Stevenson, sixty-four.' Some one else fifty, some one else forty, *and* thirty *and* twenty, and still not a mention of Annie Macdiarmid or of me. You should have *seen* her face! I shall never forget it. *Green!* and she laced her fingers in and out, and chewed, and chewed. I was too stunned to feel. The world seemed to have come to an end. Down it came – sixteen, fourteen, ten – and then at last – at bitter, long last – 'Miss Marian White, *six!* Miss Macdiar-mid, TWO!'"

Darsie stared beneath the brush, drawing a long breath of dismay.

"What *did* you do?"

"Nothing! That was where he showed himself so wise. An ordinary master would have raged and stormed, insisted upon our working for extra hours, going over and over the old ground, but he knew better. He just banged all the books together, tucked them under his arm, and called out: 'No more work! Put on your hats and run off home as fast as you can go, and tell your mothers from me to take you to the Waxworks, or a Wild Beast show. Don't dare to show yourselves in school again until Monday morning. Read as many stories as you please, but open a school book at your peril!'" /

Marian paused dramatically, Darsie peered at her through a mist of hair, and queried weakly, "Well?"

"Well – so we didn't! We just slacked and lazed, and amused ourselves till the Monday morning, and then, like giants refreshed, we went down to the fray and –"

"And what?"

"I've told you before! I got second-class honours, and the Macdiarmid came out first in all England, distinction in a dozen subjects – arithmetic among them. So now, Miss Garnett, kindly take the moral to heart, and let me hear no more nonsense about 'reviving memories.' *Your* memory needs putting to sleep, so that it may wake up refreshed and active after a good night's rest."

And Darsie weakly, reluctantly obeyed. /

Chapter XXX

Farewell to Newnham

MAY week followed hard on the Tripos that year, but Darsie took no part in the festivities. The remembrance of the tragic event of last summer made her shrink from witnessing the same scenes, and in her physically exhausted condition she was thankful to stay quietly in college. Moreover, a sad task lay before her in the packing up her belongings, preparatory to bidding adieu to the beloved little room which had been the scene of so many joys and sorrows during the last three years.

Vi Vernon, as a publicly engaged young lady, was paying a round of visits to her *fiancé's* relations, but Mr. and Mrs. Vernon had come up as usual, arranging to keep on their rooms, so that they might have the satisfaction of being in Cambridge when the Tripos List came out. With a son like Dan and a daughter like Hannah, satisfaction was a foregone conclusion; calm, level-headed creatures both of them, who were not to / be flurried or excited by the knowledge of a critical moment, but most sanely and sensibly collected their full panoply of wits to turn them to good account.

Hannah considered it in the last degree futile to dread an exam. "What else," she would demand in forceful manner – "what else are you working for? For what other reason are you here?" But her arguments, though unanswerable, continued to be entirely unconvincing to Darsie and other nervously constituted students.

The same difference of temperament showed itself in the manner of waiting for results. Dan and Hannah, so to speak, wiped their pens after the writing of the last word of the last paper, and there and then resigned themselves to their fate. They had done their best; nothing more was possible in the way of addition or alteration – for good or ill the die was cast. Then why worry? Wait quietly, and take what came along!

Blessed faculty of common sense! A man who is born with such a temperament escapes half the strain of life, though it is to be doubted whether he can rise to the same height of joy as his more imaginative neighbour, who lies awake shivering at the thought of possible ills, and can no more "wait quietly" for a momentous decision than he could breathe with comfort in a burning house.

When the morning arrived on which the results / of the Tripos were to be posted on the door of the Senate House, Darsie and Hannah had taken a last sad farewell of their beloved Newnham, and were ensconced with Mr. and Mrs. Vernon in their comfortable rooms. The lists were expected to appear early in the morning, and the confident parents had arranged a picnic "celebration" party for the afternoon.

Darsie never forgot that morning – the walk to the Senate House with Dan and Hannah on either side, the sight of the waiting crowd, the strained efforts at conversation, the dragging hours.

At long last a list appeared – the men's list only: for the women's a further wait would be necessary. But one glance at the paper showed Dan's name proudly ensconced where every one had expected it would be, and in a minute he was surrounded by an eager throng – congratulating, cheering, shaking him by the hand. He looked quiet as ever, but his eyes shone, and when Darsie held out her hand he gripped it with a violence which almost brought the tears to her eyes.

The crowd cleared away slowly, the women students retiring to refresh themselves with luncheon before beginning a second wait. The Vernons repaired to their rooms and feasted on the contents of the hamper prepared for the picnic, the father and mother abeam with pride and satisfaction, Dan obviously filled with content, and dear / old Hannah full of quips. Darsie felt ashamed of herself because she alone failed to throw off anxiety; but her knees *would* tremble, her throat *would* parch, and her eyes *would* turn back restlessly to study the clock.

"Better to die by sudden shock,
Than perish piecemeal on the rock!"[138]

The old couplet which as a child she had been used to quote darted back into her mind with a torturing pang. How much longer of this agony could she stand? Anything, anything would be better than this dragging on in suspense, hour after hour. But when once again the little party approached the Senate House, she experienced a swift change of front. No, no, this was not suspense; it was hope! Hope was blessed and kindly. Only certainty was to be dreaded, the grim, unalterable fact.

The little crowd of girls pressed forward to read the lists. Darsie peered with the rest, but saw nothing but a mist and blur. Then a voice spoke loudly by her side; Hannah's voice:

"First Class! *Hurrah!*"

Whom did she mean? Darsie's heart soared upward with a dizzy hope, her eyes cleared and flashed over the list of names. Hannah Vernon – Mary Bates – Eva Murray – many names, but not her own. /

The mist and the blur hid the list once more, she felt an arm grip her elbow, and Dan's voice cried cheerily –

"A Second Class! Good for you, Darsie! I thought you were going to fail."

It was a relief. Not a triumph; not the proud, glad moment of which she had dreamed, but a relief from a great dread. The girls congratulated her, wrung her hand, cried, "Well done!" and wished her luck; third-class girls looked envious and subdued; first-class girls in other "shops" whispered in her ear that it was an acknowledged fact that Modern Languages had had an uncommonly stiff time this year. Modern Languages who had themselves gained a first class, kept discreetly out of the way. Hannah said, "See, I was right! Are you satisfied now?" No one showed any sign of disappointment. Perhaps no one but herself had believed in the possibility of a first class.

The last band of students turned away from the gates with a strange reluctance. It was the last, the very last incident of the dear old life – the happiest years of life which they had ever known, the years which from this moment would exist but as a memory. Even the most successful felt a pang mingling with their joy, as they turned their backs on the gates and walked quietly away. /

Later that afternoon Dan and Darsie found themselves strolling across the meadows towards Grandchester. They were alone, for, the picnic having fallen through, Mr. and Mrs. Vernon had elected to rest after the day's excitement, and Hannah had settled herself down to the writing of endless letters to relations and friends, bearing the good news of the double honours.

Darsie's few notes had been quickly accomplished, and had been more apologetic than jubilant in tone, but she honestly tried to put her own feelings in the background, and enter into Dan's happiness as he confided to her his plans for the future.

"I'm thankful I've come through all right – it means so much. I'm a lucky fellow, Darsie. I've got a rattling opening, at the finest of the public schools, the school I'd have chosen above all others. Jenson got a mastership there two years ago – my old coach, you remember! He was always good to me, thought more of me than I deserved, and he spoke of me to the Head. There's a vacancy for a junior master next term. They wrote to me about it. It was left open till the lists came out, but now! now it will go through. I'm safe for it now."

"Oh, Dan, I'm so glad; I'm so glad for you! You've worked so hard that you deserve your reward. A mastership, and time to write – that's / your ambition still? You are still thinking of your book?"

"Ah, my book!" Dan's dark eyes lightened, his rugged face shone. It was easy to see how deeply that book of the future had entered into his life's plans. He discussed it eagerly as they strolled across the fields, pointing out the respects in which it differed from other treatises of the kind; and Darsie listened, and sympathised, appreciated to the extent of her abilities, and hated herself because, the more absorbed and eager Dan grew, the more lonely and dejected became her own mood. Then they talked of Hannah and her future. With so good a record she would have little difficulty in obtaining her ambition in a post as mathematical mistress at a girls' school. It would be hard on Mrs. Vernon to lose the society of both her daughters, but she was wise enough to realise that Hannah's *métier* was not for a domestic life, and unselfish enough to wish her girls to choose the most congenial *rôles*.

"And my mother will still have three at home, three big, incompetent girls!" sighed Darsie in reply, and her heart swelled with a sudden spasm of rebellion. "Oh, Dan, after all my dreams! I'm so bitterly disappointed. Poor little second-class me!"

"*Don't,* Darsie!" cried Dan sharply. He stood still, facing her in the narrow path, but now / the glow had gone from his face; it was twisted with lines of pain and anxiety. "Darsie! it's the day of my life, but it's all going to fall to pieces if you are sad! You've done your best, and you've done well, and if you are a bit disappointed that you've failed for a first yourself, can't you – can't you take any comfort out of *mine?* It's more than half your own. I'd never have got there by myself!"

"Dan, dear, you're talking nonsense! What nonsense you talk! What have *I* done? What *could* I do for a giant like you?"

Dan brushed aside the word with a wave of the hand.

"Do you remember when we were talking last year, beside the fire, in the old study one afternoon, when all the others were out, talking about poor Percival, and your answer to a question I asked? '*He needs me, Dan!*' you said. I argued very loftily about the necessity of a man standing alone and facing his difficulties by himself, and you said that was true, but only a part of the truth. I've found that out for myself since then. If that was true of Percival, it is fifty times truer of me! *I* need you, Darsie! I shall always need you. I've not a penny-piece in the world, except what my father allows me. I shall probably always be poor. For years to come I shall be grinding away as a junior master. Even / when the book is written it can never bring much return in a monetary sense, but success will come in the end, I'll *make* it come! And when it does, it will belong to you as much as to me. You'll remember that?"

"Yes.... Thank you, Dan!" The answer came in a breathless gasp. Darsie's big eyes were fixed upon Dan's face in rapt, incredulous gaze. The cramp of loneliness had loosened from her heart; the depression had vanished; a marvellous new interest had entered into her life; she was filled with a beatific content.

"I'll remember! I'll be proud to remember. But – I don't understand!"

"I don't understand myself," said Dan simply. "I only know it is true. So don't get low, Darsie, and don't be discouraged. You're in a class by yourself, and all the honours in the world couldn't improve you. And now that's over, and we start afresh!"

It was like Dan to hurry back with all speed to more practical talk. Darsie understood, and was satisfied. They stood together for another moment looking back on the massed towers and spires of Cambridge, then slowly, reluctantly, turned away.

A new life lay ahead, its outline vague and undefined like that of the landscape around, but the sun was shining. It shone full on their young faces, as they went forward, hand in hand. /

EDITORIAL NOTES

1.   *THE RELIGIOUS TRACT SOCIETY*: Founded in 1799, the Religious Tract Society soon branched out from publishing tracts to more general Christian literature. They were also the publishers of the *Girl's Own Paper*, in which *A College Girl* originally appeared in serial form. A novel like this was probably also aimed at the 'reward' market, i.e. to be given as a prize at school or Sunday school.

2.   *the tale of two terraces*: This is probably a reference to the 1859 novel *A Tale of Two Cities* by Charles Dickens (1812–70), a novel with which Vaizey would have expected her audience to be familiar.

3.   *quarter-day*: Vaizey refers here to the four days per year when rents were usually due, and financial transactions (such as the girls' allowances) took place.

4.   *like the man in Rider Haggard*: H. Rider Haggard (1856–1925) was the author of many adventure novels, often set in exotic locations and featuring colonizing heroes. His stories include *King Solomon's Mines* (1885) and *She* (1887).

5.   *like the Bible one*: The story of Daniel, who was thrown into a lion's den for continuing to pray to God, and survived unscathed, featured widely in collections of Bible stories for children at the period. See Daniel 6.

6.   *High School*: see note 55 to Volume 1. I have found no record of the 'Royal Institute', but presumably it refers to a boys' day-school.

7.   *the time of the great servants' strike*: During this period domestic service was the biggest occupation of women in England and Wales. I have found no record of a widespread strike in London in this period, although newspapers of the time reported similar strikes in regional England and Russia.

8.   *a telegraph*: Invented in the 1830s, the telegraph network was well-developed by this period.

9.   *an airship*: The first engine-powered airship flight took place in 1852. By the early twentieth century, airships were relatively well known, often through public demonstrations by companies such as Zeppelin. Airships fell out of favour after the Hindenburgh disaster of 1937.

10. *a juggins*: a fool.

11. *Benger's food*: Benger's food was a wheat-based powder that was mixed with milk and drunk to aid digestion. It was produced well into the twentieth century.

12. *the sweet old ballad*: I have been unable to trace this source.

13. *neuralgia*: nerve pain.

14. Good Words: A periodical founded in 1860, *Good Words* was overtly religious, aimed at evangelicals and considered to be an 'improving' publication that could be read on Sundays. This magazine, and the general shabbiness of the 'study', is perhaps meant to

suggest the Vernons' humble origins.

15. *ink-splashed drugget*: A drugget was a heavy piece of cloth, usually designed to protect carpets.

16. '*All unsuspecting of their doom the little victims played*': This is probably a reference to the 1742 poem 'Ode on a Distant Prospect of Eton College' by Thomas Gray (1716–71), which reads 'Alas! regardless of their doom, / The little victims play' (ll. 51–2).

17. *Earley ... Oxholm*: Earley is a town in Berkshire, not far from Silchester, which features the remains of a roman amphitheatre. I have been unable to identify 'Oxholm'.

18. *a real swagger lunch just for once*: 'Swagger' used as an adjective in this period meant fashionable or showy.

19. *her little Kodak*: Darsie is probably carrying a Kodak Brownie camera, an inexpensive model sold from 1900.

20. *Hyde Park ... Buckingham Palace*: Vaizey clearly assumes that her readers would be familiar with London locations.

21. *patience on a monument*: From the 1601 play *Twelfth Night* by William Shakespeare (1564–1616): 'She sat like patience on a monument, / smiling at grief' (Act 2, Scene 4, ll. 112–13). Ironically, in the play this refers to a young woman's unrequited passion; Vaizey here uses it to describe a young man.

22. sine qua non: literally 'without which not' (Latin), i.e. an indispensable action.

23. *makes cowards of us all*: This is possibly a reference to the line in *Hamlet* (1603): 'Thus conscience does make cowards of us all' (Act 3, Scene 1, l. 84).

24. *a muff*: see note 6 to Volume 2.

25. *Newnham*: Newnham College, Cambridge, founded in 1871 and one of the two women's colleges at the university. The Vernons' expectations of both their son and daughter going to Cambridge would have been seen as extremely progressive during the period.

26. *Better to die by sudden shock ... on a rock*: Darsie appears to be misquoting 'The Giaour', an 1813 poem by Lord Byron (1788–1824), which reads 'Better to sink beneath the shock / Than molder piecemeal on the rock' (ll. 969–70). This quotation is perhaps designed to indicate Darsie's robust and romantic attitude towards life.

27. *oilclothed hall*: During this period, oilcloth was used as a cheap floor covering. Again, this emphasizes the Garnetts' relative lack of money.

28. *visit to Arden*: There is no Arden in Buckinghamshire, although there are several villages in Warwickshire with 'Arden' in their names. Vaizey is perhaps alluding here to the Forest of Arden in the 1600 play *As You Like It* by William Shakespeare (1564–1616) where the exiled Rosalind flees and eventually finds love.

29. '*Fight the good fight*': A reference to 'Fight the Good Fight with all thy Might', an 1863 hymn by John Samuel Bewley Monsell (1811–75).

30. '*Run the straight race through ... seek His Face*': see note 29, above.

31. *Plasmon biscuits*: Plasmon biscuits were manufactured with dried milk, and designed to be particularly nutritious. This taste appears to chime with Aunt Maria's taste for Benger's food. See note 11, above.

32. *barouche*: a four-wheeled horse-drawn carriage with a collapsible roof.

33. moire antique: an expensive type of watered silk.

34. *pompadour*: This hairstyle was fashionable in the early twentieth century and takes its name from Louis XV's Mistress Madame de Pompadour (1721–64). The hair is swept up and back off the face.

35. "*prunes and prism*" *decorum*: This is a reference to the character of Mrs General in the 1857 novel *Little Dorrit* by Charles Dickens (1812–70). Mrs General suggests that the

Dorrit girls say these words in order to form their mouths into attractive shapes, suggesting snobbery and superficiality.

36. *governess cart*: a small two-wheeled horse-drawn cart.
37. *rummy*: odd or peculiar.
38. *In Birchester*: It appears that Vaizey has invented this town, which seems to be somewhere in the Midlands.
39. *Callous youth, and crabbed age*: This is probably a reference to the anonymous poem 'The Passionate Pilgrim' of 1599, which begins with the lines 'Crabbed Age and Youth / Cannot live together'. It has been suggested that William Shakespeare (1564–1616) may be the author of the poem. This reference continues Darsie's habit of slightly misquoting or paraphrasing works.
40. *a poor little flapper*: The word 'flapper' in 1913 suggested a young girl in her late teens, often with her hair down. The word had connotations of flightiness but not necessarily the suggestion of loose morals that it would acquire by the 1920s.
41. *a washing dress*: The word 'washing' here implies that the fabric could be washed without undue damage.
42. *Shetland shawl*: a woollen shawl made of knitted lace, fashionable in the nineteenth century. Darsie rejects the shawl because it is no longer fashionable.
43. *the former veto against bicycle riding*: see note 33 to Volume 2.
44. *"alone among the roses"*: This is possibly a reference to the 1879 poem 'Among the Roses' by Lizzie F. Baldy, which contains the lines 'And you and I were all alone / Among the roses' (ll. 15–16). However, due to the relative obscurity of this poem, Vaizey may just be using quotation marks to indicate a general poetic atmosphere.
45. *being dragged out of the millpond*: This incident may be a reference to the 1860 novel *The Mill on the Floss* by George Eliot (1819–80), in which the proto-feminist heroine Maggie Tulliver, who has been denied education and agency, eventually drowns in the river after an act of heroism. Vaizey may be suggesting here that Darsie, unlike the high-spirited Maggie, will be able to realize her own dreams.
46. *a young Medusa*: In classical mythology, Medusa was a monster with hair made of snakes, whose gaze could turn onlookers into stone.
47. *held on like a Briton*: Ralph's imperial rhetoric is characteristic of the period.
48. *the mater*: Ralph uses the Latin term for 'mother' here, reflecting his public-school background.
49. *the ranks of women blue-stockings*: see note 143 to Volume 1.
50. *clock-golf ... yeomanry sports, blue bands*: Clock-golf is a form of lawn golf that uses a round green that looks like a clock-face. 'Yeomanry sports' appears to refer to sports on horseback; the early twentieth century saw many public exhibitions of yeomanry sports, for example at Blenheim Palace in 1911. The colours appear to refer to the bands' uniforms.
51. *dog-cart*: a small carriage, by this period probably not drawn by dogs, with two seats back to back.
52. *too awfully fagging*: too tiring.
53. *Honest Ingin*: Usually spelled 'Injun', this slang expression suggests honesty.
54. *China crape shawl*: This refers to crepe de Chine, an expensive type of fine silk that has a crisped or minutely wrinkled surface.
55. *oxydized buckle with a cairngorm in the centre*: 'Oxidized' probably refers to oxidized silver, which was popular at the time. A cairngorm is a semi-precious stone of yellow or wine colour, often used to decorate highland costume.

56. *in an Arabian night adventure*: A reference to *One Thousand and One Nights,* which was first translated into English in the eighteenth century. By the period depicted here it was well known to children, and references to it frequently appear in women's university fiction. See note 143 to Volume 1.

57. *"Submit thy way unto the Lord ... thy path"*: Although it appears that Aunt Maria is quoting, I have not been able to find any record of this phrase.

58. *goodness and mercy have followed me all the days of my life*: A reference to Psalm 23:6: 'Surely goodness and mercy shall follow me all the days of my life'.

59. *'the peace of God, which passeth understanding'*: see Philippians 4:7: 'And the peace of God, which passeth all understanding, shall keep your hearts and minds through Christ Jesus'.

60. *the porters rushed in a body to attend to the male students*: This chimes with other descriptions of arrival in Cambridge in women's university fiction. For another example, see *In Statu Pupillari* in Volume 1 of the present edition.

61. *Vice-President of a Woman's College*: In reality, Newnham has a Principal and Vice-Principal, not a President. The description of the room here recalls Meade's description of Miss Silence's study in *The Girls of Merton College*.

62. *as bedroom and study combined*: Darsie's bedroom at Newnham is historically accurate. During this period only Girton provided girls with a separate bedroom and study. L. T. Meade commented on this difference in her 1893 article on Newnham in *Atalanta*: 'At Newnham, on the contrary, students have, as a rule, only one room a-piece, which has to do duty as study, sitting-room and bedroom combined'. Meade points out, however, that Newnham was also cheaper than Girton ('Newnham College', *Atalanta*, 7 (1893–4), pp. 525–9.)

63. *taken the Longs*: It is not clear exactly what Vaizey means here. The 'Long' usually refers to the long summer vacation, but she seems to be suggesting some sort of examination.

64. *taking the Tripos in two parts*: Triposes were frequently divided into Part I and Part II, with Part I taken after two years and Part II after three or four.

65. *a pass degree*: During this period undergraduates could work towards an Honours Degree, which would result in first-, second- or third-class honours, or a pass degree (women were not eligible for the pass degree). The pass degree was often sought by wealthy or aristocratic students.

66. *coaches*: see note 16 to Volume 1.

67. *a pelican in the wilderness*: This is a reference to Psalm 102:6: 'I am like a pelican of the wilderness: I am like an owl of the desert'.

68. *gyp-room*: College servants at Cambridge in this period were called 'gyps'. The term 'gyproom' is still in use today.

69. *the famous ten o'clock "cocoas"*: Many accounts of Newnham life during this period mention the after-dinner 'cocoa' institution. E. Terry, a student in 1902, remembered that the origin of this custom lay in a benefactor to the college who had left money so that each student received half a pint of milk to drink each evening after her studies ('Social Customs', in A. Phillips (ed.), *A Newnham Anthology* (Cambridge: Cambridge University Press, 1979), pp. 53–5, on p. 53).

70. *'coffin'...'burry'...'farce'*: I have found no traces of these words being used in other descriptions of the period; they may be accurate, or Vaizey may have invented them. However, the general layout of the rooms and furniture are accurate. As one Newnham student observed about her room in 1920, 'We had very pleasant furniture: we had a bed, of course, and a table, two upright chairs, and armchair, a writing desk ... a wash-stand behind an-

other screen in another corner, and an oak chest in which we kept anything we felt like' (K. D. McKeag, 'A Corner Room in Old Hall', in Phillips (ed.), *A Newnham Anthology*, pp. 143–7, on p. 144.)

71. *there's an auction on to-night*: I have found few other references to auctions of this type, except in L. T. Meade's *A Sweet Girl Graduate* (London: A. L. Burt, 1891), in which the college authorities disapprove.

72. *Senior Classic*: see note 159 to Volume 1.

73. *the late lamented poet*: A reference to William Cowper (1731–1800), whose poem 'The Task' (1785) contains the lines 'the cups, / That cheer but not inebriate' (Book IV, ll. 39–40).

74. *an object of vertu*: an object of interest for its historical and artistic properties.

75. *Alma Tadema*: Lawrence Alma-Tadema (1836–1912), a Dutch painter popular in England. Alma-Tadema was known for his classical subjects, particularly his depictions of the decadent Roman Empire. For the girls in Darsie's generation, this may have seemed old-fashioned and Victorian.

76. *'The Maiden's Dream'*: This probably refers to the 1505 painting 'Allegory of Chastity' by the Venetian artist Lorenzo Lotto (1480–1556). One of the strengths of *A College Girl* lies in Vaizey's ability to showcase the female students' good-natured banter about their sequestration in female colleges.

77. *the Botticelli*: The auctioneer refers here to paintings by Sandro Botticelli (1445–1510), whose paintings continue the theme of daintiness and femininity implied by the earlier works.

78. *an Oxford Frame*: a frame in which the edges of all four sides protrude beyond the corners.

79. *What is home without an aspidistra*: The auctioneer's comments and the girls' laughter here underscore the aspidistra's reputation as the pre-eminent plant of the Victorian middle-class home.

80. *handsome cretonne*: Cretonne was a heavy cotton or linen cloth often used in upholstery.

81. *the physical strain of the hockey-field*: see note 18 to Volume 2.

82. *'What's your shop?'*: 'shop' refers to Tripos subject.

83. *"Fic"*: I have been unable to trace this.

84. *with one of the younger dons as chaperon*: see note 15 to Volume 2.

85. *Top-hole ... topping*: slang of the period, meaning 'excellent'.

86. *Scrum*: presumably short for 'scrumptious'.

87. *the monarch of all she surveyed*: A reference to 'The Solitude of Alexander Selkirk', a 1782 poem by William Cowper (1731–1800). Vaizey's frequent references to Cowper suggests his continuing popularity among her teenage audience and in school readers.

88. *King's College Chapel*: The visit to King's College Chapel is a stock plot event of Cambridge fiction. See note 45 to Volume 1.

89. *Anne Boleyn*: Second wife of Henry VIII, famously executed in 1536. Vaizey may be referring obliquely to the difficulties women face.

90. *Silver Street*: a real street in Cambridge.

91. *Two men looked out ... the other stars!"*: A common saying. I have been unable to trace the original source.

92. *Divinity Hall*: This probably refers to the Divinity Schools building, now part of St John's College, built in 1878–9 by the architect Basil Champneys (1842–1935).

93. *A future profession*: Darsie's astonishment here is historically accurate. Accounts of the time stress that most Newnham students were preparing to earn their own livings. L.

T. Meade put it poetically in 1893: 'The greater portion of them are obliged by circumstances to prepare for the battle for daily bread' ('Newnham College', *Atalanta*, 7 (1893–
4), p. 529).

94. *isn't it best to work in one's own home*: Women's university fiction often reflects this tension between home-life and careers for women, which was a complex issue during the period. Vaizey appears here to be suggesting, perhaps disingenuously, that women students
would also be content going back home, perhaps to appease her critics.

95. *the fire drill*: The fire brigades at both Girton and Newnham during this period were well-
publicized. See note 60 to Volume 2.

96. *Clough Hall*: Again, Vaizey uses a real college building. Clough Hall was built in 1888.

97. *Portia*: The heroine of the play *The Merchant of Venice* (1596–8) by William Shakespeare
(1564–1616). At one point Portia disguises herself as a lawyer's apprentice and argues
convincingly in court, highlighting Darsie's intelligence and independent spirit.

98. *a turnip lantern*: a jack o'lantern.

99. *Don't ask a third-year girl to dance*: During this period Newnham was still influenced
by the 'propping' (proposing) system, in which senior girls 'propped' junior ones – that
is, asked them to call them by their first names. M. G. Wallas remembered that in 1917
'second and third-years still "propped" to freshers' ('A Restless Generation', in A. Phillips
(ed.), *A Newnham Anthology*, pp. 116–19, on p. 118).

100. *the heroine of the hour*: This is historically accurate; Ann Phillips quotes an anonymous
student in 1892 who remembered what she called a 'rag dance ... with a prize for the most
original outfit' ('A Rag Dance', *A Newnham Anthology*, pp. 36–7, on p. 36).

101. *Topsy*: Topsy is a famous child character from the 1852 novel *Uncle Tom's Cabin; or, Life
Among the Lowly* by Harriet Beecher Stowe (1811–96). The casual racism here is unfortunately typical of fiction of this period.

102. *Il faut souffrire pour étre – célèbre*: It is necessary to suffer in order to be famous. A reference to the well-known French adage 'Il faut souffrire pour être belle' – one must suffer
to be beautiful.

103. *politicals*: see note 9 to Volume 1.

104. *breakfasts at the Orchard*: This is probably a reference to the Orchard Tea Garden, a popular tea shop that opened in Grantchester in 1897.

105. *the Professional Chaperon*: see note 15 to Volume 2.

106. *Grange Road*: Again, Vaizey uses real Cambridge places. Mrs Reeve's house is relatively
close to Newnham.

107. couleur de rose: rose-coloured.

108. *past the tower gateway of Trinity ... homelike shelter of their own dear Newnham*: Again,
Vaizey refers to real colleges here.

109. *Let no dog bark!*: Another reference to *The Merchant of Venice* (1596–8) by William
Shakespeare (1564–1616), Act, I Scene 1, when Gratiano describes people who take
themselves overly seriously: 'I am Sir Oracle, / And when I ope my lips, let no dog bark!'
(ll. 96–7). This is a less flattering comparison for Darsie than Vaizey's earlier Portia
reference.

110. raconteuse: story-teller.

111. *Britain's Boys*: As far as I can determine, no such magazine or book exists, but Vaizey
presumably modelled this title after other publications like *Boys of England* or the *Boy's
Own Paper*.

112. *rinking party*: 'Rinking' usually meant roller or ice skating; probably ice skating here,
given the season.

113. *Tripos*: see note 64, above.

114. *humped*: I have been unable to trace this word's slang meaning – presumably Vaizey means it to suggest tense or overly protective.

115. *Mrs. Dick*: This is probably a reference to Mr Dick, a childlike but intuitive character in the 1850 novel *David Copperfield* by Charles Dickens (1812–70).

116. *Auld Lang Syne*: song from a 1788 poem by Robert Burns (1759–96). The song is particularly fitting for *A College Girl*, with its preoccupation with the development of childhood friendships.

117. *Divinity Schools*: see note 92, above.

118. *"Mays"*: examinations given in May.

119. *Minerva*: Vaizey's don is aptly named for the Roman goddess of wisdom.

120. *terpsichorean mistress*: a dancing mistress. Terpsichore was the Muse of dancing.

121. *the canaders*: university slang for Canadian-style canoes.

122. *"Shop"*: see note 82, above.

123. *Cambridge May week*: see note 117 to Volume 1.

124. *Masonic Ball*: The Masonic Ball is listed along with individual college balls during Cambridge May Weeks throughout the late nineteenth century. Presumably it was sponsored by the Masons.

125. *Not until the three programmes were filled to the last extra*: Dance programmes were given out at balls, where partners could sign up for dances. An 'extra' was added on at the end.

126. *"bumping"*: see note 127 to Volume 1.

127. *turning turtle*: turning upside-down.

128. *swimming-tent*: I have been unable to trace this word; I assume it refers to some sort of cordoned-off area of the river or a structure like a bathing machine.

129. *near San Francisco at the time of the earthquake and fire*: A reference to the San Francisco earthquake of 1906, in which 3,000 people died.

130. *Lent term*: see note 151 to Volume 1.

131. *Be good, sweet maid ... charming*: see note 88 to Volume 2.

132. *She was Prime Minister!*: see note 9 to Volume 1.

133. *St. Columba's*: This presumably refers to St Columba's Church in Cambridge, built in 1891, which has several large halls.

134. *"How far high failure overleaps the bounds of low successes"*: This is a quotation from the 1877 poem 'The Epic of Hades: Marsayas' by Sir Lewis Morris (1833–1907).

135. *"sat at High"*: They sat at high table with the dons, on a raised dais.

136. *The Cambridge Senior*: a local examination administered to high school students.

137. rageur: a 'rager' or bad-tempered teacher.

138. *Better to die by sudden shock ... rock*: see note 26, above.